GROWING COOLER

THE EVIDENCE ON URBAN DEVELOPMENT AND CLIMATE CHANGE

REID EWING

KEITH BARTHOLOMEW

STEVE WINKELMAN

JERRY WALTERS

DON CHEN

WITH

Geoffrey Anderson

James B. Grace

Barbara McCann

David Goldberg

COOPERATING ORGANIZATIONS

ULI–the Urban Land Institute
1025 Thomas Jefferson Street, N.W.
Washington, D.C. 20007-5201

Library of Congress Cataloging-in-Publication Data

Growing cooler : evidence on urban development and climate change / Reid Ewing . . . [et al.].
    p. cm.
 Includes bibliographical references.
 ISBN 978-0-87420-082-9 (alk. paper)
1. Urban transportation—Environmental aspects—United States. 2. Urbanization—Environmental aspects—United States. 3. City planning—United States. 4. Climatic changes—United States. I. Ewing, Reid H.
 HE308.G76 2008
 363.738'7460973091732—dc22

                 2008007227

10 9 8 7 6 5 4 3 2 1
Printed in the United States of America

ULI Project Staff

Rachelle L. Levitt
Executive Vice President, Global Information Group
Publisher/Project Director

Nancy H. Stewart
Director, Book Program
Managing Editor

Lori Hatcher
Managing Director, Book Marketing

Julie D. Stern
JDS Communications
Manuscript Editor

Betsy VanBuskirk
Art Director

Sharri Wolfgang
Auras Design
Designer

Craig Chapman
Director, Publishing Operations

The views and opinions in this book represent those of the authors, and not necessarily those of the Urban Land Institute.

About ULI—the Urban Land Institute

The mission of the Urban Land Institute is to provide leadership in the responsible use of land and in creating and sustaining thriving communities worldwide. ULI is committed to

- Bringing together leaders from across the fields of real estate and land use policy to exchange best practices and serve community needs;
- Fostering collaboration within and beyond ULI's membership through mentoring, dialogue, and problem solving;
- Exploring issues of urbanization, conservation, regeneration, land use, capital formation, and sustainable development;
- Advancing land use policies and design practices that respect the uniqueness of both built and natural environments;
- Sharing knowledge through education, applied research, publishing, and electronic media; and
- Sustaining a diverse global network of local practice and advisory efforts that address current and future challenges.

Established in 1936, the Institute today has some 40,000 members worldwide, representing the entire spectrum of the land use and development disciplines. ULI relies heavily on the experience of its members. It is through member involvement and information resources that ULI has been able to set standards of excellence in development practice. The Institute has long been recognized as one of the world's most respected and widely quoted sources of objective information on urban planning, growth, and development.

About the Authors

Reid Ewing is a research professor at the National Center for Smart Growth, University of Maryland; an associate editor of the *Journal of the American Planning Association;* a columnist for *Planning* magazine; and a fellow of the Urban Land Institute. Earlier in his career, he served two terms in the Arizona legislature, analyzed urban policy issues at the Congressional Budget Office, and lived and worked in Ghana and Iran. His *Best Development Practices* is one of the best-selling books in the American Planning Association's 30-year history, and his 2003 article on sprawl and obesity is the most widely reported planning study ever.

Keith Bartholomew is an assistant professor of urban planning in the University of Utah's College of Architecture + Planning. An environmental lawyer, he worked for ten years as the staff attorney for 1000 Friends of Oregon, where he directed "Making the Land Use, Transportation, Air Quality Connection" (LUTRAQ), a nationally recognized research program examining the interactive effects of community development and travel behavior.

Steve Winkelman is director of the Transportation Program at the Center for Clean Air Policy (CCAP). He coordinated transportation analyses of climate change plans for New York and several other states, culminating in the *CCAP Transportation Emissions Guidebook*, which quantifies savings from 40 transportation policies. In February 2007, Steve launched a national discussion, "Linking Green-TEA and Climate Policy," to craft policy solutions that address travel demand.

Jerry Walters is a principal and chief technical officer with Fehr & Peers Associates, a California-based transportation planning and engineering firm. He directs integrated land use/transportation research and planning for public entities and real estate development interests throughout the United States and abroad.

Don Chen is a program officer at the Ford Foundation. He is founder and former executive director of Smart Growth America (SGA), and has worked for the Surface Transportation Policy Project, the World Resources Institute, and the Rocky Mountain Institute. He has been featured in numerous news programs and publications; has lectured in North America, Europe, Australia, and Asia; and has written for many magazines and journals, including "The Science of Smart Growth" for *Scientific American*.

Acknowledgments

The authors wish to thank the following individuals for contributions to this publication. The lead reviewers from the urban planning field were Arthur "Chris" Nelson, Virginia Polytechnic Institute, and Robert Cervero, University of California at Berkeley. From the climate community, the lead reviewers were Deron Lovaas, Natural Resources Defense Council, and Michael Replogle, Environmental Defense. James B. Grace of the U.S. Geological Survey provided assistance with structural equations modeling and coauthored Chapter 8.

Other reviewers included Robert Dunphy from the Urban Land Institute; Geoffrey Anderson, Ilana Preuss, Megan Susman, and John Thomas of the U.S. Environmental Protection Agency; Stephen Godwin, Transportation Research Board; Megan Lewis, American Planning Association; Lee Epstein, Chesapeake Bay Foundation; Greg LeRoy, Good Jobs First; Todd Litman, Victoria Transport Institute; Matthew Johnston, Environmental and Energy Study Institute; Peter Pollock, Lincoln Institute of Land Policy; Robert Johnston, University of California at Davis; Mark Muro, Brookings Institution; Scott Bernstein, Center for Neighborhood Technology; Peter Newman, Murdoch University; Brian Orland, Penn State University; Naomi Friedman, Metropolitan Washington Council of Governments; Shelley Poticha and Mariia Zimmerman, Reconnecting America; John Holtzclaw, Sierra Club; Kurt Culbertson, American Society of Landscape Architects; Rich McClintock, University of Colorado at Denver; Kaid Benfield, Natural Resources Defense Council; Larry Frank, University of British Columbia; and Judy Corbett, Local Government Commission.

Many individuals were consulted on the policy chapter, including Marty Spitzer and Suzanne Reid from the Center for Clean Air Policy; Gordon Garry, Sacramento Area Council of Governments; Dean Grandin, city of Orlando; Bob Stacey, 1000 Friends of Oregon; Michael Ronkin, formerly with the Oregon Department of Transportation; John Kari, Metropolitan Council; Carolina Gregor, San Diego Association of Governments; James Erkel, Minnesota Center for Environmental Advocacy; Ben Spinelli, New Jersey Office of Smart Growth; Gil Kelley, city of Portland; John Rahaim, city of Seattle; Stuart Cohen, Transportation and Land Use Coalition of the Bay Area; Panama Bartholomy, California Energy Commission; Anthony Eggert, California Air Resources Board; Royce Hanson, Montgomery County Planning Board; Tim Marx, Minnesota Housing Finance Agency; Gary Toth, formerly with the New Jersey Department of Transportation; Steve Adams, Florida Department of Environmental Protection; Karl Moritz, Maryland-National Capital Park and Planning Commission; and Nicholas Donohue, Office of the Governor of Virginia.

Stephanie Potts and Kate Rube of Smart Growth America and Tamar Shapiro of the Governors' Institute helped with logistics. Shala White and Meghan Ewing produced graphic materials. The U.S. Environmental Protection Agency (EPA) and the William and Flora Hewlett Foundation funded the research.

We also would like to extend our special thanks to two people. *Growing Cooler* would still be languishing on my hard drive were it not for Julie Stern of JDS Communications and Rachelle Levitt of the Urban Land Institute. Julie edited the entire manuscript with uncanny attention to detail, a light hand, and patience and good humor with multiple authors occasioning multiple revisions. Rachelle embraced the concept of the book from day one, and gently but firmly pushed to get the book into circulation early in the climate policy debate.

Reid Ewing
College Park, Maryland

Contents

1

Overview

The phrase "you can't get there from here" has a new application. For climate stabilization, a commonly accepted target for the year 2050 would require the United States to cut its carbon dioxide (CO_2) emissions by 60 to 80 percent below 1990 levels. Carbon dioxide levels have been increasing rapidly since 1990, and so would have to level off and decline even more rapidly to reach this target level by 2050. This publication demonstrates that the U.S. transportation sector cannot do its fair share to meet this target through vehicle and fuel technology alone. We have to find a way to sharply reduce the growth in vehicle miles driven across the nation's sprawling urban areas, reversing trends that go back decades.

This publication is based on an exhaustive review of existing research on the relationship among urban development, travel, and the CO_2 emitted by motor vehicles. It provides evidence on and insights into how much CO_2 savings can be expected with compact development, how compact development is likely to be received by consumers, and what policy changes will make compact development possible. Several related issues are not fully examined in this publication. These include the energy savings from more efficient building types, the value of preserved forests as carbon sinks, and the effectiveness of pricing strategies—such as tolls, parking charges, and mileage-based fees—when used in conjunction with compact development and expanded transportation alternatives.

The term "compact development" does not imply high-rise or even uniformly high density, but rather higher average "blended" densities. Compact development also features a mix of land uses, development of strong population and employment centers, interconnection of streets, and the design of structures and spaces at a human scale.

THE BASICS

Scientific consensus now exists that greenhouse gas accumulations due to human activities are contributing to global warming with potentially catastrophic consequences (IPCC 2007). International and domestic climate policy discussions have gravitated toward the goal of limiting the temperature increase to 2°C to 3°C by cutting greenhouse gas emissions by 60 to 80 percent below 1990 levels. The primary greenhouse gas is carbon dioxide, and every gallon of gasoline burned produces about 20 pounds of CO_2.

Driving Up CO$_2$ Emissions

The United States is the largest emitter worldwide of the greenhouse gases (GHGs) that cause global warming. Transportation accounts for a full third of CO$_2$ emissions in the United States, and that share is growing, rising from 31 percent in 1990 to 33 percent today. It is hard to envision a "solution" to the global warming crisis that does not involve slowing the growth of transportation CO$_2$ emissions in the United States.

The Three-Legged Stool Needed to Reduce CO$_2$ from Automobiles

Transportation CO$_2$ reduction can be viewed as a three-legged stool, with one leg related to vehicle fuel economy, a second to the carbon content of the fuel itself, and a third to the amount of driving or vehicle miles traveled (VMT). Energy and climate policy initiatives at the federal and state levels have pinned their hopes on shoring up the first two legs of the stool, through the development of more efficient vehicles (such as hybrid cars) and lower-carbon fuels (such as biodiesel fuel). Yet a stool cannot stand on only two legs.

As the research compiled in this publication makes clear, technological improvements in vehicles and fuels are likely to be offset by continuing, robust growth in VMT. Since 1980, the number of miles Americans drive has grown three times faster than the U.S. population, and almost twice as fast as vehicle registrations (see Figure 1-1). Average automobile commute times in metropolitan areas have risen steadily over the decades, and many Americans now spend more time commuting than they do vacationing.

FIGURE 1-1
Growth of Population, Vehicle Registration, and VMT in the United States relative to 1980 Values

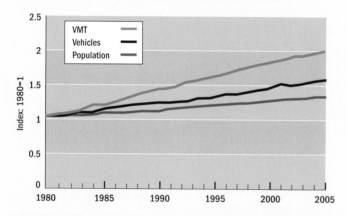

SOURCE: Federal Highway Administration (FHWA). "Vehicle Registrations, Fuel Consumption, and Vehicle Miles of Travel as Indices," *Highway Statistics 2005.* Washington, D.C.: U.S. Department of Transportation, 2006, http://www.fhwa.dot.gov/policy/ohim/hs05/htm/mvfvm.htm.

This raises some questions, which this report addresses. Why do we drive so much? Why is the total distance we drive growing so rapidly? And what can be done to alter this trend in a manner that is effective, fair, and economically benign?

The growth in driving is due in large part to urban development, or what some refer to as the built environment. Americans drive so much because we have given ourselves little alternative. For 60 years, we have built homes ever farther from workplaces, located schools far from the neighborhoods they serve, and isolated other destinations—such as shopping—from work and home. From World War II until very recently, nearly all new development has been planned and built on the assumption that people will use cars every time they travel. As a larger and larger share of our built environment has become automobile dependent, car trips and distances have increased, and walking and public transit use have declined. Population growth has been respon-

FIGURE 1-2
Projected Growth in CO$_2$ Emissions from Cars and Light Trucks

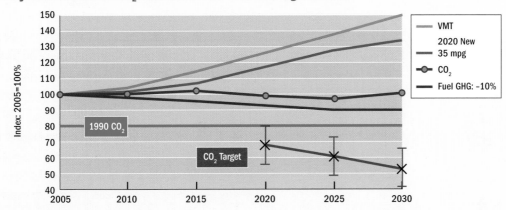

SOURCE: S. Winkelman (Center for Clean Air Policy) calculations based on EIA's *Annual Energy Outlook 2008 (Early Release)* and the Energy Independence and Security Act of 2007.

sible for only a quarter of the increase in vehicle miles driven over the last couple of decades. A larger share of the increase can be traced to the effects of a changing built environment, namely to longer trips and people driving alone.

As with driving, land is being consumed for development at a rate almost three times faster than population growth. This expansive development has caused CO$_2$ emissions from cars to rise even as it has reduced the amount of forest land available to absorb CO$_2$.

How Growth in Driving Cancels Out Improved Vehicle Fuel Economy

Conventional pollutants can be reduced in automobile exhaust with sophisticated emission control systems such as catalytic converters, on-board computers, and oxygen sensors. In contrast, CO$_2$ is a fundamental end product of burning fossil fuels; there is no practical way to remove or capture it from moving vehicles. At this point in time, the only way to reduce CO$_2$ emissions from vehicles is to burn less gasoline and diesel fuel.

An analysis by Steve Winkelman of the Center for Clean Air Policy, one of the coauthors of this publication, finds that CO$_2$ emissions will continue to rise, despite technological advances, as the growth in driving is projected to overwhelm planned improvements in vehicle efficiency and fuel carbon content from the Energy Independence and Security Act of 2007 (U.S. Congress 2007). The act requires pas-senger vehicle fuel economy improvements to at least 35 miles per gallon (mpg) for new passenger vehicles by 2020, which would lead to a 34 percent increase in fleet-wide fuel economy by 2030 (green line in Figure 1-2). The act also sets renewable fuel requirements that Winkelman calculates would reduce lifecycle GHG emissions by 10 percent by 2025 (purple line). Absent growth in driving, these measures would reduce CO$_2$ emissions from cars and light trucks by 23 percent below current levels.

Even when these more stringent standards for vehicles and fuels fully penetrate the market, however, transportation-related emissions still would far exceed target levels for stabilizing the global climate. The U.S. Department of Energy's Energy Information Administration (EIA) forecasts a 48 percent increase in driving between 2005 and 2030 (orange line in Figure 1-2), outpacing the projected 23 percent increase in population (EIA 2008).[1] The rapid increase in driving would overwhelm both the increase in vehicle fuel economy and the lower carbon fuel content required by the Energy Independence and Security Act of 2007. Carbon dioxide emissions from cars and light trucks would remain at 2005 levels (blue line), or 26 percent above 1990 levels (light blue line) in 2030. For climate stabilization, the United States must bring the CO_2 level to approximately 33 percent below 1990 levels by 2030 to be on a path to a CO_2 reduction of 60 to 80 percent by 2050 (red line).

As the projections show, the United States cannot achieve such large reductions in transportation-related CO_2 emissions without sharply reducing the growth in the number of miles driven.

Changing Development Patterns to Slow Global Warming

Recognizing the unsustainable growth in driving, the American Association of State Highway and Transportation Officials (AASHTO), representing state departments of transportation, is urging that the growth of vehicle miles driven be cut in half. How does a growing country—one with 300 million residents and another 120 million on the way by mid-century—slow the growth of vehicle miles driven? Aggressive measures certainly are available, including imposing ever stiffer fees and taxes on driving and parking or establishing no-drive zones or days. Some countries are experimenting with such measures. However, many in this country would view these measures as punitive, given the reality that most Americans do not have a viable alternative to driving. The body of research surveyed here shows that much of the rise in vehicle emissions can be curbed simply by growing in a way that will make it easier for Americans to drive less. In fact, the weight of the evidence shows that, with more compact development, people drive 20 to 40 percent less, at minimal or reduced cost, while reaping other fiscal and health benefits.

How Compact Development Helps Reduce the Need to Drive

Better community planning and more compact development help people live within walking or bicycling distance of some of the destinations they need to get to every day—work, shops, schools, and parks, as well as transit stops. If they choose to use a car, trips are short. Rather than building single-use subdivisions or office parks, communities can plan mixed-use developments that put housing within reach of these other destinations. The street network can be designed to interconnect, rather than end in culs-de-sac and funnel traffic onto overused arterial roads. Individual streets

FIGURE 1-3
Housing within One-Quarter Mile of Commercial Centers for Contrasting Development Patterns in Seattle

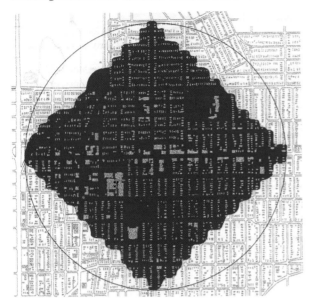 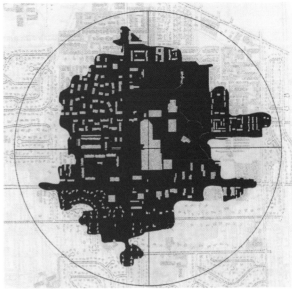

SOURCE: A.V. Moudon, P.M. Hess, M.C. Snyder, and K. Stanilov. "Effects of Site Design on Pedestrian Travel in Mixed-Use, Medium-Density Environments." *Transportation Research Record.* Vol. 1578, 1997, pp. 48–55.

can be designed to be "complete," with safe and convenient places to walk, bicycle, and wait for the bus. Finally, by building more homes as condominiums, townhouses, or detached houses on smaller lots, and by building offices, stores and other destinations "up" rather than "out," communities can shorten distances between destinations. This makes neighborhood stores more economically viable, allows more frequent and convenient transit service, and helps shorten car trips.

This type of development, which has seen a resurgence in recent years, goes by many names, including "walkable communities," "new urbanist neighborhoods," and "transit-oriented developments" (TODs). "Infill" and "brownfield" developments put unused parcels in urban areas to new uses, taking advantage of existing infrastructure and nearby destinations. Some "lifestyle centers" are now replacing single-use shopping malls with open-air shopping on connected streets with housing and office space above stores. And many communities have rediscovered and revitalized their traditional town centers and downtowns, often adding more housing to the mix. These varied development types are collectively referred to in this publication as "compact development" or "smart growth."

How We Know That Compact Development Will Make a Difference: The Evidence

As these forms of development have become more common, planning researchers and practitioners have documented the fact that residents of compact, mixed-use, transit-served communities drive less than their counterparts in sprawling communities. Studies have looked at the issue from varying angles. They have:

FIGURE 1-4

Average Daily Vehicle Miles Traveled

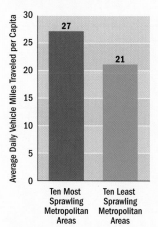

SOURCE: R. Ewing, R. Pendall, and D. Chen. *Measuring Sprawl and Its Impact.* Washington, D.C.: Smart Growth America/U.S. Environmental Protection Agency, 2002, p. 18.

■ compared travel statistics for regions and neighborhoods of varying compactness and auto orientation;

■ analyzed the travel behavior of individual households in various settings; and

■ simulated the effects on travel of different future development scenarios at the regional and project scales.

Regardless of the approach, researchers have found significant potential for compact development to reduce the miles that residents drive.

A comprehensive sprawl index developed by coauthor Reid Ewing of the National Center for Smart Growth at the University of Maryland ranked 83 of the largest metropolitan areas in the United States by their degree of sprawl, measured in terms of population and employment density, mix of land uses, strength of activity centers, and connectedness of the street network (Ewing, Pendall, and Chen 2002, 2003). Even accounting for income and other socioeconomic differences, residents drove about 25 percent less in the more compact regions. In sprawling Atlanta and Raleigh, residents racked up more than 30 miles driving each day for every person living in the region. In more compact Boston and Portland, Oregon, residents drove less than 24 miles per person per day.

This finding holds up in studies that focus on the travel habits of individual households. The link between urban development patterns and individual or household travel has become the most heavily researched subject in urban planning, with more than 100 rigorous empirical studies completed. These studies have been able to account for factors such as the tendency of higher-income households to make more and longer trips than lower-income families.

One of the most comprehensive studies, conducted in King County, Washington, by Larry Frank of the University of British Columbia (Frank, Kavage, and Appleyard 2007), found that residents of the most walkable neighborhoods drive 26 percent fewer miles per day than those living in the most sprawling areas. A meta-analysis of many of these types of studies shows that people living in places with twice the density, diversity of uses, accessible destinations, and interconnected streets drive about a third less than otherwise comparable residents of low-density sprawl.

Many studies have been conducted by or in partnership with public health researchers interested in how the built environment can be better designed to encourage daily physical activity. These studies show that residents of communities designed to be walkable both drive fewer miles and also make more trips by foot and bicycle, which improves individual health. A recent literature review found that 17 of 20 studies, all dating from 2002 or later, have established statistically significant links between some aspect of the built environment and obesity.

Two other types of studies also find strong associations between development patterns and driving: simulations that predict the impacts of various growth options for entire regions and simulations that predict the impacts of individual development projects when sited and designed in different ways. In regional growth simulations, planners compare the effect of a metropolitan-wide business-as-usual scenario with more compact growth options. Coauthor Keith Bartholomew of the University of Utah analyzed 23 of these studies and found that compact scenarios generate up to one-third fewer miles driven than business-as-usual scenarios (Bartholomew 2005, 2007). The better-performing scenarios are those with higher degrees of land use mixing, infill development, and population density, as well as a larger amount of expected growth. Under a plausible set of assumptions, the reduction of miles driven with compact development would be 18 percent by 2050. Even this may be on the low side, since the travel models used in these studies only crudely account for travel within neighborhoods and disregard walk and bike trips entirely.

Atlantic Station today.

Of the project-level studies, one of the best known evaluated the impact of building a very dense, mixed-use development at an abandoned steel mill site in the heart of Atlanta versus spreading the equivalent amount of commercial space and number of housing units in the prevailing patterns at three suburban locations. Analysis using travel models enhanced by coauthor Jerry Walters of Fehr & Peers Associates (Walters, Ewing, and Allen 2000), and supplemented by the U.S. Environmental Protection Agency's Smart Growth Index (to capture the effects of site design) found that the infill location would generate about 36 percent less driving and emissions than the outlying comparison sites. The results were so compelling that the development was deemed a transportation control measure by the federal government for the purpose of improving the region's air quality.

The Atlantic Station project in Midtown Atlanta has become a highly successful reuse of central city industrial land. An early evaluation of travel by residents and employees of Atlantic Station suggests even larger VMT reductions than projected originally. On average, Atlantic Station residents are estimated to generate eight VMT per day, and employees to generate 11 VMT per day. These estimates compare favorably with a regional average VMT of more than 32 miles per person per day, among the highest in the nation.

The Potential of Smart Growth

The potential of smart growth to curb the rise in GHG emissions will, of course, be limited by the amount of new development and redevelopment that takes place over

WHAT SMART GROWTH WOULD LOOK LIKE

How would this shift to compact development change U.S. communities? Many more developments would look like the transit-oriented developments and new urbanist neighborhoods already going up in almost every city in the country, and these developments would fill in vacant lots, replace failing strip shopping centers, and revitalize older town centers, rather than displacing forests or farmland. Most developments would no longer be single-use subdivisions or office parks, but would mix shops, schools, and offices together with homes. They might feature ground-floor stores and offices with living space above, or townhomes within walking distance of a retail center. Most developments would be built to connect seamlessly with the external street network.

The density increases required to achieve the changes proposed in this publication would be moderate. In 2003, the average density of residential development in U.S. urban areas was about 7.6 units per acre. As a result of shifting market demand, new developments between 2007 and 2025 would average 13 units per acre, and the average density of metropolitan areas overall would rise to approximately nine units per acre.

Two recent publications—*This is Smart Growth* (Smart Growth Network 2006) and *Visualizing Density* (Campoli and MacLean 2007)—provide a glimpse of what this future might look like.

the next few decades, and by the share of it that is compact in nature. A great deal of new building will take place as the U.S. population grows to 420 million in 2050. According to the best available analysis, by Arthur "Chris" Nelson of Virginia Tech, 89 million new or replaced homes—and 190 billion square feet of new offices, institutions, stores, and other nonresidential buildings—will be constructed through 2050. If Nelson's forecasts are correct, two-thirds of the development on the ground in 2050 will be built between 2007 and then. Pursuing smart growth is a low-cost climate change strategy, because it involves shifting investments that have to be made anyway.

Smart Growth Meets Growing Market Demand for Choice

There is no doubt that moving away from a fossil fuel–based economy will require many difficult changes. Fortunately, smart growth is a change that many Americans will embrace. Americans are demanding more choices in where and how they live, and changing demographics will accelerate this change in demand.

While prevailing zoning and development practices make sprawling development easier to build, developers who make the effort to create compact communities are encountering a responsive public. In 2003, for the first time in the country's history, the sales price per square foot for attached housing—that is, condominiums and townhouses—was higher than that of detached housing. The real estate analysis firm Robert Charles Lesser & Co. has conducted a dozen consumer preference surveys in suburban and urban locations[2] for a variety of builders to help them design their projects. In every location examined, about one-third of respondents prefer smart growth housing products and communities. Other studies by the National Association of Homebuilders, the National Association of Realtors, the Fannie Mae Foundation, high-production builders, and university researchers have corroborated these results—some estimating even greater demand for smart growth housing products. When smart growth also offers shorter commutes, it appeals to another one-quarter of the market, because many people are willing to trade lot or house size for shorter commutes.

Because the demand is greater than the current supply—according to a study by Chris Leinberger of the Brookings Institution—the price-per-square-foot values of houses in mixed-use neighborhoods show price premiums ranging from 40 to 100 percent, compared to houses in nearby single-use subdivisions.

This market demand is only expected to grow over the next several decades, as the share of households made up of older Americans rises with the aging of the baby boomers. Through 2025, households without children will account for close to 90 percent of new housing demand, and single-person households will account for one-third. Nelson projects that the demand for attached and small-lot housing will exceed the current supply by 35 million units (71 percent), while the demand for large-lot housing actually will fall short of the current supply.

FIGURE 1-5
2003 Housing Supply versus 2025 Housing Demand

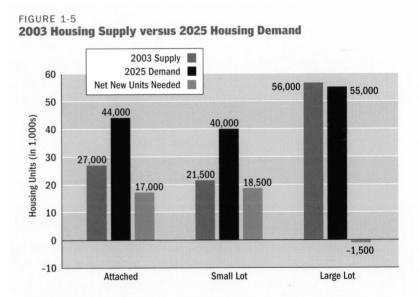

SOURCE: A.C. Nelson. "Leadership in a New Era." *Journal of the American Planning Association.* Vol. 72, Issue 4, 2006, pp. 393–407.

Total Estimated VMT Reduction and Total Climate Impact

When viewed in total, the evidence on land use and driving shows that compact development will reduce the need to drive between 20 and 40 percent, as compared with development at the outer suburban edge with isolated homes, workplaces, and other destinations. So, as a rule of thumb, it is realistic to assume a 30 percent cut in VMT with compact development.

Making reasonable assumptions about growth rates, the market share of compact development, and the relationship between VMT and CO_2, smart growth could, by itself, reduce total transportation-related CO_2 emissions from current trends by 7 to 10 percent in 2050. This reduction is achievable with land use changes alone. It does not include additional reductions from complementary measures, such as higher fuel prices and carbon taxes, peak-period road tolls, pay-as-you drive insurance, paid parking, and other policies designed to make drivers pay more of the full social costs of auto use.

This estimate also does not include the energy saved in buildings with compact development, or the CO_2-absorbing capacity of forests preserved by compact development. Whatever the total savings, it is important to remember that land use changes provide a permanent climate benefit that would compound over time. The second 50 years of smart growth would build on the base reduction from the first 50 years, and so on into the future. More immediate strategies, such as gas tax increases, do not have this degree of permanence.

The authors calculate that shifting 60 percent of new growth to compact patterns would save 79 million metric tons of CO_2 annually by 2030. The savings over that period equate to a 28 percent increase in federal vehicle efficiency standards, generating one-half of the cumulative savings of the new 35 mpg CAFE standards. Every resident of a compact neighborhood would provide the environmental benefit expected from, say, driving one of today's efficient hybrid cars. This effect would be compounded, of course, if the resident also drove such an efficient car whenever he or she chose to make a vehicle trip. Smart growth would become an important "third leg" in the transportation sector's fight against global warming, along with more efficient vehicles and lower-carbon fuels.

A Climate-Sparing Strategy with Multiple Payoffs

Addressing climate change through smart growth is an attractive strategy because, in addition to being in line with market demand, compact development provides many other benefits. Documented co-benefits include preservation of farmland and open space, protection of water quantity and quality, improvement of health by providing more opportunities for physical activity, and reduction of road and other infrastructure costs. For example, the Envision Utah scenario planning process resulted in a compact growth plan that will save the region about $4.5 billion in infrastructure spending, leave 171 square miles of additional open space, and reduce per capita water use by more than 10 percent.

Among the co-benefits of compact development, perhaps the most important is greater energy security. Compact development uses less energy per capita than does sprawl. As the world approaches and then passes peak production of conventional oil, in the face of ever-rising demands, Americans in compact urban areas will be better able to weather the economic storm of rapidly rising gasoline prices. Moreover, to the degree that the United States makes the transition to compact development, the country as a whole will be less dependent on regions of the world that are unstable, hostile, and/or especially vulnerable to terrorist attacks.

Finally, unlike hydrogen and cellulosic ethanol, which get a lot of attention in the climate change debate as substitutes for gasoline, the "technology" of compact, walkable communities exists today, as it has in one form or another for thousands of years. We can begin using this technology in the service of a cooler planet right now.

FIGURE 1-6
World Oil Production in the Best and Worst Cases*

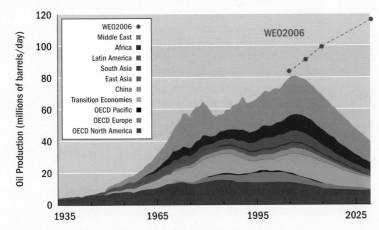

* The International Energy Agency's optimistic forecast in *World Energy Outlook* (IEA 2007) shows worldwide oil production continuing to rise (the WEO line on top), while the sobering assessment of the Energy Watch Group in *Crude Oil: The Supply Outlook* suggests that oil production already has peaked (the curve on the bottom). Most forecasts lie between these two extremes, with the peak production of conventional oil occurring between now and 2020 (Hirsch et al. 2005). While oil substitutes such as liquified coal, oil shale, and tar sands will fill some of the gap, they are more expensive than conventional oil and worse from the standpoint of global warming potential.

SOURCE: Energy Watch Group. *Crude Oil: The Supply Outlook*. Ottobrunn, Germany: October 2007, http://www.energywatchgroup.org/fileadmin/global/pdf/EWG_Oilreport_10-2007.pdf.

The Combined Effect of Compact Development, Transportation Investments, and Road Pricing

Accurately forecasting the implications of compact development for VMT requires an understanding of the network of interactive effects of population growth, land use, transportation investments, and road pricing on driving patterns. Analyses of historical data make it clear that VMT responds to a variety of forces in a complex way. Growth of metropolitan areas during the past 20 years has been characterized by an actual decrease in population density, as urbanized areas have expanded faster than population. This trend has started to reverse itself, but current conditions reflect the legacy of this era of sprawl.

During this period, the emphasis in the majority of urbanized areas has been on increasing highway capacity and the result has been a steady rise in VMT that has exceeded population growth (see Figure 1-2). Increases in average income during this period have contributed to substantially greater use of and reliance on personal vehicles. Rising personal income, while positive in other respects, has worked to promote sprawl, discourage mass transit ridership, and increase VMT.

During the decade from 1985 to 1995, decreases in inflation-corrected gas prices appear to have contributed to increases in VMT. During the past ten-year period, however, gas prices have increased as has traffic congestion, and both of these forces have begun to create pressures to reduce VMT.

Nationally, mass transit has contributed relatively little thus far to reducing reliance on personal vehicle use in the majority of urbanized areas. Increasingly, cities are attempting to build more mass transit capacity, and it is clear that such a development could act to reduce VMT if the right set of associated circumstances prevails. Internal

FIGURE 1-7
Urban VMT Reduction under a Low-Carbon Scenario (2030)

	Elasticities of VMT with Respect to Policy Variables	Change in Annual Growth Rates of Policy Variables (Percent above/below Trend)	Effect on Annual VMT Growth Rate (Percent below Trend)
Population density	–0.30	1	–7.7
Highway lane miles	0.55	–1	–11.4
Transit revenue miles	–0.06	2.5	–4.6
Real fuel price	–0.17	2.7	–14.4
Total effect	NA	NA	–38.1

forces such as further increases in traffic congestion and delays, along with sustained elevated fuel prices, can be expected to automatically produce reductions in VMT as they affect personal decisions. A deliberate strategy of compact development and smart growth has the potential to reverse historic trends to an even greater degree.

In Chapter 8, we mathematically model the interactions described above using a statistical technique called structural equation modeling (SEM) and relying on historical data for 84 urbanized areas. Two models were estimated with our combined dataset: a cross-sectional model for 2005 and a longitudinal model for the two ten-year periods between 1985 and 2005. The cross-sectional model was used to capture long-term relationships between transportation and land use. Each urbanized area has had decades to arrive at quasi equilibrium among density, road capacity, transit capacity, and VMT. However, there is not enough spatial variation in fuel prices across the United States to detect effects on VMT in a cross-sectional sample. So a longitudinal analysis was required to capture short- and medium-term responses to fuel price fluctuations.

Together, the cross-sectional and longitudinal models give us a sound basis for deducing the elasticities of urban VMT with respect to different urban variables. An elasticity is the percentage change in one variable, such as VMT, with respect to a 1 percent change in another variable, such as density or average gasoline price. Using reasonable assumptions about future density, average gasoline price, and other variables, we project that under a trend scenario, urban VMT in the United States will experience a rise of 48 percent by 2030 and 102 percent by 2050, leaving the nation far off a climate-stabilizing CO_2 path. In contrast, under a low-carbon scenario of higher densities, higher gasoline prices, less highway expansion, and more transit service, the nation can come close to a climate-stabilizing CO_2 path by 2030 (see Figure 1-7).

Policy and Program Recommendations

Intentionally or not, many current public policies increase sprawl, auto dependence and, hence, GHG emissions. Many local zoning codes require low-density, single-use development. Public spending frequently supports development at the urban fringe rather than in already developed areas. Transportation policies remain focused on accommodating the automobile. Implementing an effective smart growth strategy for climate stabilization will require reorienting these and many other policies and programs.

Here, we summarize key policy initiatives at each level of government that could form the basis for this policy transformation. The specifics of these initiatives can be found in Chapter 9.

Federal Actions

Enact a "Green-TEA" Transportation Act. Beginning in 1991 with the Intermodal Surface Transportation Efficiency Act (known as ISTEA), federal surface transportation acts have put increasing emphasis on alternatives to the automobile, as well as on community involvement, environmental goals, and coordinated planning. The next surface transportation bill, scheduled for adoption in 2009, could bring yet another paradigm shift by emphasizing environmental performance, climate protection, and green development. We refer to this proposed new legislation as "Green-TEA."

The key feature of Green-TEA would be a requirement that states and metropolitan areas achieve articulated national goals when spending federal transportation funds. These goals would include GHG emission reductions necessary for eventual climate stabilization, "fix-it-first" prioritization for transit and highway rehabilitation and maintenance, and "complete streets" that provide for all transportation modes.

Other Green-TEA provisions would:

- create state and metropolitan funding formulas with incentives for reducing transportation demand instead of rewarding increased driving, as current legislation does;
- eliminate funding and procedural inequities between highway and transit projects;
- give deteriorating roads, bridges, and transit systems priority in funding, limiting highway expansion until existing facilities are brought up to reasonable standards;
- require any subsequent highway expansions to meet economic, transportation, and climate performance standards;
- provide direct project funding for metropolitan planning organizations (MPOs) instead of routing federal funds through state departments of transportation;
- provide technical assistance to MPOs and state and local governments, including improved data, models, and scenario planning tools to help in developing and implementing smart growth solutions; and
- establish a new National Transportation System Administration to oversee a national high-speed rail network and integrate that network with the nation's aviation system.

Extend Transportation Conformity Requirements to GHGs. In *Massachusetts v. EPA*, the U.S. Supreme Court affirmed the EPA's authority and duty to regulate GHG emissions under the current federal Clean Air Act. The EPA could meet its obligation by adopting national GHG reduction targets, requiring states to develop state implementation plans for meeting these targets, and mandating that state and metropolitan transportation plans and programs conform to state implementation plans.

Use Cap and Trade to Support Smart Growth. Many Congressional proposals for climate stabilization would authorize a national cap-and-trade market system similar to those in use in Europe and under development in several states. The revenues generated from auctioning allowances under these systems could be used to support smart growth. Uses of funds might include providing technical assistance to MPOs and state and local governments, including improved data, models, and scenario planning tools; a "Smart Location Tax Credit" targeted at compact development; and support for travel alternatives such as transit, bicycling, and pedestrian infrastructure that are important complements to compact development. Although land development is unlikely to become a regulated activity (like electrical power generation) under cap-and-trade systems, it may have a role to play in "offset" markets. It could be included as an allowable offset in any cap-and-trade climate legislation.

State Actions

Adopt and Suballocate VMT Reduction Targets. In the absence of federal leadership, many states have adopted goals for GHG reduction. These goals could be translated into VMT reduction targets. The targets could be proportionally allocated to metropolitan regions within a state, and each MPO could be charged with developing a plan for meeting its respective target. VMT targets could even be suballocated to localities.

Align State Spending with Climate and Smart Growth Goals. After adopting targets, states will want to ensure that funding programs—whether carried out directly by the state or executed through grants to local governments—support such targets. States can begin by analyzing the criteria used to distribute all state and federal funds in housing, economic development, water and sewer infrastructure, schools, transportation, and recreation. States could earmark and distribute at least a portion of these funds according to local performance in meeting GHG and VMT reduction targets.

Adopt a Statewide "Complete Streets" Policy and Funding Program.
A complete streets policy would require that pedestrian and bicycle facilities be provided on all new and reconstructed streets and highways, and that pedestrian and bicyclists' needs be considered in routine roadway operation and maintenance. To create complete communities, the policy might mandate that new streets

be interconnected and culs-de-sac be discouraged so that travel distances for pedestrians and bicyclists are minimized.

Regional Actions

Give Funding Priority to Compact, Transit-Served Areas. By giving funding priority to compact, transit-served areas, MPOs can help reduce GHG emissions. In concert with local governments, MPOs would designate "priority funding areas" where local governments have planned for compact development. In addition to receiving priority for public funds, areas could qualify for streamlined development approvals and other financial incentives.

Establish a Regional Transfer of Development Rights Program. Transfer of development rights (TDR) programs enable landowners to sell their development rights to other landowners through a market-based system. Effectively crafted, TDR programs can help reduce VMT by directing growth to compact, transit-served areas and away from low-density greenfield sites, thus reducing the need for long-distance travel. While TDR programs typically have been administered by local governments, a regional TDR program likely would encompass more rural and urban areas, thereby providing greater market opportunities for TDR transfers.

Create a Carbon Impact Fee for New Development. Suburban and exurban development has a cost advantage over urban infill development because of low land costs and subsidized infrastructure. Regulatory reforms alone cannot overcome this advantage. For decades, governments have charged impact fees on new development to offset the costs of schools, libraries, sewers, parks, and transportation. Creating and implementing a regional CO_2 emissions impact fee would internalize carbon impacts into development costs, thereby rewarding best development practices and raising the price of carbon-inefficient development. Fee revenues could be used to help fund transit, bicycling facilities, sidewalks and other pedestrian amenities, and similar projects in compact areas.

Local Actions

Change the Development Rules. Local regulations often prohibit the type of climate-friendly, compact development discussed in this book. Outdated land development codes—often from the 1970s or earlier—effectively mandate sprawl by restricting the mix of land uses and requiring large amounts of parking as well as large minimum building setbacks. Many localities have tried to address these issues on a development-by-development basis, granting exceptions to the rules through arduous review and approval processes. Instead, a better approach would be to amend local policies and regulations—including general plans, zoning and subdivision ordinances, parking standards, annexation rules, adequate public facilities requirements, and design guidelines—to facilitate smart growth through normal approval processes. They also should consider ways that permitting processes might be accelerated for compact development projects that meet specified standards.

Channel Growth into Compact Development Areas. With surprising regularity, MPOs and localities have settled on a common approach to VMT reduction—channeling growth into dense, walkable areas that can be efficiently served by transit, and giving these areas priority for infrastructure funding. This is the idea behind "smart growth areas" in the San Diego region, "urban development areas" in Virginia, and "metropolitan activity centers" in Orlando. Public infrastructure, amenities, and good urban design will guarantee that such areas are attractive places to live, work, and shop.

Provide for Workforce Housing near Jobs. In most metropolitan areas, the cost of housing declines with distance from job centers and other desired destinations, while the cost of transportation increases. With gasoline costs rising, the financial tradeoff between a longer commute and less-expensive housing is changing, and the potential savings from living in a convenient location with transportation choices is becoming a more important aspect of affordability. Local governments could make the provision of affordable "workforce" housing a condition of approval for large-scale residential and commercial developments. In addition, localities could give priority to transit accessibility when allocating housing assistance funds.

The Organization of this Book

Chapter by chapter, this book addresses the impacts of the following:

- emerging market and policy trends on urban development;
- vehicular travel on GHG emissions;
- urban development on vehicular travel;
- residential preferences on urban development and travel;
- highway building on urban development and travel;
- urban development on residential energy use;
- the combination of urban development, transit enhancements, and roadway pricing on vehicular travel; and, finally
- policy options to encourage compact development and reduce vehicular travel.

$$2$$

Emerging Trends in Planning, Development, and Climate Change

The United States cannot reduce carbon dioxide (CO_2) emissions in 2050 by 60 to 80 percent below 1990 levels—a commonly accepted target for climate stabilization—unless the transportation sector contributes, and the transportation sector cannot do its fair share through vehicle and fuel technology alone. The increase in vehicular travel across the nation's sprawling urban areas needs to be dramatically reduced, reversing trends that go back decades.

Background

The transportation sector accounts for 28 percent of total greenhouse gas (GHG) emissions in the United States and 33 percent of the nation's energy-related CO_2 emissions (EIA 2006, p. xvi; EIA 2007a, p. 15). It has pulled ahead of the industrial sector as the main contributor of CO_2 (see Figure 2-1). The United States, in turn, is responsible for 22 percent of CO_2 emissions worldwide and close to a quarter of worldwide GHG emissions (EIA 2007b, p. 93). It is hard to envision a "solution" to the global warming crisis that does not involve slowing the growth of transportation CO_2 emissions in the United States.

The transportation sector's CO_2 emissions are a function of vehicle fuel efficiency, fuel carbon content, and VMT, factors sometimes referred to as a "three-legged stool." Energy and climate policy initiatives at the federal and state levels have focused almost exclusively on technological advances in vehicles and fuels, the first two legs. Yet, there is a growing recognition that managing VMT has to be part of the solution, that the third leg is needed to support the stool.

THREE CRITICAL QUESTIONS

This book asks and answers three critical questions facing the urban planning profession, the land development community, and federal, state, and local policy makers:

- What reduction in vehicle miles traveled (VMT) is possible in the United States with compact development rather than continuing urban sprawl?
- What reduction in CO_2 emissions will accompany such a reduction in VMT?
- What policy changes will be required to shift the dominant land development pattern from sprawl to compact development?

17

FIGURE 2-1

U.S. Carbon Dioxide Emissions by End Use

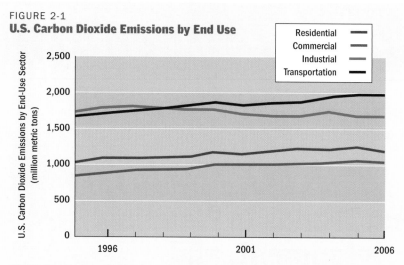

SOURCE: Energy Information Administration (EIA). *U.S. Carbon Dioxide Emissions from Energy Sources: 2006 Flash Estimate.* Washington, D.C.: U.S. Department of Energy, 2007a.

In *A Call for Action*, the U.S. Climate Action Partnership (USCAP)—made up of major U.S. corporations and environmental groups—includes promoting "better growth planning" (USCAP 2007). The United Nations Intergovernmental Panel on Climate Change (IPCC 2007c, p. 20) lists "influenc[ing] mobility needs through land use regulations and infrastructure planning" among policies and measures shown to be effective in controlling GHG emissions. California's Climate Action Team (2007) expects "smart land use and intelligent transportation" to make the second-largest contribution toward meeting the state's ambitious GHG reduction goals.

The architects of the principal GHG stabilization framework are banking on major changes in urban development and travel patterns. "The task of holding global emissions constant would be out of reach, were it not for the fact that all the driving and flying in 2056 will be in vehicles not yet designed, most of the buildings that will be around then are not yet built, the locations of many of the communities that will contain these buildings and determine their inhabitants' commuting patterns have not yet been chosen . . ." (Socolow and Pacala 2006).

A recent report by the U.S. Environmental Protection Agency (EPA) finds: "By themselves, individual approaches incorporating vehicle technologies, fuels, or transportation demand management (TDM) approaches could moderately reduce, but not flatten, emissions from now until 2050. Most of the system approaches analyzed, by contrast, could . . . nearly flatten the entire U.S. transportation sector emissions, despite the passenger vehicle category representing only half of the sector's emissions" (Mui et al. 2007). In other words, all three legs of the policy stool will be required to moderate transportation CO_2 emission levels.

The Nature of Compact Development

This publication makes the case for compact development—or its alias, smart growth—rather than continued urban sprawl. It does so in the context of global climate change.

The term "compact development" does not imply high-rise or even uniformly high-density development. A discussion of alternatives to urban sprawl always seems to gravitate toward high-density development, and leads to fears that more compact development will result in the "Manhattanization" of America. That is not what this book is about.

According to data provided by Chris Nelson of Virginia Tech, the blended average density of residential development in the United States in 2003 was about 7.6 units per net acre (see Figure 2-2). This estimate includes apartments, condominiums, and townhouses, as well as detached single-family housing on both small and large lots. A net acre is an acre of developed land, not including streets, school sites, parks, and other undevelopable land.

Because of changing demographics and lifestyle preferences, Nelson projects a significant change in market demand by 2025. The mix of housing stock required to meet this demand would have a blended density of approximately nine units per net acre. Given the excess of large-lot housing already on the ground relative to 2025 demand, all net new housing built between now and then would have to be attached or small-lot detached units (not including replacement of large-lot housing). The density of new and redeveloped housing would average about 13 units per net acre. That is a typical density for a townhouse development. Apartments and condos boost the average, while single-family detached housing lowers it.

The role of density, however, should not be overemphasized. As important as density is, it is no more fundamental to compact development than are the mixing of land uses, the development of strong population and employment centers, the inter-

Alternative futures, circa 2056.

CREDIT: © *Scientific American* (From R. Socolow and S. Pacala, "A Plan to Keep Carbon in Check." *Scientific American*, September 2006, pp. 50–57)

FIGURE 2-2
Projections of Housing Demand and Density in 2025

	Density (units per net acre)	2003 Units*	2025 Units*	Difference*
Attached	20	27,000	44,000	17,000
Small-lot detached	7	22,000	40,000	18,000
Large-lot detached	2	57,000	56,000	–1,000
Average blended density (per net acre)		7.6	9.1	13.3

*In thousands.

SOURCE: A.C. Nelson. "Leadership in a New Era." *Journal of the American Planning Association*, Vol. 72, Issue 4, 2006, pp. 393–407.

FIGURE 2-3
Nature of Compact Development versus Sprawl

Compact Development	Sprawl
Medium to high densities	Low densities
Mixed uses	Single uses
Centered development	Strip development
Interconnected streets	Poorly connected streets
Pedestrian- and transit-friendly design	Auto-oriented design

SOURCES: R. Ewing. "Is Los Angeles–Style Sprawl Desirable?" *Journal of the American Planning Association*, Vol. 63, 1997, pp. 107–126; R. Ewing, R. Pendall, and D. Chen. *Measuring Sprawl and Its Impact*. Washington, D.C.: Smart Growth America/U.S. Environmental Protection Agency, 2002.

connection of streets, and the design of structures and spaces at a human scale (see Figure 2-3). Images of compact development are available in *This is Smart Growth* (Smart Growth Network 2006) and *Visualizing Density* (Campoli and McLean 2007).

Urban Sprawl and Transportation

In 1997, the *Journal of the American Planning Association* (JAPA) carried a pair of articles on the merits of urban sprawl versus compact development (Gordon and Richardson 1997; Ewing 1997). The authors debated the characteristics, causes, and costs of sprawl, and briefly discussed cures. Gordon and Richardson's lead article—titled "Are Compact Cities a Desirable Planning Goal?"—argued that U.S. real estate markets are producing what consumers want; that the social, economic, environmental, and geopolitical impacts of that development are benign; and hence that there is no need for urban planning intervention in markets. Most relevant to concerns over global climate change, the authors contended that a "global energy glut" and vehicle emission controls rendered compact development unnecessary.

Ewing's counterpoint—"Is Los Angeles–Style Sprawl Desirable?"—defined sprawl broadly as 1) leapfrog or scattered development, 2) commercial strip development, or 3) large expanses of low-density or single-use development, as in sprawling bedroom communities, and compact development as the reverse. The article argued that U.S. real estate markets have many imperfections that cause them to "fail," that the social welfare costs of such failures are enormous, and that urban planning interventions therefore are warranted. Particularly relevant to the global climate change debate is the following:

> While the best case envisioned by [Gordon and Richardson] has the real price of gasoline holding steady, it is the worst case that worries others . . . . The fact that the most recent large-scale war fought was in the Persian Gulf is itself a testament to the risk of relying on the political stability of this region for a commodity [oil] so essential to economic activity . . . . Being unregulated, carbon dioxide

FIGURE 2-4
Growth of Population and Urbanized Land Area by Census Region between 1982 and 1997

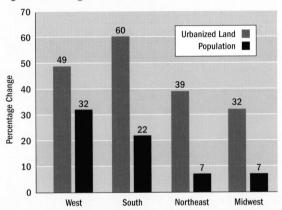

SOURCE: W. Fulton, R. Pendall, M. Nguyen, and A. Harrison. "Who Sprawls Most? How Growth Patterns Differ Across the U.S." Washington, D.C.: Brookings Center on Urban and Metropolitan Policy, 2001.

FIGURE 2-5
Growth of VMT, Vehicle Registrations, and Population in the U.S. relative to 1980 Values

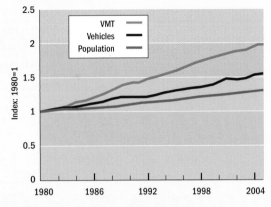

SOURCE: Federal Highway Administration (FHWA). "Vehicle Registrations, Fuel Consumption, and Vehicle Miles of Travel as Indices." *Highway Statistics 2005*, Washington, D.C.: U.S. Department of Transportation, 2006, http://www.fhwa.dot.gov/policy/ohim/hs05/htm/mvfvm.htm.

emissions represent a bigger threat to national welfare than do regulated emissions. There is now a near-consensus within the scientific community that carbon dioxide build-up in the atmosphere is causing global climate change, and that the long-term effects could be catastrophic.

A decade later, there seems to be little doubt that the "worst case" is upon us. The urbanized area of the United States has grown more than twice as fast as metropolitan population, as urban development sprawled outwards unchecked (see Figure 2-4). This development pattern has boosted VMT and reduced the amount of forest land available to absorb CO_2.

Vehicle miles traveled in the United States have grown three times faster than population, and almost twice as fast as vehicle registrations (see Figure 2-5). In one analysis, 36 percent of the VMT growth was explained by increasing trip length (see Figure 2-6), caused in large part by changing development patterns. Another 17 percent was explained by shifts to automobile trips from other modes of transportation, which also were caused in part by development patterns. Yet another 17 percent was due to lower vehicle occupancy, as rates of carpooling declined. Only 13 percent of the growth in VMT was explained by population growth. Using comparable methodology, we estimate that one-third of the national growth in VMT between 1990 and 2001 was due to longer vehicle trips.[1]

Vehicle miles traveled have grown more than twice as fast as highway capacity in urbanized areas of the United States. In all 85 urbanized areas for which statistics are available, highways became more congested between 1982 and 2005 (Schrank

FIGURE 2-6
Factors Explaining VMT Growth between 1983 and 1990

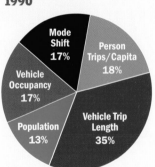

SOURCE: A.E. Pisarski. *Travel Behavior Issues in the 90s.* Washington, D.C.: Federal Highway Administration, 1992, p. 10.

FIGURE 2-7
Growth of Annual Hours of Delay per Capita

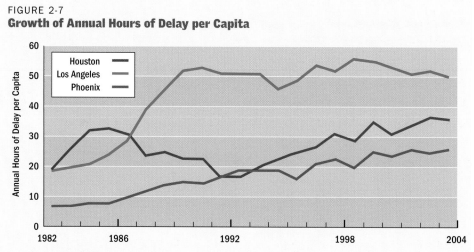

SOURCE: D. Schrank and T. Lomax. *The 2007 Urban Mobility Report*. College Station: Texas Transportation Institute, 2007, http://mobility.tamu.edu/ums/.

and Lomax 2007). This is true even in regions that struggled to keep pace with VMT growth and appeared to succeed for a time (see Figure 2-7). Highway building itself induces more traffic and urban sprawl, in a never-ending cycle. (This will be discussed in greater detail in Chapter 6, "Induced Traffic and Induced Development.")

Carbon dioxide emissions from the transportation sector have grown while regulated pollutant emissions actually declined, thanks to improved fuel and engine technology (see Figure 2-8).[2] There is no catalytic converter for CO_2, as CO_2 and water are basic end products of fossil fuel combustion. Carbon dioxide emissions are propor-

FIGURE 2-8
Change in Transportation Emissions in the United States Relative to 1995 Values

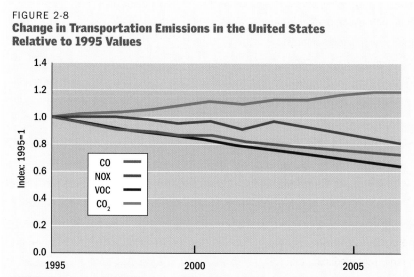

SOURCE: Environmental Protection Agency (EPA). "National Emissions Inventory (NEI) Air Pollutant Emissions Trends Data." Washington, D.C., undated, www.epa.gov/ttn/chief/trends/.

tional to gasoline consumption and, during this period, improvements in vehicle fuel efficiency were overwhelmed by the growth in VMT. Under business-as-usual policies, VMT growth will continue to outstrip technological advances. (See Chapter 3, "The VMT/CO_2/Climate Connection," for more details.)

The United States is home to only 5 percent of the world's population, but U.S. residents own almost a third of the world's cars, which account for 45 percent of the CO_2 emissions generated by cars worldwide (see Figure 2-9). U.S. cars play a disproportionate role in global warming because they are less fuel efficient than cars elsewhere in the world, and also because they are driven farther.

Changing Consumer Demand

There are many reasons why smart growth may be the "low-hanging fruit" in the struggle against climate change. The main reason is the large and growing consumer demand for homes in compact neighborhoods. The real estate analysis firm Robert Charles Lesser & Co. (RCLCO) has conducted a dozen consumer preference surveys for urban and suburban builders to help them design their projects.[3] The RCLCO surveys have shown that about one-third of the respondents at every location are interested in smart growth housing (Logan 2007). Preference varies by geography, economic and demographic fundamentals, and buyer profiles; life stage and income are key variables. Other studies by the National Association of Home Builders (NAHB), the National Association of Realtors (NAR), the Fannie Mae Foundation, high-production builders, and university researchers have corroborated these results, with some estimating even greater demand for compact development (Myers and Gearin 2001).

Perhaps the best national assessment of the demand for compact development is the National Survey on Communities, conducted for Smart Growth America (a nonprofit advocacy group) and the NAR (Belden Russonello & Stewart 2004). In this survey, respondents were given a choice between communities labeled "A" and "B." Community A was described as having single-family homes on large lots, no sidewalks, shopping and schools located a few miles away, commutes to work of 45 minutes or more, and no public transportation. In contrast, community B was described as having a mix of single-family and other housing, sidewalks, shopping and schools within walking distance, commutes of less than 45 minutes, and nearby public transportation.

Overall, 55 percent of Americans expressed a preference for community B, the smart growth community. This community appealed to 61 percent of those who were thinking of buying a house within the next three years. Commuting time had a significant influence on respondents' preferences. About a third of the respondents said they would choose the smart growth design if commutes were comparable, while another quarter preferred such a design if it also meant being closer to work.

Bolstering these results, a national consumer survey by the global public relations company Porter Novelli found that 59 percent of U.S. adults now "support the

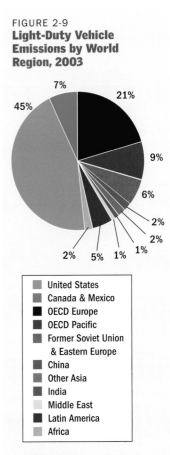

FIGURE 2-9
Light-Duty Vehicle Emissions by World Region, 2003

- United States
- Canada & Mexico
- OECD Europe
- OECD Pacific
- Former Soviet Union & Eastern Europe
- China
- Other Asia
- India
- Middle East
- Latin America
- Africa

SOURCE: J. DeCicco and F. Fung. *Global Warming on the Road: The Climate Impact of America's Automobiles.* Washington, D.C.: Environmental Defense, 2006.

FIGURE 2-10
Attractions of a Smart Growth Community*

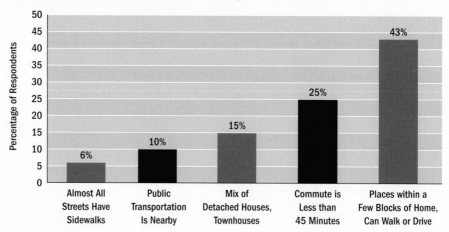

* For those choosing the smart growth community. The question was "Look at the community you selected and choose the ONE most appealing characteristic of that community for you."
SOURCE: Belden Russonello & Stewart. *National Survey on Communities*. Washington, D.C.: National Association of Realtors and Smart Growth America, October 2004, www.brspoll.com/Reports/Smart%20Growth.pdf.

development" of compact communities (defined in detail in the survey itself). Half would now be interested in living in a compact community (Handy et al. in press). Levels of support were high among all groups except rural residents. More impressive than the absolute levels of support was the increase in support between survey years 2003 and 2005, a statistically significant 15 percent. The smart growth community was described identically and questions were phrased identically in the two survey years.[4] The authors attribute the increase to media coverage of sprawl and its impacts.

When it comes to housing demand, demographics is destiny. As baby boomers become empty nesters and retirees, they are exhibiting a preference for compact, walkable neighborhoods. So are single adults and married couples without children. These trends likely will accelerate, because the baby boom generation represents America's largest generational cohort. By 2020, the number of individuals turning 65 years of age will skyrocket to more than 4 million per year. Between 2007 and 2050, the share of the U.S. population older than 65 years of age will grow from 12.8 to 20.7 percent (Figure 2-11).

Growth in households without children (including one-person households) also will rise dramatically. From 2000 to 2025, households without children will account for 88 percent of total growth in households. Thirty-four percent will be one-person households. By 2025, only 28 percent of households will have children (Nelson 2006).

Beyond demographics, cultural changes also are at work in the housing market, particularly among Generation Xers who are now fully engaged in homebuying. According to research by Yankelovich, a leading marketing services consultancy, Gen Xers value face-to-face relationships with neighbors and neighborhood charac-

FIGURE 2-11
U.S. Population Pyramids for 2000 and 2050

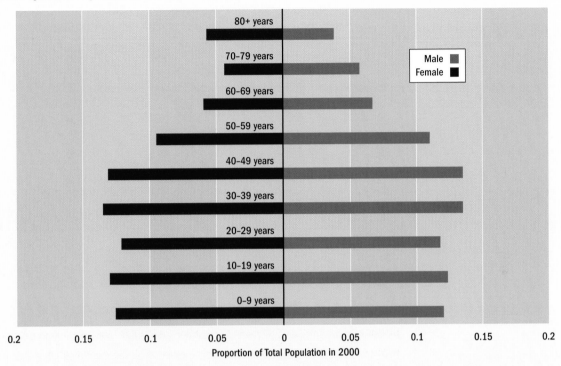

Proportion of Total Population in 2000

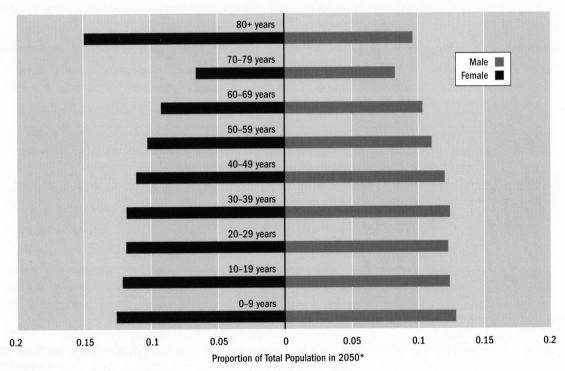

Proportion of Total Population in 2050*

*Estimated.
SOURCE: U.S. Census Bureau. "U.S. Interim Projections by Age, Sex, Race, and Hispanic Origin."
Washington, D.C., 2004, www.census.gov/ipc/www/usinterimproj/.

FIGURE 2-12
2003 Housing Supply versus 2025 Housing Demand

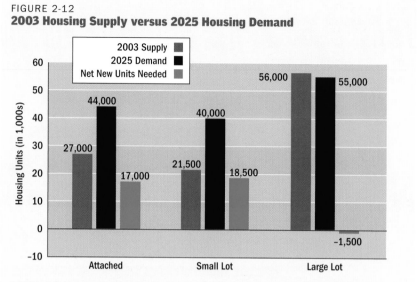

SOURCE: A.C. Nelson. "Leadership in a New Era." *Journal of the American Planning Association.* Vol. 72, Issue 4, 2006, pp. 393–407.

teristics such as sidewalks and nearby recreational facilities. Yankelovich president J. Walker Smith discussed these findings at the June 2004 NAHB conference, noting that "planned communities that foster togetherness and neighborhood life will resonate with this generation" (NAHB 2004). Another industry analyst, Brent Harrington of DMB Associates, reports that Gen Xers are looking for more diverse and compact communities characterized by smaller but better-designed homes as well as shopping and schools in more central locations, reflecting an "extreme disillusionment with the bland, vanilla suburbs" (Anderson 2004).

Nelson projects that by 2025, the demand for attached and small-lot housing will exceed the current supply by 35 million units (71 percent), while the demand for large-lot housing will fall short of the current supply (see Figure 2-12). If he is correct, the United States already has too much of the "big stuff."

These trends are visible now: Downtown and in-town housing tops the list of hot markets each year in the Urban Land Institute's *Emerging Trends in Real Estate* (ULI and PricewaterhouseCoopers 2005, 2006, 2007). In addition, new urban and smart growth communities are in such high demand that they not only command a price premium at the point of purchase, but also hold their premium values over time (Eppli and Tu 1999, 2007; Leinberger 2007).

In addition to changing demographics, lifestyle, and housing preferences, changes in travel behavior and needs are being carefully watched. The nonprofit association AARP has made transportation and quality-of-life matters one of its top policy issues to tackle in the next decade. The AARP is concerned because roughly one in five people over 65 years of age does not drive at all, and more than half drive only occasionally (STPP 2004). Older adults who lose their ability to drive remain at home most days, losing much of their independence and the ability to access essential services.

AARP surveys suggest that most people want to "age in place" (Bayer and Harper 2000; Mathew Greenwald & Associates 2003—see Figure 2-13). In most areas where older Americans are aging in place, alternatives to the automobile are limited. In fact, according to a national poll, only 45 percent of Americans over 65 live in close proximity to public transportation (Mathew Greenwald & Associates 2003).

A majority of respondents to another poll said that they would prefer to walk more throughout the day rather than drive everywhere (see Figure 2-14). The elderly are particularly inclined to walk when conditions are right (Mathew Greenwald & Associates 2003). These results, plus the high cost of special transportation services, are reasons for making sure older people can easily access transit and live in safe, walkable communities.

FIGURE 2-13
Americans Want to Age in Place*

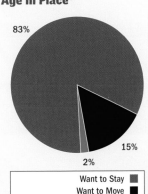

83%

15%

2%

| Want to Stay ■ |
| Want to Move ■ |
| Don't Know or Refuse to Answer ■ |

* Agreement with the statement: "What I would really like to do is stay in my current residence for as long as possible" among those 45 years of age and older.
SOURCE: A. Bayer and L. Harper. *Fixing to Stay: a National Survey of Housing and Home Modification Issues.* Washington, D.C.: American Association of Retired Persons (AARP), May 2000.

FIGURE 2-14
Americans Want to Walk More*

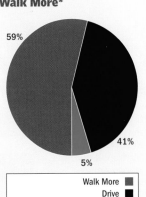

59%

41%

5%

| Walk More ■ |
| Drive ■ |
| Don't Know or Refuse to Answer ■ |

*The question was: "Please tell me which of the following statements describe you more: A) If it were possible, I would like to walk more throughout the day either to get to specific places or for exercise, or B) I prefer to drive my car wherever I go."
SOURCE: Belden Russonello & Stewart. *Americans' Attitudes Toward Walking and Creating Better Walking Communities.* Washington, D.C.: Surface Transportation Policy Project, April 2003, www.transact.org/ library/reports_pdfs/pedpoll.pdf.

Changing Public Priorities

The urban planning field has been overtaken by movements that promote alternatives to conventional auto-oriented sprawl. Planners now advocate urban villages, neotraditional neighborhoods, transit-oriented developments (TODs), mixed-use activity centers, jobs/housing balance, context-sensitive highway designs, and traffic calming.

Alternative models of land development are everywhere. A 2003 listing shows 647 new urbanist developments in some state of planning or construction (New Urban News 2003), even though the new urbanist movement began only 12 years earlier. *Transit-Oriented Development in the United States: Experiences, Challenges, and Prospects* identifies 117 TODs on the ground or substantially developed as of late 2002 (Cervero et al. 2004). The first TOD guidelines were issued about a decade earlier. In 2004, there were more than 100 lifestyle centers (open-air shopping centers fashioned after main streets) in the United States, a 35 percent increase from 2000 (Robaton 2005). The U.S. Green Building Council's new rating and certification system for green development, Leadership in Energy and Environmental Design for Neighborhood Development (LEED-ND), generated 370 applications from land developers, many more than expected by the program sponsors.

This series of photographs illustrates alternative models of land development. Top left: Southern Village, a new urbanist village in North Carolina; top right: transit-oriented development in Bethesda, Maryland; middle left: CityPlace, a lifestyle center in West Palm Beach, Florida; middle right: redevelopment/infill (so-called "refill") in St. Paul, Minnesota; bottom left: green development in Prairie Crossing, Illinois; bottom right: Stapleton, a "new town in town" in Denver, Colorado.

Recognizing the unsustainable growth in driving, the American Association of State Highway and Transportation Officials, representing state departments of transportation, recently called for VMT growth through 2055 to be cut by half (AASHTO 2007). Such unlikely allies as the Institute of Transportation Engineers and the Congress for the New Urbanism have teamed up to develop new context-sensitive street standards for walkable communities (see the illustration on the facing page). At the local level, several hundred traffic-calming programs have been created in the past decade; the term traffic calming was not even used in the United States until the mid-1990s (Ewing, Brown, and Hoyt 2005).

Loss of farmlands and natural areas—and the public benefits they provide—are behind a number of planning initiatives. The Maryland Smart Growth Program was motivated primarily by the rate at which the urban footprint was expanding into

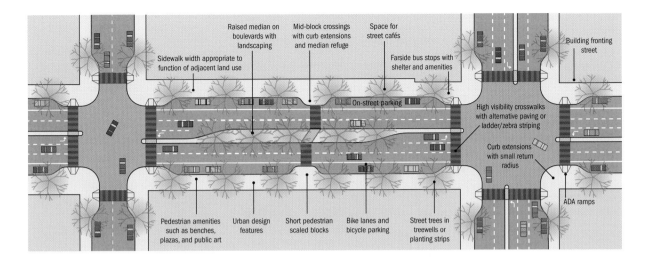

Elements of a context-sensitive urban highway.

CREDIT: Kimley-Horn and Associates et al. "Context Sensitive Solutions in Designing Major Urban Thoroughfares for Walkable Communities-Proposed Recommended Practice." Washington, D.C.: Institute of Transportation Engineers, 2006, www.ite.org/bookstore/RP036.pdf.

resource areas (see Figure 2-15). Nationally, most urbanized areas have seen their land area expand much faster than their population (Fulton et al. 2001).

Fiscal constraints at the state and local levels are prompting governments to look for less expensive ways to meet infrastructure and service needs. Compact growth is less expensive to serve than sprawl, by an estimated 11 percent nationally for basic infrastructure (Burchell et al. 2002). The per capita costs of most services decline with density and rise as the spatial extent of urbanized land area increases (Carruthers and Ulfarsson 2003). The Envision Utah scenario planning process resulted in the selection of a compact growth plan that will save the region about $4.5 billion (17 percent) in infrastructure spending compared with a continuation of sprawling development (Envision Utah 2000). A major impetus for growth management is the desire to hold down public service costs.

The U.S. obesity epidemic and associated mortality, morbidity, and health care costs have added to the momentum for walkable communities. Circa 2000, a new

FIGURE 2-15
Parcel Development in Maryland, 1900 to 1960 (left) and 1961 to 1997 (right)

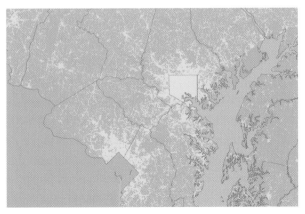
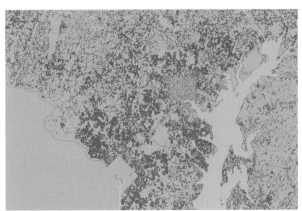

SOURCE: Maryland Department of Planning.

FIGURE 2-16
National Opinion Poll Results

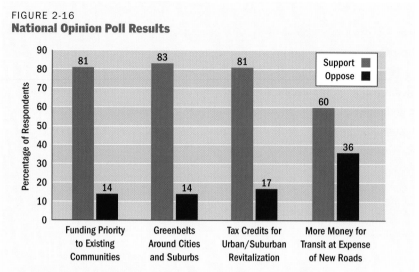

SOURCE: Belden Russonello & Stewart. *National Survey on Growth and Land Development.* Washington, D.C.: Smart Growth America, September 2000, www.smartgrowthamerica.org/poll.pdf.

collaboration between urban planning and public health advocates, began under the banner of active living. Out of this came the Active Living by Design Program of the Robert Wood Johnson Foundation, the Active Community Environments initiative of the Centers for Disease Control and Prevention (CDC), numerous Safe Routes to School programs, and dozens of Mayors' Healthy City initiatives. A recent literature review found that 17 of 20 studies, all dating from 2002 or later, had established statistically significant links between some aspect of the built environment and the risk of obesity (Papas et al. 2007).

FIGURE 2-17
State and Local Ballot Measures Passed, 2000 Election

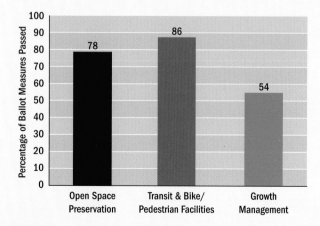

SOURCE: P. Myers and R. Puentes. "Growth at the Ballot Box: Electing the Shape of Communities in November 2000." Washington, D.C.: Brookings Center on Urban and Metropolitan Policy, 2001.

Public support for smart growth policies appears to be strong and growing (Myers 1999; Myers and Puentes 2001; American Planning Association 2002; Kirby and Hollander 2005). In a 2000 national survey, a majority of respondents favored specific policies under the general heading of smart growth (see Figure 2-16). In the 2000 election, 553 state or local ballot initiatives in 38 states focused on "issues of planning or smart growth" and high percentages passed (see Figure 2-17). In 2006, voters approved 70 percent of ballot measures supporting public transit and rejected three out of four ballot initiatives on "regulatory takings" that could have significantly crimped planning efforts (Goldberg 2007).

According to *The 2007 Growth and Transportation Survey*, sponsored by the National Association of Realtors and Smart Growth America, 75 percent of Americans believe that being smarter about development and improving public transportation is a better long-term solution for reducing traffic congestion than building new roads. Nearly half of those surveyed said improving public transit would be most effective in reducing congestion, and another 26 percent said that developing communities that reduce the need to drive would be most effective. Only one in five said building new roads is the best answer to congestion. Asked to rate potential ways to combat climate change, nearly nine in ten said they believe that new communities should be built so people can walk more and drive less; that cars, homes, and buildings should be required to be more energy efficient; and that public transportation should be improved and made more available.

The Effect of Compact Development on VMT and CO_2 Emissions

California's landmark Global Warming Solutions Act of 2006 (AB 32) calls for restoring California's GHG emissions to 1990 levels by 2020, a 25 percent reduction relative to current emissions (see Figure 2-18). The act also requires the Air Resources Board (ARB) to identify a list of "discrete early action greenhouse gas reduction measures." Once on the list, these measures are to be developed into regulatory proposals, adopted by the ARB, and made enforceable by January 1, 2010.

Pursuant to the act, the ARB released *Proposed Early Actions to Mitigate Climate Change in California* (ARB 2007). At the same time, the California Environmental

FIGURE 2-18
California's Projected GHG Emissions and Targets

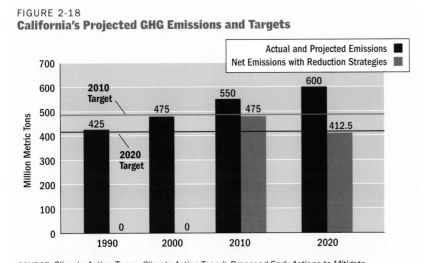

SOURCE: Climate Action Team. *Climate Action Team's Proposed Early Actions to Mitigate Climate Change in California—Draft for Public Review.* Sacramento: California Department of Environmental Quality, April 30, 2007, www.climatechange.ca.gov/climate_action_team/reports/2007-04-20_CAT_REPORT.PDF.

Protection Agency's Climate Action Team recommended 21 additional actions for which GHG emission reductions have been quantified (Climate Action Team 2007). Of all the actions on the original list, those expected to achieve the second-largest reduction (originally 18 million metric tons per year CO_2 equivalent by 2020, since lowered to 10 million metric tons) fell under the heading of "smart land use and intelligent transportation." No details were provided as to what this category of actions might entail, or how the targeted reduction might be achieved.

How much could a transition from sprawl to compact development reasonably reduce U.S. transport CO_2 levels relative to current trends? The answer is the product of the following six factors:

- market share of compact development;
- reduction in VMT per capita with compact development;
- increment of new development or redevelopment relative to the base;
- proportion of weighted VMT within urban areas;
- ratio of CO_2 to VMT reduction for urban travel; and
- proportion of transport CO_2 due to motor vehicle travel.

Each factor is discussed and quantified in turn below.

Market Share of Compact Development

The first factor that will determine CO_2 reduction with compact development is market penetration during the forecast period, 2007 to 2050. The market share of compact development in the United States is growing but probably still small (Sobel 2006). No comprehensive inventory exists.

Two factors, however, suggest that whatever the market share is today, it will increase dramatically during the forecast period. One factor is the current undersupply of compact development relative to demand (see "Changing Consumer Demand" above). "A review of existing studies on consumer demand for smart growth products as well as consumer surveys . . . consistently find that at least one third of the consumer real estate market prefers smart growth development" (Logan 2007). The other factor is changing demographics (also discussed in "Changing Consumer Demand"). "The aging of the baby boomers is an inexorable force likely to increase the number of households desiring denser residential environments" (Myers and Gearin 2001). The question is, how fast will the supply of compact development respond to this demand?

Over the long run, it is reasonable to assume that what is supplied by the development industry will roughly equal what is demanded by the market, with a time lag. This will be true, provided government policies allow and encourage it. If a third of the market currently wants the density, diversity, and design of smart growth, and almost another third wants the destination accessibility of smart growth (see "Changing Consumer Demand"), the market will be inclined to provide these product types.

Changing demographics and lifestyles will increase these proportions. The policy recommendations presented in Chapter 9 will facilitate market changes as well as

make a contribution of their own to growing market shares. We will assume that between now and 2050, the *lower bound on the proportion of compact development is
six-tenths and the upper bound is nine-tenths*, consistent with demographic trends
and the current undersupply. As discussed below in "Increment of New Development
or Redevelopment Relative to the Base," this still leaves more than 40 percent of
development as it is today, largely sprawling and auto oriented.

Reduction in VMT per Capita with Compact Development

Based on the urban planning literature reviewed in this publication, it appears that
compact development has the potential to reduce VMT per capita by anywhere from
20 to 40 percent relative to sprawl. The actual reduction in VMT per capita will depend
on two factors: how bad trend development patterns are in terms of the so-called "five
Ds" (density, diversity, design, destination accessibility, and distance to transit); and
how good alternative growth patterns are in terms of these same five Ds. The five Ds,
which are described in Chapter 4, are qualities of the urban environment that urban
planners and developers can affect, which in turn affect travel choices.

Considering all the evidence presented in Chapter 4, it is reasonable to assume
*an average reduction in VMT per capita with compact development relative to sprawl
of three-tenths*. This fraction applies to each increment of development or redevelopment but does not affect base development.

Increment of New Development or Redevelopment Relative to the Base

The cumulative effect of compact development also depends on how much new
development or redevelopment occurs relative to a region's existing development
pattern. The amount of new development and redevelopment depends, in turn, on the
time horizon and the area's growth rate. The longer the time horizon and the faster the
rate of development or redevelopment, the greater will be the regionwide percentage
change in VMT per capita.

A recent article in the *Journal of the American Planning Association* began with
the following words: "More than half of the built environment of the United States we
will see in 2025 did not exist in 2000, giving planners an unprecedented opportunity
to reshape the landscape" (Nelson 2006). Between 2005 and 2050, the number of
residential units of all types may grow from 124 million to 176 million, or a total of 52
million.[5] In addition, roughly 6 percent of the housing stock of the previous decade is
replaced each decade,[6] with about two-thirds being rebuilt on site and another third
consisting of new units built elsewhere because of land use conversions (such as a
strip mall replacing houses, with the displaced homes rebuilt elsewhere).[7] Counting
compounding effects, perhaps 37 million homes will need to be replaced entirely
through conversion processes between 2005 and 2050. The number of new plus
replaced residential units may reach 89 million units between 2005 and 2050, or
more than 70 percent of the stock that existed in 2005.

Even more dramatic is the construction of nonresidential space, largely because, on average, about 20 percent of such space turns over each decade.[8] Nonresidential space includes retail, office, industrial, government, and other structures. From 2005 to 2050, nonresidential space will expand from about 100 billion square feet[9] to about 160 billion square feet, or by 60 billion square feet.[10] In addition, about 130 billion square feet will be rebuilt; some structures will be rebuilt two or more times because their useful life is less than 20 years. Perhaps a total of 190 billion square feet of nonresidential space will be constructed between 2005 and 2050, or nearly twice the volume of space that existed in 2005.

The magnitude of development ahead suggests there may be unprecedented opportunities to recast the built environment in ways that reduce a variety of emissions, especially CO_2. Furthermore, as noted above in "Changing Consumer Demand," a very large share of this new development will be driven by emerging market forces that desire compact development, not because it reduces CO_2 emissions but rather because it is responsive to changing demographics and lifestyles.

Much of the built environment existing in 2005 will remain, of course, including most existing residential stock, institutional buildings, and high-rise structures. Nonetheless, we may assume that easily *two-thirds of development on the ground in 2050* will be developed or redeveloped between now and then.

Proportion of Weighted VMT within Urban Areas

A shift to compact development will affect *urban* VMT, not *rural* VMT. Put another way, compact development policies will affect travel within cities, not travel between cities. Two-thirds of the total VMT in the United States currently is urban. Heavy vehicles produce about four times more CO_2 emissions per mile than light vehicles, and heavy vehicles represent a higher proportion of rural VMT. Weighting VMT accordingly, 62 percent of the nation's VMT is presently urban. This estimate includes cars, trucks, and buses.

The proportion of urban VMT is growing as the United States becomes ever more urbanized. Projecting current trends out to 2050, about *four-fifths of the weighted VMT in 2050 will be urban*.

Ratio of CO_2 to VMT Reduction

Compact development may not reduce CO_2 emissions by exactly the same proportion as VMT. The reasons, discussed in Chapter 3, are the CO_2 penalties associated with cold starts and lower operating speeds in compact areas. For the project-level simulations presented in Chapter 4, the ratio of CO_2 to VMT reduction for compact development projects is 0.96. The "Synthesis" section in Chapter 3 indicates that a 30 percent reduction in VMT would be expected to produce a 28 percent reduction in CO_2. This figure factors in CO_2 penalties associated with cold starts and reduced vehicle operating speeds. Thus the ratio of CO_2 to VMT reduction would be around 0.93.

Given these two pieces of evidence, we will conservatively assume a *CO_2 reduction equal to nine-tenths of the VMT reduction*. This is the ratio of CO_2 reduction to VMT reduction for one scenario versus another in the target year, 2050. The effects of increased vehicle efficiency and fuel switching already have been incorporated into both scenarios. As shown in Figures 3-7 and 3-8, the ratio of CO_2 to VMT will decline dramatically under all scenarios. However, in the projections of this section, compact development in 2050 is being compared to trend development in 2050, not to development in the base year, 2007.

Proportion of Transportation CO_2 from Motor Vehicles

Motor vehicles (automobiles, light- and heavy-duty trucks, and buses) contributed 79 percent of transportation CO_2 emissions in 2005 (EPA 2007, Table 3-7). This percentage is increasing over time, largely because of the growth of heavy-vehicle traffic. We will assume that *motor vehicles contribute four-fifths of transportation CO_2 emissions*, with the balance coming from aircraft, ships, and trains.

Net CO_2 Reduction in Comparison to Other Actions

Projecting out to 2050, the net CO_2 reduction is estimated to be as follows:

6/10 to 9/10 (market share of compact development)

x

3/10 (reduction in VMT per capita with compact development)

x

2/3 (increment of new development or redevelopment relative to base)

x

4/5 (proportion of weighted VMT within urban areas)

x

9/10 (ratio of CO_2 to VMT reduction)

x

4/5 (proportion of transportation CO_2 from motor vehicles).

The first four terms represent the reduction in U.S. VMT with compact development as compared to continuing sprawl, while the last two terms translate the VMT reduction into a CO_2 reduction. Doing the math, compact development has the potential to reduce total U.S. VMT by 10 to 14 percent and total U.S. transportation CO_2 emissions by 7 to 10 percent.

These reductions should be put into perspective. The long-run elasticity of VMT with respect to fuel price is around –0.3 (see the review by Victoria Transport Policy Institute 2007 and meta-analysis by Graham and Glaister 2002). The VMT savings with compact development would be equivalent to a national gasoline tax hike or carbon tax of $1 or more per gallon at current prices. The CO_2 savings with compact development through 2030 would be at least as large as a 32-mile-per-gallon (mpg) corporate average fuel economy (CAFE) standard (2020 combined mpg for cars and light trucks), or one-half of the savings expected from the recently adopted 35-mpg CAFE standard. The CO_2 savings with compact development would be slightly less than if one-quarter of the projected gasoline use were replaced with petroleum diesel, biodiesel, or electricity (a replacement rate viewed as "reasonable" within a 25-year time frame, according to Pickrell 2003).

The 7 to 10 percent reduction is an end-year estimate. During the 43-year period, the cumulative drop in CO_2 emissions would be about half this amount. Yet, the very phenomenon that limits the short- and medium-term impacts of compact development—the long-lived nature of buildings and infrastructure—makes the reduction essentially permanent and compoundable. The next 50 years of compact development would build on the base reduction from the first 50 years, and so on into the future. More immediate strategies, such as gas tax increases, do not have the same degree of permanence.

The 7 to 10 percent reduction only relates to the transportation sector. Compact development, however, would reduce CO_2 emissions for other sectors as well. An order-of-magnitude estimate for the residential sector is provided in Chapter 7. Controlling for socioeconomic and climatic variables, an equivalent household uses 20 percent less primary energy for space heating and cooling in a compact area than in a sprawling one. This savings is primarily due to less exterior wall area in attached and multifamily housing, and less floor area consumed at higher densities.

The 7 to 10 percent reduction does not consider the impact of intelligent transportation systems, congestion pricing, pay-as-you-drive insurance, or other complementary strategies. These might be used to better manage existing roads and public transportation.

The VMT/CO_2/Climate Connection

A paradigm shift can occur very rapidly in the physical sciences, as the dominant scientific opinion changes in response to overwhelming evidence. Since the early 1990s, the scientific community has come to agree on the reality of climate change, on the contribution of human activity to climate change, and on the catastrophic consequences if current trends continue. Social revolutions are slower than scientific revolutions. Public opinion about global warming is changing more slowly than scientific opinion, and political action is slower still. But they, too, are changing.

The issue of climate change has risen to prominence worldwide in only 15 years, as the following timeline illustrates:

- **June 1992:** The United Nations Framework Convention on Climate Change (UNFCCC), opened for signatures at the "Earth Summit" in Rio de Janeiro, calls for stabilizing GHG concentrations in the atmosphere. The United States is a signatory.
- **December 1997:** The Kyoto Protocol to the UNFCCC establishes a set of quantified GHG emission targets for developed countries. The U.S. does not ratify the protocol.
- **June 2002:** The U.S. government acknowledges for the first time that human activity is contributing to global warming, in a report issued by the U.S. Environmental Protection Agency (EPA) over the objections of the White House.
- **September 2006:** California becomes the first state to adopt legislation—the Global Warming Solutions Act of 2006 (AB 32)—requiring regulations and market actions to reduce the state's GHG emissions to 1990 levels by 2020.
- **January 2007:** Major U.S. corporations and environmental groups, banding together as the U.S. Climate Action Partnership, call for a 10 to 30 percent reduction in CO_2 emissions within 30 years (USCAP 2007).

HARD SCIENCE

The global concern about climate change is supported by hard science. The Fourth Assessment Report of the U.N. Intergovernmental Panel on Climate Change concludes that: "Global atmospheric concentrations of carbon dioxide, methane and nitrous oxide have increased markedly as a result of human activities since 1750 and now far exceed preindustrial values determined from ice cores spanning many thousands of years."

The pace has accelerated recently:

- **April 2007:** The U.S. Supreme Court rules that the EPA has the authority to regulate GHG emissions, and has the duty to do so unless it can provide a scientific basis for not acting.
- **May 2007:** Tulsa, Oklahoma, becomes the 500th city to sign the U.S. Mayors Climate Protection Agreement to reduce greenhouse gas emissions (U.S. Conference of Mayors 2007).
- **June 2007:** In the largest international public opinion survey ever taken, most of the world identifies environmental degradation as the greatest danger—above nuclear weapons, AIDS, and ethnic hatred (Pew Research Center 2007). Global warming, in particular, is viewed as a "very serious" problem (see Figure 3-1).
- **July 2007:** Congressional lawmakers introduce more than 125 bills, resolutions, and amendments specifically addressing global climate change and GHG emissions, compared with the 106 pieces of relevant legislation introduced during the entire two-year term of the previous Congress (Pew Center on Global Climate Change 2007).
- **August 2007:** California's attorney general settles his sprawl and carbon emissions case with San Bernardino County. The county agrees to amend its general plan and create a new GHG reduction plan within 30 months to outline opportunities and strategies—especially land use decisions—to reduce GHG emissions.
- **September 2007:** President George W. Bush hosts a climate change summit for top officials from the world's major economies to come to agreement on a framework for lowering global GHG emissions in the post-Kyoto era.
- **October 2007:** Former Vice President Al Gore and the United Nations Intergovernmental Panel on Climate Change win the 2007 Nobel Peace Prize for their work raising awareness of global warming.
- **November 2007:** Six states and one Canadian province form the Midwestern Regional Greenhouse Gas Reduction Accord, agreeing to establish a cap-and-trade system to meet GHG reduction targets.
- **December 2007:** America's Climate Security Act of 2007 (S.2191, also known as Lieberman-Warner) passes out of the Senate Committee on Environment and Public Works (U.S. Congress 2007b). At United Nations–led talks in Bali, nearly 200 nations agree to launch negotiations on a successor to the Kyoto protocol, after the United States drops its opposition to a proposal that would have rich nations doing more to help poor nations control GHG emissions. And the Energy Independence and Security Act of 2007 is passed by Congress and signed into law by President Bush (U.S. Congress 2007a). The law establishes corporate average fuel economy (CAFE) standards of at least 35 miles per gallon (mpg) by 2020 and renewable fuel requirements that would cut GHGs by 10 percent.

FIGURE 3-1
World Views on Global Warming: How Serious a Problem?

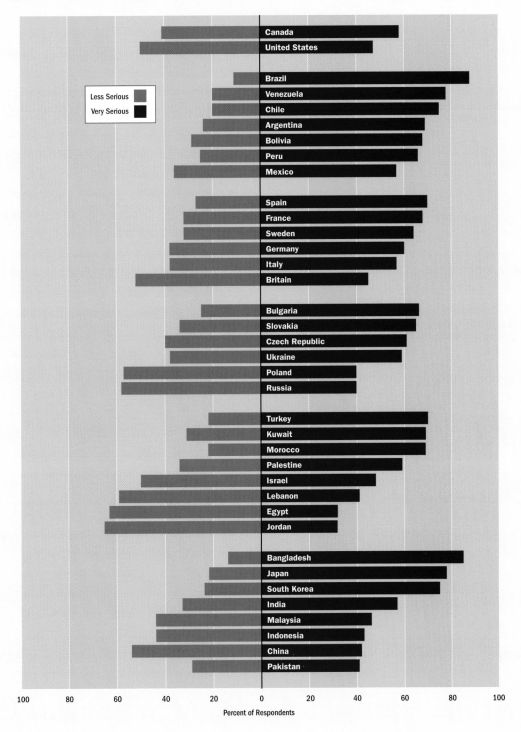

SOURCE: Pew Research Center. "47-Nation Pew Global Attitudes Survey." Global Attitudes Project, Washington, D.C., June 27, 2007, http://pewglobal.org/reports/pdf/256.pdf.

The Science of Climate Change

The global concern about climate change is supported by hard science (Greenough et al. 2001; Barnett and Adger 2003; Hegerl et al. 2007; IPCC 2007a). The Fourth Assessment Report of the U.N. Intergovernmental Panel on Climate Change (2007a, p. 2) concludes that: "Global atmospheric concentrations of carbon dioxide, methane and nitrous oxide have increased markedly as a result of human activities since 1750 and now far exceed preindustrial values determined from ice cores spanning many thousands of years." Greenhouse gas concentrations have risen from preindustrial levels of approximately 280 parts per million (ppm) CO_2 equivalent (CO_2e) to 430 ppm CO_2e (Stern 2007).[1] Rather than slowing down, the growth of atmospheric CO_2 seems to be speeding up as a result of the expanding global economy, the increasing carbon intensity of the global economy, and a decline in the efficiency of CO_2 sinks on land and oceans (Canadell et al. 2007). All the concern about GHG emissions is still just talk across most of the globe.

The result is climate change. "Warming of the climate system is unequivocal, as is now evident from observations of increases in global average air and ocean temperatures, widespread melting of snow and ice, and rising global mean sea level" (IPCC 2007a, p. 5). Eleven of the last 12 years are among the 12 warmest globally since the instrumental record began in 1850 (IPCC 2007a, p. 5).[2] Long-term changes have been observed in Arctic temperatures and ice formations, ocean salinity, droughts, heavy precipitation, heat waves, and tropical cyclone intensity (Höppe and Pielke 2006). Some of the changes, such as the shrinking of the Artic sea ice and the prolonged drought in East Africa, are quite remote from the United States. Others hit closer to home, including the increased intensity of hurricanes in the North Atlantic, the higher frequency of large wildfires in the Western United States, and the higher frequency of extreme rainstorms or snowstorms in various part of the country (Trenberth 2005; Emanuel 2005; Höppe and Pielke 2006; Westerling et al. 2006; Madsen and Figdor 2007).

With current trends, the atmospheric concentration of CO_2e is expected to rise from 430 ppm to 630 ppm by 2050. Even if GHG emissions were held at year 2000 levels, the planet would warm by 1°C over the next 100 years. Under a variety of scenarios with differing assumptions about growth, technology, and climate feedback, the likely range of warming by 2100 is between 1.1°C and 6.4°C, with a best estimate of 1.8°C to 4.0°C (IPCC 2007a, p. 12).

With a 2°C increase in global average temperature, all coral reefs are at risk of being bleached. At 3°C, more than one-third of all species will be at risk of eventual

FIGURE 3-2

Atmospheric Concentration of CO$_2$ over the Past 10,000 Years

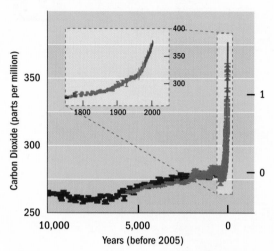

SOURCE: Intergovernmental Panel on Climate Change (IPCC). *Climate Change 2007: The Physical Science Basis, Summary for Policymakers.* Working Group I contribution of the Intergovernmental Panel on Climate Change: Fourth Assessment Report, 2007a, www.ipcc.ch/, p. 3.

FIGURE 3-3
Correlation between Sea Surface Temperature and Intensity of Hurricanes in the North Atlantic

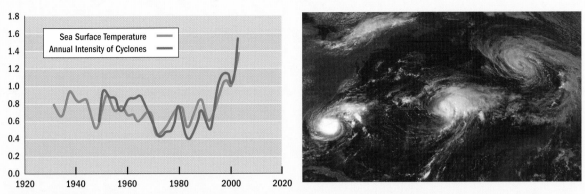

SOURCE: K. Emanuel. "Increasing Destructiveness of Tropical Cyclones over the Past 30 Years." *Nature*, Vol. 436, 2005, pp. 686–688.

FIGURE 3-4
Correlation between Spring/Summer Temperatures and Fire Frequency in the Western United States

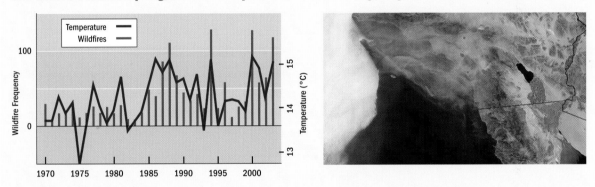

SOURCE: A.L. Westerling, H. G. Hidalgo, D. R. Cayan, and T. W. Swetnam. "Warming and Earlier Spring Increase Western U.S. Forest Wildfire Activity." *Science*, Vol. 313, August 18, 2006, pp. 940–943, http://www.sciencemag.org/cgi/rapidpdf/1128834.pdf.

FIGURE 3-5
Increase in Frequency of Extreme Rainstorms and Snowstorms in the United States

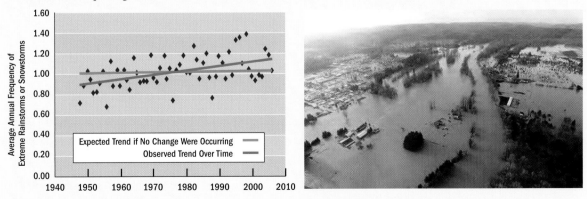

SOURCE: T. Madsen and E. Figdor. *When It Rains, It Pours: Global Warming and the Rising Frequency of Extreme Precipitation in the United States.* Boston: Environment America Research & Policy Center, December 2007, http://www.environmentamerica.org/uploads/oy/ws/oywshWAwZy-EXPsabQKd4A/When-It-Rains-It-Pours—US—WEB.pdf.

FIGURE 3-6

Global Average Surface Temperature Warming under Different Scenarios

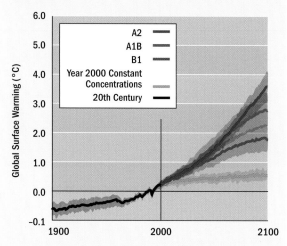

SOURCE: Intergovernmental Panel on Climate Change (IPCC). *Climate Change 2007: The Physical Science Basis, Summary for Policymakers.* Working Group I contribution of the Intergovernmental Panel on Climate Change: Fourth Assessment Report, 2007a, www.ipcc.ch/, p. 14.

extinction. With an increase of 2°C to 3°C, coastal flooding threatens to harm or displace 70 million to 250 million people, respectively, and hundreds of millions of people face an increased risk of hunger. In this same range of temperature increase, the Amazon rainforest and Great Lakes ecosystems are at risk of collapse (Meinshausen 2006). From 1°C to 4°C, a partial deglaciation of the Greenland ice sheet will occur, with the sea level destined to increase by four to six meters over centuries to millennia (IPCC 2007b, p. 17; Schellnhuber et al. 2006).

To stabilize the atmospheric GHG concentration at 450 ppm CO$_2$e and hold the global average temperature increase to 2°C, global GHG emissions will have to peak around 2015 and decline by 30 to 40 percent below 1990 levels by 2050 (Höhne, Phylipsen, and Moltmann 2007; Meinshausen and den Elzen 2005). What this global reduction means for the United States depends on the GHG emissions of other countries. The emerging consensus is that industrialized countries will need to reduce their GHG emissions by 60 to 80 percent below 1990 levels by 2050 (European Commission 2007; Helme and Schmidt 2007; Höhne, Phylipsen, and Moltmann 2007; Meinshausen and den Elzen 2005; New England Governors/Eastern Canadian Premiers 2001; Schwarzenegger 2005).

The British government's review and the IPCC report show that the less we limit GHG emissions globally in the near term, the harder it will be to stabilize them at the target concentrations later (Stern 2007; IPCC 2007c, p.15). For each five years that the peak in global emissions is delayed beyond 2015, the annual rate by which emissions must decline will increase by an additional 1 percent (Meinshausen and den Elzen 2005). One percent per year is a substantial level of effort, comparable to the reduction the United Kingdom achieved nationally after it switched all of its coal-fired power plants to natural gas in the 1990s (Helme and Schmidt 2007).

Prospects for the U.S. Transportation Sector

The transportation sector is responsible for 33 percent of U.S. CO$_2$ emissions (28 percent of U.S. GHG emissions), and its emissions are projected to grow faster than the average rate for all sectors of the economy (EIA 2007, Table A18). Passenger vehicles (cars and light trucks) are responsible for more than three-fifths of transportation sector CO$_2$ emissions.

The GHG reduction "required" from U.S. transportation is a function of the level of reductions that can be expected in other sectors of the economy to meet the 60 to 80 percent reduction target. While certain sectors of the economy may be able to reduce GHG emissions more than others, it is unlikely that they will be able to compensate for limited progress in the transportation sector. As discussed below, current policy proposals on vehicle technology and fuels would leave passenger vehicle CO_2 emissions well above 1990 levels in 2030, significantly off course for meeting the 2050 target. Reduction in travel demand will therefore become an important element of climate policy.

VMT and CO_2 Projections

U.S. fuel economy has been flat for almost 15 years, as the upward spiral of car weight and power has offset more efficient technology (Schipper 2007). In December 2007, Congress passed the Energy Independence and Security Act of 2007 (U.S. Congress 2007a), which set a CAFE standard of at least 35 mpg by 2020, a 40 percent average increase over 2007's standards of 27.5 mpg for cars and 22.5 mpg for light trucks and SUVs. The new CAFE standards will result in a 34 percent increase in fleetwide fuel economy by 2030 (green line in Figure 3-7). The energy bill also sets renewable fuel requirements that would reduce lifecycle GHG emissions by 10 percent by 2025 (purple line in Figure 3-7). Absent growth in driving, these measures would reduce CO_2 emissions from cars and light trucks by 23 percent below 2005 levels.

However, even when these more stringent standards for vehicles and fuels fully penetrate the market, transportation-related emissions still would far exceed target levels for stabilizing the global climate because of the growth in the VMT. The U.S. Department of Energy's Energy Information Administration (EIA) forecasts a 48 percent increase in driving between 2005 and 2030 (orange line in Figure 3-7), outpacing the projected 23 percent increase in population (EIA 2008, Table A7).[3] The projected VMT

FIGURE 3-7
Projected Growth in CO_2 Emissions from Cars and Light Trucks

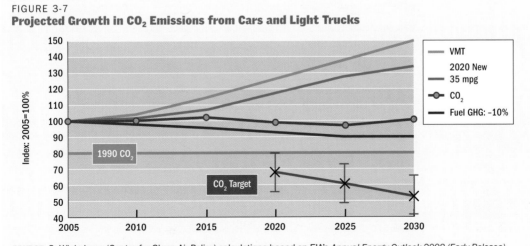

SOURCE: S. Winkelman (Center for Clean Air Policy) calculations based on EIA's *Annual Energy Outlook 2008 (Early Release)* and the Energy Independence and Security Act of 2007.

FIGURE 3-8
**Projected Growth in CO$_2$ Emissions from Cars and Light Trucks,
Assuming More Stringent Nationwide Vehicle and Fuel Standards***

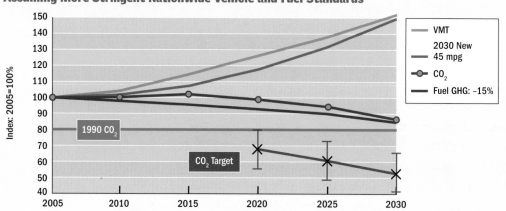

*Extrapolating trends from Figure 3-7 with new passenger vehicle fuel economy of 45 mpg in 2030 and low carbon fuel
standard of –15 percent in 2030.
SOURCE: See Figure 3-7.

increase represents a slowdown relative to historic VMT growth rates, but is within the
likely range for future VMT growth (Polzin 2006). The rapid increase in driving would
overwhelm both the increase in vehicle fuel economy and the lower carbon fuel content required by the energy act. Carbon dioxide emissions from cars and light trucks
would remain at 2005 levels (dark blue line in Figure 3-7), or 26 percent *above* 1990
levels in 2030 (light blue line in Figure 3-7). For climate stabilization, the United
States must bring the CO$_2$ level to 33 percent *below* 1990 levels by 2030 to be on
path to a CO$_2$ reduction of 60 to 80 percent by 2050 (red line in Figure 3-7).

If the fuel economy and fuel carbon content trends represented in Figure 3-7
were extended through to 2030, so that new vehicle fuel economy would increase
to 45 mpg (green line in Figure 3-8) and fuel carbon content would decrease to 15
percent below current levels (purple line), then 2030 CO$_2$ emissions (dark blue line)
would be reduced to 14 percent below 2005 levels, or 8 percent above 1990 levels.
Clearly, lowering transportation CO$_2$ emissions to 60 to 80 percent below 1990 levels
by 2050 would require even greater improvements in vehicles, fuels and, almost certainly, reductions in VMT per capita.

Other Influences on CO$_2$ Emissions

Carbon dioxide emissions are a function not only of VMT but also of numbers of vehicle trips (VT) and vehicle operating speeds. The number of vehicle trips is directly
related to the number of vehicle starts, while average vehicle operating speed is a
proxy for the entire driving cycle (starts, acceleration, cruising speed, deceleration, and
stops). Both affect vehicle operating efficiency and CO$_2$ emissions per vehicle mile.

Vehicle Trip Frequencies

Starting a vehicle when it is cold uses more energy and emits more CO_2 than does starting the vehicle after it has warmed up. For an average car in California, the California Air Resources Board EMFAC model shows cold start emissions of 213 grams CO_2 after a 12-hour soak.[4] To put this in context, an average passenger car emits 386 grams of CO_2 per mile when traveling at an average speed of 30 miles per hour.[5]

Still, any cold start penalty associated with compact development is likely to be small. From the EMFAC model, CO_2 emissions from *all* vehicle starts (cold, intermediate, and hot) account for just 3.3 percent of total annual passenger vehicle CO_2 emissions in California.[6] Moreover, while there has been some speculation in the literature that compact development could increase trip frequencies, the weight of evidence suggests otherwise. Overall trip rates appear to depend largely on household socioeconomics and demographics. Controlling for these influences, vehicle trip rates are lower in compact areas because some of a household's daily trips shift from the automobile to other modes (Ewing, DeAnna, and Li 1996; Ewing and Cervero 2001).

Vehicle Operating Speeds

Compact development policies could have secondary effects on CO_2 emissions by lowering (or raising) average vehicle speeds. Motor vehicles with internal combustion engines are most efficient at an average speed of about 45 miles per hour, with lower efficiency and higher CO_2 emission rates for speeds above and below this "sweet spot" (see Figure 3-9).

FIGURE 3-9
CO_2 Emission Rate versus Average Vehicle Speed*

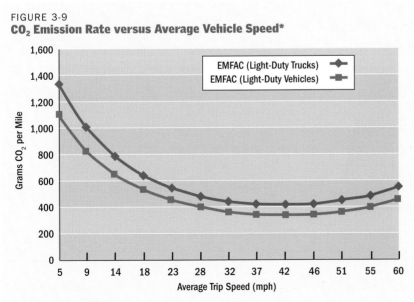

*Data include all model years in the range 1965 to 2007. The magnitude of the curve (not the shape) is a function of temperature and humidity assumptions, in this case 80°F and relative humidity of 50 percent.

SOURCE: Data from EMFAC 2007, V2.3 Nov. 1, 2006, provided by Jeff Long, California Air Resources Board, April 2007.

The data in Figure 3-9 come from the California Air Resources Board EMFAC model and represent average speed for vehicle trips that have been calibrated to reflect real-world driving behavior, including acceleration, starts, idling, and so forth.

Can we therefore conclude that it would be most efficient to design cities and roadways to maximize vehicle operating efficiency? No, because the efficiency gained by designing roads for high average speeds would be negated by an increase in miles traveled. Development can and would become ever more dispersed. The phenomena of induced traffic and induced development are discussed in Chapter 6. Moreover, the most efficient speed for today's cars is probably higher than the most efficient speed for tomorrow's cars. Emission rate curves for hybrid vehicles, in particular, look different, because these vehicles experience less of a low-speed emissions penalty.

Synthesis

With the transition from sprawl to compact development, both VMT and VT would be expected to decline, though by different percentages. The result would be a drop in CO_2 emissions per capita. Vehicle trips would decline as travelers shift from the automobile to alternative modes, and VMT would decline as mode shifts occur and as automobile trips get shorter. Vehicle operating speeds also might decline, and would

FIGURE 3-10
Close Relationship between VMT per Household and CO₂ Emissions in the Chicago Metropolitan Area

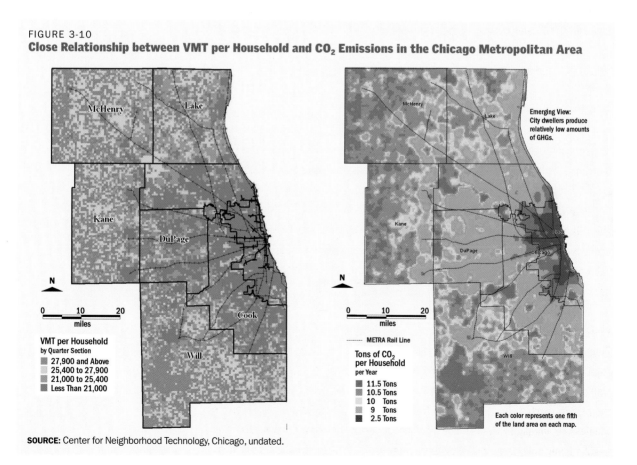

SOURCE: Center for Neighborhood Technology, Chicago, undated.

have an opposite effect on CO_2 emissions per capita. Compact development could mean lower cruising speeds and more stop-and-go driving, hence higher emissions per mile traveled (assuming conventional vehicle technology).

We can get a sense of the magnitude of these effects based on available information. All else being equal, there is a one-to-one relationship between VMT and CO_2 emissions; a 30 percent reduction in VMT will result in a 30 percent reduction in CO_2 emissions.

Let us posit that regional density will be 50 percent higher in 2050 under compact development than with current trends, a reasonable assumption given the data presented in "The Effect of Compact Development on VMT and CO_2 Emissions" in Chapter 2. Given an elasticity of peak-hour speed with respect to density of –0.15 (derived from Chapter 4, "Sprawl versus Congestion"), the average peak-hour vehicle operating speed might decline by 7.5 percent (–0.15 x 50 percent) with compact development. If so, average daily speed would decline by 3 percent, since the morning and afternoon peak periods represent two-fifths of average daily traffic in metropolitan areas. Such a decline would cause a 2 percent increase in CO_2 emissions per mile at typical urban speeds (see "Vehicle Operating Speeds" above). Therefore, if compact development reduced VMT by 30 percent, lowered average vehicle operating speed by 3 percent, and had no effect on vehicle trips, the net impact would be a 28 percent drop in CO_2 emissions.[7]

The next chapter addresses the extent to which compact urban development can reduce VMT and associated CO_2 emissions.

The Limits of Technology

There is a popular belief that new fuel sources will solve our energy security and GHG problems. This belief was reinforced by President George W. Bush's announcement of an Advanced Energy Initiative in his 2006 State of the Union address. The initiative focuses on the development and deployment of three technologies: plug-in hybrid electric vehicles (PHEVs), cellulosic ethanol fuel, and hydrogen fuel cell vehicles (FCVs) (National Economic Council 2006). As outlined below, each of these technologies holds substantial promise for long-term GHG emission reduction. Each, however, also faces technological and other challenges to widespread deployment in the near and medium terms.

Electricity

Plug-in hybrid electric vehicles (PHEVs) can be driven in both electric-only and hybrid (that is, with a fuel-powered engine) modes. They can be plugged into a standard wall outlet to recharge. PHEVs differ from standard hybrid-electric vehicles now on the market (such as Toyota's Prius) in that they rely to a much greater degree on electrical power. Ideally, PHEVs can use electricity for up to 40 miles of travel, relying on gasoline only on longer trips. PHEV technology could result in significant reductions in

FIGURE 3-11
Global Warming Emissions, PHEVs Compared to Other Mid-Sized Cars

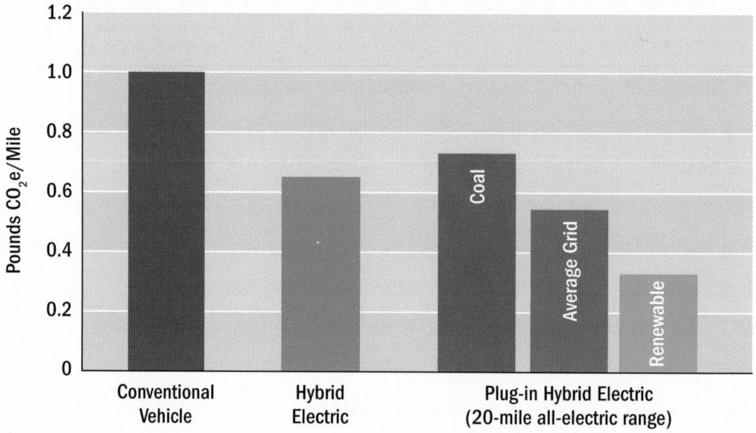

SOURCE: Natural Resources Defense Council (NRDC). *Climate Facts: The Next Generation of Hybrid Cars.* San Francisco, 2007, http://www.nrdc.org/energy/plugin.pdf.

FIGURE 3-12
**Emissions Ratios,
Electric/Gasoline**

GHGs	0.73
Total VOC	0.07
Total CO	0.02
Total NOx	0.69
Total PM10	1.18
Total SOx	2.25
Urban VOC	0.01
Urban CO	0.00
Urban NOx	0.10
Urban PM10	0.61
Urban SOx	0.19

SOURCE: M. Kintner-Meyer, K. Schneider, and R. Pratt. *Impacts Assessment of Plug-In Hybrid Vehicles on Electric Utilities and Regional U.S. Power Grids: Part 1: Technical Analysis.* Richland, Washington: Pacific Northwest National Laboratory, 2007, http://www.pnl.gov/energy/eed/etd/pdfs/phev_feasibility_analysis_combined.pdf.

overall GHG emissions compared to those of conventional gasoline-powered vehicles. The precise reduction depends on the power source used to generate the electricity for charging the vehicle's battery (see Figure 3-11).

A recent report from the U.S. Department of Energy (DOE) estimates that with the nation's current power generation mix, immediate deployment of PHEVs would reduce GHGs by as much as 27 percent. Moreover, much of the shift to PHEVs could be supported by existing unused power capacity in the U.S. power grid during off-peak hours. Without adding new generating facilities, this capacity could recharge as many as 158 million light-duty vehicles, about 73 percent of the nation's 2007 fleet (Kintner-Meyer, Schneider, and Pratt 2007).

As attractive as PHEV technology is, however, several environmental, economic, and engineering barriers stand in the way of its near-term deployment. First, while GHG emissions likely would decrease—as would emissions of volatile organic compounds (VOCs) and carbon monoxide (CO)—emissions of oxides of sulfur (SOx) and particulate matter (PM) would increase (see Figure 3-12). Although the calculated urban emissions of these pollutants are lower than for the status quo, the effects of SOx emissions (such as acid rain) are experienced at a multistate scale. Additionally, because SOx emissions are capped, power generators likely would need to install supplemental emission reduction technology or purchase offsetting emission credits.

More fundamental is the technological challenge of creating batteries capable of delivering the necessary electrical power at an affordable cost. Current estimates show as much as a $34,000 price premium for PHEV battery systems (U.S. Department of Energy 2007). The extra cost at the time of purchase would be offset by reduced energy costs associated with replacing liquid fuels with electricity, but these savings would justify a purchase price that is only a fraction of the estimated premium. The DOE has computed the acceptable price premium to be in the range of $1,700 to $3,400, considering regional price differences for electricity and gasoline, and fuel efficiencies of existing vehicles. Compared with a Toyota Prius, current electricity prices in California justify no added cost for PHEV technology assuming a gasoline price of $2.50/gallon, and only a $500 premium with a gas cost of $3.00/gallon (see Figure 3-13).

Because of these engineering/economic barriers, the DOE concludes that substantial commercial deployment of PHEV by 2016 (per the Advanced Energy Initiative) is highly uncertain (U.S. Department of Energy 2007).

Biofuels

Biofuels are produced from plant-based sugars through fermentation and distillation. The main attraction of biofuels is their ability to substitute for imported oil, a nonrenewable and politically volatile resource. Biofuels also have the potential to reduce emissions of GHGs and other pollutants.

Current commercial production of ethanol utilizes corn kernels or sugar cane as the fuel source. Plant cellulose from sources such as switchgrass and wood biomass also can serve as the basis for ethanol production and may have more potential to reduce GHG emissions. Cellulosic fuel is the focus of current energy planning efforts (see, for example, California Energy Commission 2007a; National Economic Council 2006).

A Union of Concerned Scientists study (2007) reports a range of GHG emissions for corn-based ethanol of +21 percent to –53 percent compared to gasoline emissions, depending on the energy source used in the ethanol production process. Emissions from cellulosic ethanol are estimated at 88 percent below those from gasoline (see Figure 3-14). A recent California Energy Commission study concludes that corn-based E85 reduces GHG emissions between 15 and 36 percent, compared to advanced reformulated gasoline (RFG3) (California Energy Commission 2007b). The same blend made from cellulosic sources reduces emissions by 60 to 72 percent.

Such estimates are not without their detractors. Researchers at Cornell University and the University of California at Berkeley have demonstrated that when the energy used to create fertilizers, pesticides, and farming and distilling equipment is included in the calculation, ethanol requires more energy from fossil fuels than it delivers itself. According to these researchers, the energy penalties associated with ethanol from corn, switchgrass, and wood biomass are 29, 45, and 57 percent, respectively (Pimentel and Patzek 2005).

FIGURE 3-13
Life Cycle Cost Analysis for a PHEV Compared with a Toyota Prius with 56 mpg Mixed City-Highway Fuel Economy*

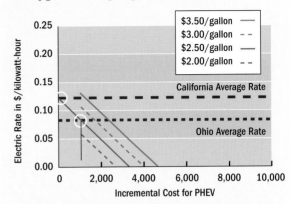

*Diagonal lines denote break-even costs.
SOURCE: M. Scott, M. Kintner-Meyer, D. Elliott, and W. Warwick. *Impacts Assessment of Plug-In Hybrid Vehicles on Electric Utilities and Regional U.S. Power Grids: Part 2: Economic Assessment.* Richland, Washington: Pacific Northwest National Laboratory, 2007, http://www.pnl.gov/energy/eed/etd/pdfs/phev_feasibility_analysis_combined.pdf.

FIGURE 3-14
Life Cycle Global Warming Pollution Relative to Gasoline

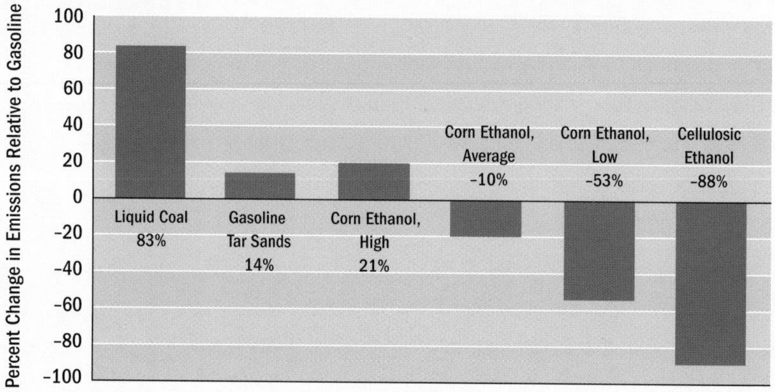

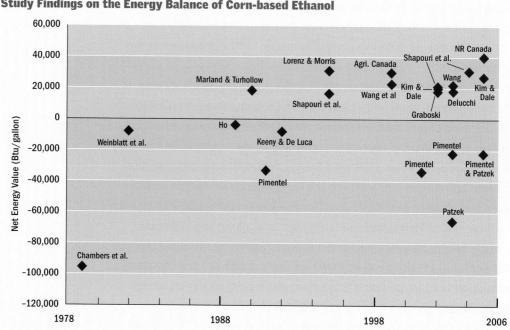

SOURCE: Union of Concerned Scientists. *Biofuels: An Important Part of a Low-Carbon Diet.* Cambridge, Massachusetts, 2007, http://www.ucsusa.org/assets/documents/clean_vehicles/ucs-biofuels-report.pdf.

The wide variation in study findings (see Figure 3-15) reflects the diversity of analytical approaches. The key differences across these studies are the models used and whether and how to account for the impacts of land use changes, co-products (using processing wastes as the basis for other products), and the manufacture of fertilizers and production and processing equipment (Farrell and Sperling 2007).

FIGURE 3-15
Study Findings on the Energy Balance of Corn-based Ethanol

SOURCE: Wang, M. "Energy and Greenhouse Gas Emissions Impacts of Fuel Ethanol." Presentation to the NGCA Renewable Fuels Forum, The National Press Club, August 23, 2005, http://www.transportation.anl.gov/pdfs/TA/349.pdf.

Biofuels also present technological challenges. Although it is technically feasible to power an appropriately designed vehicle with 100 percent ethanol, the ethanol fuels currently available in the United States are comprised of blends of ethanol and gasoline. One such fuel, E85—which is 85 percent ethanol and 15 percent gasoline—is commercially available in some parts of the country (primarily in the Midwest), but can only be burned in vehicles designed for that fuel. A 10 percent ethanol/90 percent gasoline mix known as E10, on the other hand, is available more broadly and can be burned in conventional vehicles.

Finally, the conversion of land from agricultural production to fuel feedstock raises market and humanitarian issues. Replacing 10 percent of the transportation petroleum consumed in the United States with biofuel (ethanol and biodiesel) is estimated to require converting 30 percent of the nation's farmland to fuel crops, a shift that will have unknown effects on food prices and worldwide availability (Pearce 2006).

Hydrogen

Hydrogen-powered fuel cell vehicles (FCVs) use hydrogen to electrochemically produce electricity, which then is used to power the vehicle. These vehicles are estimated to be two to three times more energy efficient than conventional gasoline-powered vehicles—and on par with advanced hybrids—and the only vehicle-based emission they produce is water. Yet, strictly speaking, hydrogen is not a fuel, but rather an energy carrier that transmits energy from a production facility to a vehicle. This provides a high degree of flexibility in the feedstocks—that is, the raw materials—that can be used to create the hydrogen and in the energy that can be used for that purpose. That flexibility, however, means that the GHG emission impacts of FCVs can vary widely, depending on the types of feedstocks and processing energy sources used (see Figure 3-16). A study sponsored by the California Energy Commission sets the range of possible GHG emission reductions, compared to conventional vehicles, at 26 to 91 percent (TIAX 2007).

Of the three technologies focused on in the Advanced Energy Initiative, commercialization of hydrogen-powered FCVs faces the greatest challenges (California Energy Commission 2005). Barriers exist in three areas: on-board hydrogen storage, hydrogen fueling infrastructure, and consumer cost.

The first barrier, on-board storage, is tied to the relatively low energy density of hydrogen fuels compared to gasoline. Depending on the storage method, hydrogen has only one-quarter to one-half the energy density by volume of gasoline. This means that it requires substantially more space to store comparable amounts of energy. With current technology, the hydrogen tanks required to accommodate the driving ranges of gasoline-powered vehicles (approximately 300 miles) are larger than the trunk of a mid-sized car (U.S. Department of Energy 2006). The excessive size required to store this energy also would result in excessive weight, which would reduce vehicle energy efficiency. Despite ten years of focused research on this issue, little progress has been made (Felderhoff et al. 2007).

FIGURE 3-16

Estimated "Well-to-Wheels" GHG Emissions for 2012 Hydrogen Vehicles Using Different Feedstock and Processing Methods*

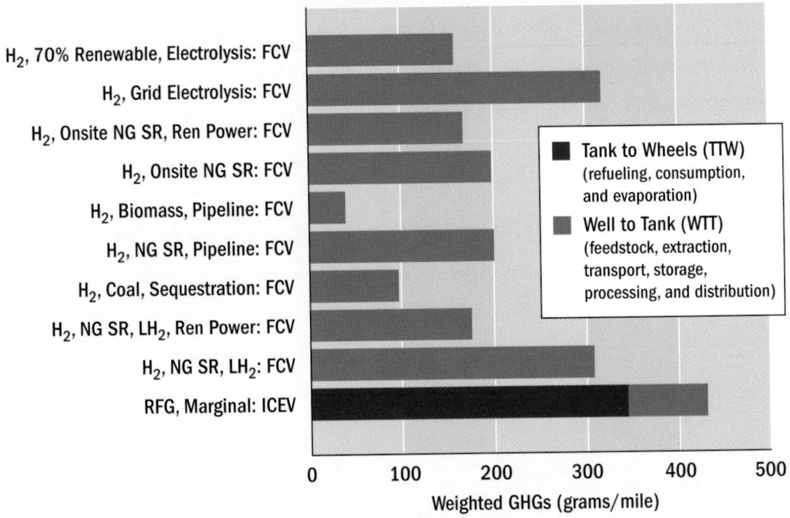

* The full fuel cycle is the combination of WTT and TTW, which is commonly referred to as a wells-to-wheels analysis.

SOURCE: TIAX. *Full Fuel Cycle Assessment: Well-to-Wheels Energy Inputs, Emissions, and Water Impacts.* Sacramento: California Energy Commission, 2007, http://www.energy.ca.gov/2007publications/CEC-600-2007-002/CEC-600-2007-002-D.PDF.

The second barrier, fueling infrastructure, suffers from a "Catch-22." The penetration of hydrogen FCVs into the nation's vehicle fleet will be slow; even the most aggressive scenario under consideration puts FCVs at only 1.1 percent of the fleet in 2020 (Melendez and Milbrandt 2006). The small number of FCVs on the road will make creating a ubiquitous or even reasonably convenient network of refueling stations cost prohibitive. The lack of such a network, however, likely would have a dampening effect on the vehicle retail market, effectively discouraging new car buyers from selecting an FCV.

Overcoming this no-win situation would be expensive. A base-level refueling network of 284 stations along interstate highways would provide a station every 50 miles east of the Mississippi River and every 100 miles west of the river. Only 24 million people—about 8 percent of the population—would be within five miles of these stations. Yet the cost of providing this network is estimated to be as much as $850 million, about $3 million per station (Melendez and Milbrandt 2006).

Consumer cost is the third significant barrier. Current gasoline vehicle technology generates energy at $25 to $35 per kilowatt. The U.S. Department of Energy estimates that to be cost competitive, FCV technology will need to deliver energy at the midpoint of that range ($30/kW). The price per kilowatt from FCV technology in 2004 was estimated to be $176, almost six times the DOE target price (TIAX 2004). This effectively adds almost $9,000 to the vehicle purchase price. Moreover, current prototype hydrogen FCVs are reported to cost up to $1 million per vehicle. The California Energy Commission sets a low estimate for the "consumer payback period" on FCVs—the length of time it takes for an FCV's reduced fuel costs to equal the added purchase costs—at 20 years, assuming a gasoline price of $4/gallon (California Energy Commission 2007b). This is well beyond the four-year payback period consumers customarily will accept.

Deployment and Market Penetration

Interwoven with the technological challenges outlined above is the question of market penetration. Solving the multiple engineering problems associated with alternative fuels and vehicles will not reduce GHGs if such technologies are not widely accepted by consumers and auto manufacturers. The demise of the electric car in California, despite a state mandate and a well-performing vehicle, illustrates the importance of buy-in by both parties. The documentary *Who Killed the Electric Car?* comes to the inescapable conclusion that General Motors contributed to the failure of its own product.

A 2003 scenario analysis for the U.S. Department of Energy and Natural Resources Canada evaluated two very different strategies for bringing GHG emissions down to 2000 levels by the year 2050. The "Go Your Own Way" (GYOW) scenario depends entirely on innovations in fuel and vehicle technologies and deep market penetration by those technologies (see Figures 3-17 and 3-18). Under the GYOW

FIGURE 3-17
2050 Transportation Fuel/Vehicle Policy & Technology Scenarios

	Base	Greening the Pump (GtP)	Go Your Own Way (GYOW)
Light-vehicle (LV) VMT	2002 rates to 2020 with decline in rate of growth post-2020	15% less than Base by 2015	Same as Base
LV sales	2002 through 2020; 2015–2020 growth rate applied through 2050	Same as Base	Same as Base
New car/light truck split	50%/50% in 2010, then constant	62%/38% in 2050	42%/58% in 2050
New car/light truck mpg	28.7%/21.4% constant	42%/31% in 2050	59%/44% in 2050
% Hybrids/FCVs of new LVs	0%/0%	10%/0% in 2050	30%/50% in 2050
E10 in LVs	Continuation of current	Mandatory by 2020	Mandatory by 2020
E85 in LVs	None	20% of LVs sold use E85 in 2050	30% of LVs sold use E85 in 2050
Compressed natural gas/liquefied petroleum gas in LVs	None	3% by 2025	None

SOURCE: U.S. Department of Energy and Natural Resources Canada. *Study of North American Transportation Energy Futures*. Washington, D.C., 2003, www.nrel.gov/analysis/seminar/docs/2003/es_3-13-03.ppt.

FIGURE 3-18
GHG Emissions for Several Transportation Fuel/Vehicle Policy and Technology Scenarios

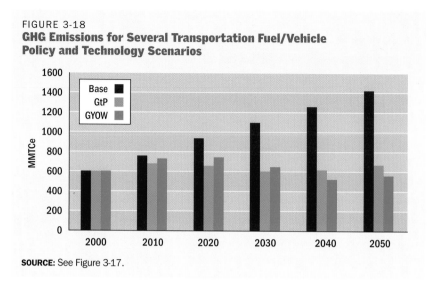

SOURCE: See Figure 3-17.

scenario, new car/light truck fuel efficiency would achieve levels more than double today's CAFE standards, with proportional increases in heavy vehicle fuel efficiency. Thirty percent of new light vehicles would be hybrids, 50 percent would be hydrogen FCVs, and 30 percent would burn E85 ethanol. The estimated cumulative vehicle and fuel costs of GYOW would be $1.2 trillion higher (in year 2000 undiscounted dollars) than in the base case. The "Greening the Pump" (GtP) scenario, by contrast, takes a more incremental approach to technology deployment, assuming only a 50 percent hike in fuel efficiency. Ten percent of new vehicles in GtP would be hybrids and 20 percent would burn E85; none would be FCVs. Nevertheless, the GtP scenario achieves nearly the same level of GHG reduction as GYOW. It does so by incorporating a 15 percent reduction in VMT, equivalent to that achievable by 2030 with land use measures. And the GtP scenario achieves target levels with vehicle and fuel costs that are $2.8 trillion lower than the base case, as opposed to $1.2 trillion higher than the base case with the purely technological approach of GYOW.

As this study demonstrates, relying solely on technological advances to stabilize vehicle GHG emissions requires heroic engineering and marketing achievements that are hard to defend and are unsupported by recent experience (U.S. Department of Energy and Natural Resources Canada 2003).

4

The Urban Development/VMT Connection

Four different empirical literatures inform the discussion of urban development and its impacts on VMT, the primary determinant of transportation-related CO_2 emissions (see list at right).

    In this chapter, we review each literature in turn and present order-of-magnitude effect sizes. For two literatures—disaggregate travel studies and regional simulation studies—the sample of studies is large enough to permit meta-analyses of study results. A meta-analysis is a special kind of literature synthesis, conducted most often in scientific fields. It is more than a literature review, as it generalizes across studies quantitatively, taking individual studies as units of analysis and combining study results to arrive at average effect sizes and confidence intervals.

    The different literatures provide a consistent picture. Compact development has the potential to reduce VMT per capita by anywhere from 20 to 40 percent relative to sprawl. The actual reduction in VMT per capita will depend on the specific form of compact development, as outlined in the following sections.

Aggregate Travel Studies

For decades, it has been known that compact areas have lower levels of automobile use per capita and greater use of alternative modes of transportation than do sprawling areas. They also tend to generate shorter trips. The combined effect is significantly less VMT per capita in compact areas (see Figure 4-1). This fact has been documented most famously by Peter Newman and Jeffrey Kenworthy (1989a, 1989b, 1999, 2006, 2007) and by John Holtzclaw and colleagues (1991, 1994, 2002). This

FOUR EMPIRICAL LITERATURES

- Aggregate travel studies, such as sprawl index research conducted for Smart Growth America;
- Disaggregate travel studies, such as Smart Growth Index elasticity estimates;
- Regional simulation studies, such as Portland's LUTRAQ (Land Use, Transportation, Air Quality) study; and
- Project simulation studies, such as the EPA's Atlantic Station study.

FIGURE 4-1
Vehicle Miles Traveled per Household for Neighborhoods in the San Francisco Metropolitan Area

SOURCE: Holtzclaw, J., R. Clear, H. Dittmar, D. Goldstein, and P. Haas. "Location Efficiency: Neighborhood and Socioeconomic Characteristics Determine Auto Ownership and Use—Studies in Chicago, Los Angeles and San Francisco." *Transportation Planning and Technology,* Vol. 25, 2002, pp. 1–27.

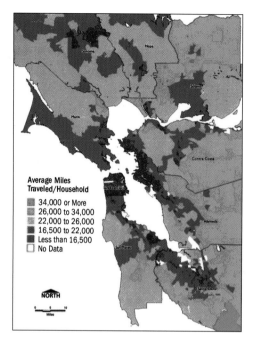

same-shaped exponential decline in vehicular travel with density is found in many data series (see Figures 4-2 and 4-3 for communities in the Baltimore area and for higher-income cities worldwide).

Four facts, however, preclude broad generalizations about urban development patterns and fuel consumption or CO_2 emissions. First, dense areas may experience more congestion and lower travel speeds than sprawling areas, hence lower vehicle fuel economy for whatever VMT they produce. Second, dense areas may have different population characteristics than sprawling areas, differences that could confound urban development and travel relationships. Third, density is only one aspect of urban form, albeit an important one. Urban sprawl is defined more broadly as any development pattern in which homes, workplaces, stores, schools, and other activities are widely separated from one another. Fourth, any relationships that appear in aggregate statistics for neighborhoods, cities, or metropolitan areas would not necessarily apply to individual households, the ultimate travel decision makers.[1]

In a paper entitled "The Transport Energy Trade-Off: Fuel-Efficient Traffic versus Fuel-Efficient Cities," Newman and Kenworthy (1988) addressed the first of these qualifiers. They concluded that the lower VMT in compact areas overwhelms any effect of lower vehicle fuel economy (see Figure 4-4). They subsequently substantiated this relationship for many other places (Newman 2006; Newman and Kenworthy 2006, 2007).

The second qualifier is not so easily dismissed. In Figures 4-2 through 4-4, residential density is not the only characteristic that distinguishes Taneytown from Charles Street in the Baltimore metropolitan area, or one higher-income city from another, or the inner and outer portions of the New York metropolitan area. Culture, socioeconomics, demographics, transit availability, and even gas prices could account for most or all of the differences in per capita vehicle use. Critics of these early stud-

FIGURE 4-2
Vehicle Miles Traveled per Capita versus Residential Density for Baltimore Neighborhoods

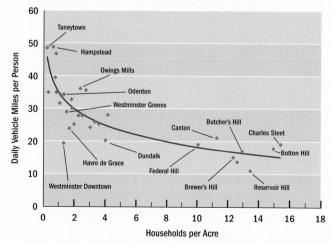

SOURCE: Baltimore Metropolitan Council, 2001 Travel Survey.

FIGURE 4-3
Vehicle Kilometers Traveled per Capita versus Activity Intensity for 58 Higher-Income Cities

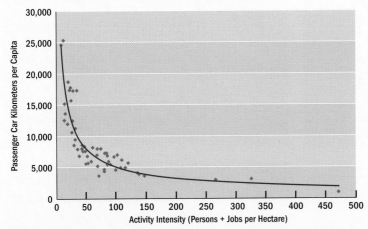

SOURCE: P.W.G. Newman and J.R. Kenworthy, "Urban Design to Reduce Automobile Dependence." *Opolis: An International Journal of Suburban and Metropolitan Studies,* Vol. 2, Issue 1, 2006, pp. 35–52.

FIGURE 4-4
Per Capita Gasoline Consumption in Inner and Outer Portions of the New York Metropolitan Area

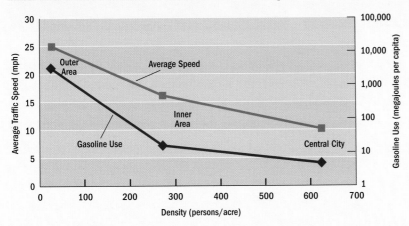

SOURCE: P.W.G. Newman and J.R. Kenworthy. "The Transport Energy Trade-Off: Fuel-Efficient Traffic versus Fuel-Efficient Cities." *Transportation Research A,* Vol. 22A, Issue 3, 1988, pp. 163–174.

ies argued, correctly, that until these other factors were controlled, the independent effect of urban development patterns would be unknown and unknowable (Gomez-Ibanez 1991; Gordon and Richardson 1989). Recent aggregate studies have done a better job of controlling for confounding influences, and still found strong relationships between urban form and VMT (Cameron et al. 2003, 2004; van de Coevering and Schwanen 2006).

Likewise, the third qualifier also is not easily dismissed. If poor accessibility is the common denominator of sprawl, then sprawl is more than low-density development.

Sprawling development patterns include low-density and single-use development (top left), uncentered strip development (top right), scattered and leapfrog development (bottom left), and sparse street networks (bottom right).

The term also encompasses scattered or leapfrog development, commercial strip development, and single-use development such as bedroom communities. In scattered or leapfrog development, residents and service providers must pass vacant land on their way from one developed area to another. In classic strip development, consumers must pass other uses on the way from one store to the next; this is the antithesis of multipurpose travel to an activity center. In a single-use development, of course, different uses are located far apart as a result of the segregation of land uses. Poor accessibility also could be a product of fragmented street networks that separate urban activities more than need be (see the photos of sprawling development patterns above).

The fourth qualifier has led to a host of studies using disaggregate travel data; that is, data for individuals or households. Such studies are summarized in the following section of this chapter, "Disaggregate Travel Studies." For now, the focus is on aggregate relationships, where the unit of analysis is the place.

Measuring Urban Sprawl

Around 2000, the first attempts were made to measure the extent of urban sprawl. They were crude. For example, *USA Today*—on the basis of an index introduced in its February 22, 2001, issue—declared: "Los Angeles, whose legendary traffic congestion and spread-out development have epitomized suburban sprawl for decades, isn't so sprawling after all. In fact, Portland, OR, the metropolitan area that enacted the nation's toughest antigrowth laws, sprawls more." Indeed, according to *USA Today*'s index, even the New York metropolitan area sprawls more than Los Angeles (Nasser and Overberg 2001).

The most notable feature of these early studies was their failure to define sprawl in all its complexity. Several researchers created measures of urban sprawl that focused on density (Fulton et al. 2001; Malpezzi and Guo 2001; Lopez and Hynes 2003; Burchfield et al. 2005). Density has the big advantage of being easy to measure with available data. Judged in terms of average population density, Los Angeles looks compact; it is the endless, uniform character of the city's density that makes it seem so sprawling. Another notable feature of these studies was the wildly different sprawl ratings given to different metropolitan areas by different analysts. With the exception of Atlanta, which always seems to rank among the most sprawling, the different variables used to measure sprawl led to very different results. In one study, Portland was ranked as most compact and Los Angeles was far down the list. In another, their rankings were essentially reversed.

Meanwhile, others were developing more complete measures of urban sprawl. Galster et al. (2001) characterized sprawl in eight dimensions: density, continuity,

Endless uniform density in Los Angeles.

concentration, clustering, centrality, nuclearity, mixed use, and proximity. The condition—sprawl—was defined as a pattern of land use that has low levels in one or more of these dimensions. Each dimension was operationally defined, and six of the eight were quantified for 13 urbanized areas. New York and Philadelphia ranked as the least sprawling of the 13, and Atlanta and Miami as the most sprawling.

Since then, Galster and his colleagues have extended their sprawl measures to 50 metropolitan areas, and are closing in on 100. Their recent work confirms the multidimensional nature of sprawl. In one study, metropolitan areas were ranked in 14 dimensions, some related to population, others to employment, and still others to both (Cutsinger et al. 2005). The 14 dimensions were reduced to seven factors through principal components analysis. Metropolitan areas ranking near the top on one factor were likely to rank near the bottom on another. Los Angeles, for example, ranked second on both "mixed use" and "housing centrality," but 48th on "proximity" and 49th on "nuclearity." With so many variables and esoteric names, this type of analysis can get very confusing.

Building on this work, Cutsinger and Galster (2006) identified four distinct sprawllike patterns among the 50 metropolitan areas: 1) deconcentrated, dense areas; 2) leapfrog areas; 3) compact, core-dominant areas with only moderate density; and 4) dispersed areas. Since none of the 50 metropolitan areas exhibited uniform sprawllike patterns in all dimensions, the authors judged it incorrect to treat sprawl as a single phenomenon.

Multidimensional sprawl indices also were developed for the U.S. EPA and Smart Growth America. They defined sprawl as any environment with 1) a population widely dispersed in low-density residential development; 2) a rigid separation of homes, shops, and workplaces; 3) a lack of major employment and population concentrations downtown or in suburban town centers and other activity centers; and 4) a network of roads marked by very large block size and poor access from one place to another. These indices were used to measure sprawl for 83 of the nation's largest metropolitan areas (Ewing, Pendall, and Chen 2002, 2003).

Principal components analysis was used to reduce 22 land use and street network variables to four factors representing these four dimensions of sprawl, each factor being a linear combination of the underlying operational variables.[2] The four factors represent a balanced scorecard of sprawl indicators. "Density" and "mix," while correlated, are very different constructs, as are "centeredness" and "street accessibility." The four factors were combined into an overall metropolitan sprawl index.

All sprawl indices were standardized, with mean values of 100 and standard deviations of 25. The indices were constructed so that the more compact a metropolitan area was, the larger its index value would be. More sprawling metropolitan areas had smaller index values. Thus, in 2000, the relatively compact Portland, Oregon, metropolitan area had an index value of 126, while the slightly smaller Raleigh-Durham metropolitan area had an index value of 54 (see photographs at right).

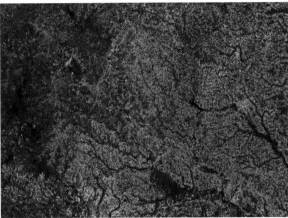

WWW.MAPS.GOOGLE.COM

Relating Urban Sprawl to Travel Outcomes

The study for the EPA and Smart Growth America analyzed relationships between sprawl and various travel outcomes. The overall sprawl index showed strong and statistically significant relationships to six outcome variables. All relationships were in the expected directions. As the index increases (that is, as sprawl decreases), average vehicle ownership, daily VMT per capita, the annual traffic fatality rate, and the maximum ozone level decrease to a significant degree. At the same time, shares of work trips by transit and walk modes increase significantly.

The significance of these relationships rivaled or, in some cases, actually exceeded that of the sociodemographic control variables. The index was the only variable that rose to the level of statistical significance for walk share of work trips and maximum ozone level, and had the strongest association to daily VMT per capita and the annual traffic fatality rate. It had secondary, but still highly significant, associations with average vehicle ownership and transit share of work trips.

Obviously, these relationships are not independent of each other. The lower level of vehicle ownership in dense metropolitan areas contributes to higher mode shares for alternatives to the automobile. These, in turn, contribute to lower VMT, which contributes to lower traffic fatalities and ozone levels. Because of the different data sources, units of analysis, and sample sizes, it would be treacherous to model the causal paths among these outcome variables. But, intuitively, they should be related as indicated.

Sprawl versus VMT

The relationship between the overall metropolitan sprawl index and VMT per capita is plotted in Figure 4-5. The simple correlation is significant. The more compact an area (the larger the index value), the lower the VMT per capita. In 2000, the relatively compact Portland, Oregon, metropolitan area generated 23.6 VMT per capita, while the sprawling Raleigh-Durham metropolitan area produced 31.0 VMT per capita, a difference of 24 percent.

Satellite photographs show the relatively compact Portland, Oregon, metropolitan area at left, and the sprawling Raleigh-Durham metropolitan area at right. Photographs are at the same scale.

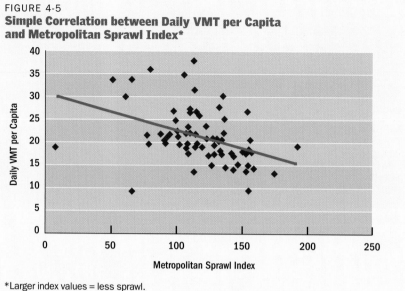

FIGURE 4-5
Simple Correlation between Daily VMT per Capita and Metropolitan Sprawl Index*

*Larger index values = less sprawl.

SOURCE: R. Ewing, R. Pendall, and D. Chen. *Measuring Sprawl and Its Impact.* Washington, D.C.: Smart Growth America/U.S. Environmental Protection Agency, 2002.

Recall that the overall sprawl index is composed of four factors: density, mix, centeredness, and street accessibility (as discussed earlier in this chapter, in "Measuring Urban Sprawl"). The density factor has the strongest and most significant relationship to travel and transportation outcomes (see Figure 4-6). To illustrate the effect of density, a 50-unit increase in the density factor (from one standard deviation below average to one standard deviation above average) is associated with a drop of 10.75 daily VMT per capita (50 x –0.215). That is, controlling for metropolitan population, per capita income, and other factors, the difference between low- and high-density metropolitan areas is more than 10 VMT per capita per day, or 40 percent. Fifty units is roughly the difference in density between San Francisco (denser) and Washington, D.C. (less dense).

The centeredness factor has the next most significant environmental influence on travel and transportation outcomes. The relationship between degree of centering and VMT per capita is just short of significant at the 0.05 level. A 50-unit increase in the centeredness factor (from one standard deviation below the average to one standard deviation above) is associated with a 2.3 daily VMT per capita (50 x –0.0462), about one-quarter the change associated with the density factor. The two effects are additive. Fifty units is roughly the difference in degree of centering between New York (more centered) and Philadelphia (less centered).

Sprawl versus Congestion

It has been argued that the dispersal of jobs and housing allows residents to live closer to their workplaces than they could if jobs were concentrated in downtown and

FIGURE 4-6
Transportation Outcomes versus Sprawl Factors*

	Vehicles per Household	Transit Share of Work Trips	Walk Share of Work Trips	Mean Travel Time to Work	Annual Delay per Capita	VMT per Capita	Fatalities per 100,000 Population	Peak Ozone Level
Density factor	– –	++	++			– –	–	– –
Mix factor				–			–	+
Centers factor	– –	++	++	–	–	–	–	–
Streets factor				++	++			
Metro population		+		++	+			++
Average household size	+			++	++			
Percentage of working age	++				++	+		
Per capita income		++		++			–	
Adjusted R2	0.56	0.67	0.36	0.61	0.63	0.28	0.44	0.40

*+ indicates a positive relationship significant at the 0.05 probability level; ++ a positive relationship significant at the 0.01 probability level; – a negative relationship significant at the 0.05 probability level; and – – a negative relationship significant at the 0.01 probability level.
SOURCE: See Figure 4-5.

other centers. It also has been argued that the dispersal of jobs and housing eases traffic congestion by dispersing origins and destinations. These effects, if dominant, would lead to shorter trips and less congestion in sprawling metropolitan areas. But the dispersal of jobs and housing also may result in jobs/housing imbalances across the region, cross commuting, and significantly more VMT per capita than with more compact urban development. The average commute has been getting steadily longer in miles and minutes (Hu and Reuscher 2004). The net effect of sprawl on traffic congestion is unclear a priori.

Evidence from aggregate travel studies suggests that density aggravates congestion, but not much. One study found little relationship between density and commute time in the largest urban areas (Gordon, Kumar, and Richardson 1989): "Travel times may be long in high- or low-density cities (e.g., New York or Houston) or short (e.g., Los Angeles or Dallas)." Basically, shorter trips and mode shifts in dense areas largely offset any effect of lower speeds.

Another study found that congestion rises with population density for counties in California (Boarnet, Kim, and Parkany 1998). Urbanized counties as a group are more congested than rural counties. However, this same study found "surprisingly congested counties that are either rural or on the fringe of urban areas." These fringe counties generate a lot of VMT. We reanalyzed congestion data from that study and, excluding one outlier, computed an elasticity of congestion with respect to density of 0.14.

The Texas Transportation Institute's Urban Mobility database for 85 urbanized areas also shows a weak relationship between density and congestion (Schrank and

Lomax 2007). TTI measures congestion in terms of a travel time index; that is, the ratio of travel time in the peak period to travel time at free-flow conditions. A value of 1.30 indicates that a ten-minute free-flow trip takes, on average, 13 minutes in the peak period. In a cross-sectional analysis for 2005, the last year in the series, the elasticity of travel time with respect to population density is 0.066. This elasticity estimate controls for population size because bigger cities have more congestion regardless of their urban form. In a longitudinal analysis for the same 85 urbanized areas using TTI data from 1982 and 2005, the elasticity of change in travel time with respect to change in density is 0.058. This analysis controlled for population growth because fast-growing areas have more congestion regardless of how they grow.

Such studies have been criticized for focusing on only one dimension of sprawl: "Other land use dimensions are less well studied in a comparative framework . . . while it is believed that land use patterns may play an important role in mitigating or slowing the growth of congestion in urban areas, few studies have explored the relationship between land use and congestion across more than a small number of urban areas or examined multiple measures of land use beyond population density" (Sarzynski et al. 2006).

In the Smart Growth America study, average commute time and annual traffic delay per capita were found to be a function primarily of metropolitan area population, and secondarily of other sociodemographic variables (Ewing, Pendall, and Chen 2002, 2003). The four sprawl factors pulled in opposite directions, essentially canceling each other out. After controlling for population size and other influences, the overall sprawl index did not appear to have an effect on average commute time or annual traffic delay per capita.

Using the same sprawl index as Ewing, Pendall, and Chen (2002), Kahn (2006) divided metropolitan areas into four categories and found that, relative to workers in compact metropolitan areas, workers in sprawling areas commute an extra 1.8 miles each way. But their commute is still 4.3 minutes shorter; the extra commute distance is more than offset by higher travel speeds. Indeed, commute speed is estimated to be 9.5 mile per hour higher in the sprawling metropolitan areas.

Why is there a difference in the sprawl versus commute-time relationship between two studies that test the same sprawl index? The first study uses U.S. Census commute data, the second American Housing Survey commute data. The first study treats sprawl as a continuous variable, the second as a categorical variable. Whatever their differences, both studies suggest higher VMT in sprawling metropolitan areas than in compact ones.

Another recent study, by Galster and colleagues, related seven dimensions of sprawl to traffic congestion for 50 large metropolitan areas in 2000 (Sarzynski et al. 2006). Controlling for 1990 levels of congestion and changes in an urban area's transportation network and relevant demographics, the study found that density and housing centrality were positively related to year 2000 delay per capita and that housing/job proximity was negatively related to year 2000 commute time.

Differences between this and earlier studies may be due to the use of a lagged model structure, different land use measures, or a different sample of metropolitan areas. Since Sarzynski et al. were unable to study the effect of land use changes between 1990 and 2000 (for lack of sprawl indices for 2000), it is hard to interpret the coefficients of a lagged model. Relationships to delay could be bogus in all of these studies, since the delay measure used by everyone comes from the TTI *Annual Mobility Report* and is imputed rather than actually measured in the field. Considering all the evidence from aggregate travel studies, it is reasonable to assume some drop in average travel speeds with rising density. From this literature, we cannot draw any conclusions about travel speeds versus land use mix or other dimensions of urban form.

Disaggregate Travel Studies

Land use/travel studies date from the early 1960s, when urban density was first shown to affect auto ownership, trip rates, and travel mode shares. Around 1990, researchers began to use disaggregate travel data for individuals or households; made some effort to account for other influences on travel behavior, particularly the socioeconomic status of travelers; and tested a wider variety of local land use variables than had earlier studies.

The relationship between urban development patterns and individual or household travel has become the most heavily researched subject in urban planning. There are now more than 100 empirical studies that have been conducted with a degree of rigor—that is, with decent sample sizes, sociodemographic controls, and statistical tests to determine the significance of the various effects (see literature reviews by Badoe and Miller (2000); Crane (2000); Ewing and Cervero (2001); Saelens, Sallis, and Frank (2003); and Heath et al. (2006)). The vast majority of these studies show significant relationships between development patterns and travel behavior. Today, only the direction of causality and strength of effects seems to be seriously debated.

When funding from public health sources became available after 2000, planning researchers morphed into physical activity researchers, and the literature grew even further (see reviews by Frank (2000), Frank and Engelke (2001, 2005), Lee and Moudon (2004), Owen et al. (2004), Badland and Schofield (2005), and Handy (2006)). Both types of physical activity—for transportation and for exercise—were studied together for the first time, and the physical environment was measured comprehensively in terms of development patterns and physical activity settings (see Figure 4-7). A special Winter 2006 issue of the *Journal of the American Planning Association* was devoted to this new research. Again, nearly all studies show significant relationships. And, again, the debate is mainly over the direction of causality and effect sizes.

FIGURE 4-7
Causal Pathways Linking the Built Environment to Health

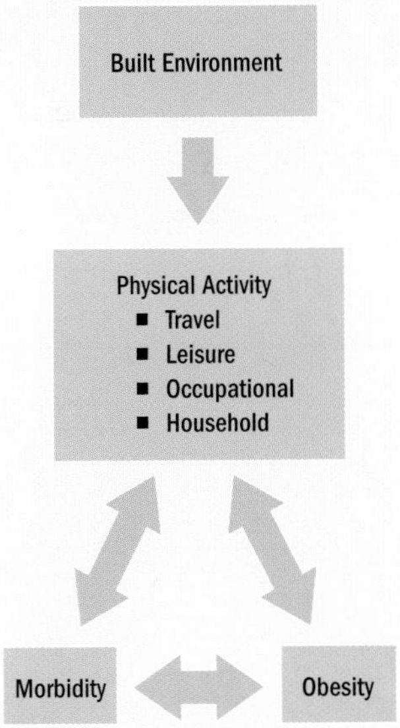

SOURCE: R. Ewing, T. Schmid, R. Killingsworth, A. Zlot, and S. Raudenbush. "Relationship Between Urban Sprawl and Physical Activity, Obesity, and Morbidity." *American Journal of Health Promotion*, Vol. 18, Issue 1, 2003, pp. 47–57.

FIGURE 4-8
Neighborhoods with Different Designs and Travel Characteristics in Chapel Hill, North Carolina

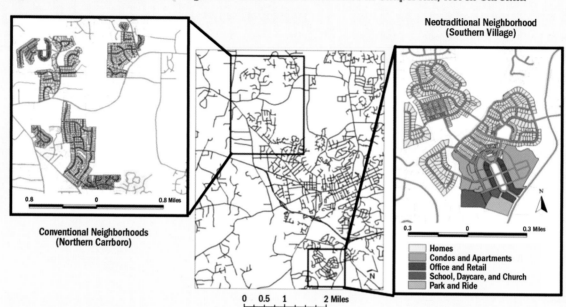

SOURCE: A.J. Khattak and D. Rodriquez. "Travel Behavior in Neo-Traditional Neighborhood Developments: A Case Study in USA." *Transportation Research Part A,* Vol. 39, 2005, pp. 481–500.

Different Geographic Scales

Dealing with individual and household travel behavior, disaggregate travel studies typically have measured the built environment at the scale of the individual's or the household's neighborhood (see Figure 4-8). This is both a strength and a weakness of such studies.

The obvious strength is the ability to capture variations in the built environment—and related travel behavior—across a metropolitan area. Since something like 70 to 75 percent of all urban trips have an individual's home at one end or the other, the residential neighborhood is clearly the most relevant single geography for disaggregate travel research.

The weakness of such studies is the extended size of the typical adult or adolescent's activity space. The average length of U.S. trips is 6.8 miles, taking residents well beyond their neighborhoods. The average walk trip is 0.7 mile, again beyond the confines of a neighborhood. By previous estimates, between 40 and 60 percent of all trips taken by household members are part of multistop tours. Several studies have found that mode choice depends on the built environments at both the trip origin (home) and its destination (work or shopping).

The appropriate geographic scale for travel research is far from clear, and can only be determined empirically. Ideally, different scales would be tested against VMT in the same study, and more than one scale would be represented in forecasting models.

Measuring the Five Ds

The concept of sprawl seems particularly tailored to large areas such as metropolitan areas and their component counties. The degree to which employment is concentrated in central business districts or suburban centers, for example, is a characteristic of an entire metropolitan area, not of an individual community or neighborhood. Yet there are analogous measures for subareas as small as neighborhoods, and these analogous measures have been studied in depth for their relationships to trip frequency, trip distance, mode choice, and trip chaining (that is, the linking of trips into tours).

In travel research, urban development patterns have come to be characterized by "D" variables. The original "three Ds," coined by Cervero and Kockelman (1997), are density, diversity, and design. The Ds have multiplied since then, with the addition of destination accessibility and distance to transit. If we could think of an appropriate label, parking supply and cost might be characterized as a sixth D.

Density usually is measured in terms of persons, jobs, or dwellings per unit area. Diversity refers to land use mix. It often is related to the number of different land uses in an area and the degree to which they are "balanced" in land area, floor area, or employment. Design includes street network characteristics within a neighborhood (see Figure 4-9). Street networks vary from dense urban grids of highly interconnected, straight streets to sparse suburban networks of curving streets forming "loops and lollipops." Street accessibility usually is measured in terms of average block size, proportion of four-way intersections, or number of intersections per square mile. Design also is measured in terms of sidewalk coverage, building setbacks, street

FIGURE 4-9
Housing within One-Quarter Mile of a Commercial Center for Contrasting Development Patterns in Seattle

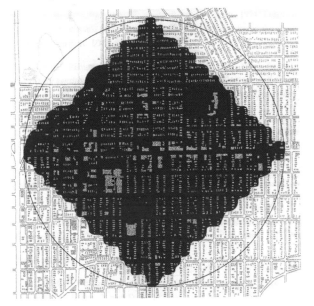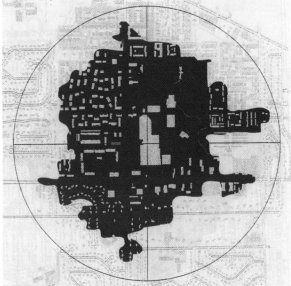

SOURCE: A.V. Moudon, P.M. Hess, M.C. Snyder, and K. Stanilov et al. "Effects of Site Design on Pedestrian Travel in Mixed-Use, Medium-Density Environments." *Transportation Research Record,* Vol. 1578, 1997, pp. 48–55.

widths, pedestrian crossings, presence of street trees, and a host of other physical variables that differentiate pedestrian-oriented environments from auto-oriented ones.

Destination accessibility is measured in terms of the number of jobs or other attractions reachable within a given travel time, which tends to be highest at central locations and lowest at peripheral ones. Distance to transit usually is measured from home or work to the nearest rail station or bus stop by the shortest street route. Where exact addresses are not known, distance to transit is represented by transit route density or stop spacing.

D Variables versus VMT and VT

The D variables have a significant effect on the overall VMT and VT (vehicle trips) of individuals and households, mostly through their effect on the distance people travel and the modes of travel they choose (Ewing and Cervero 2001). Trip frequencies appear to be primarily a function of travelers' socioeconomic and demographic characteristics and secondarily a function of the built environment; trip lengths are primarily a function of the built environment and secondarily of socioeconomic and demographic characteristics; and mode choices depend on both, though probably more on socioeconomics.

Trip lengths are generally shorter at locations that are more accessible, have higher densities, or feature mixed uses. This holds true for both the home end (that is, residential neighborhoods) and nonhome end (activity centers) of trips. Alternatives to the automobile claim a larger share of all trips at higher densities and in mixed-use areas. Walk mode shares can rise to 20 percent or more in mixed-use neighborhoods even without high-quality transit service (see Figure 4-10).

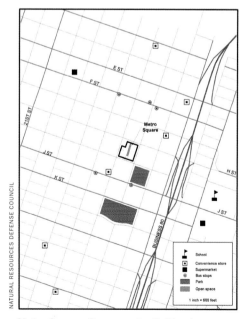

Metro Square, Sacramento, California

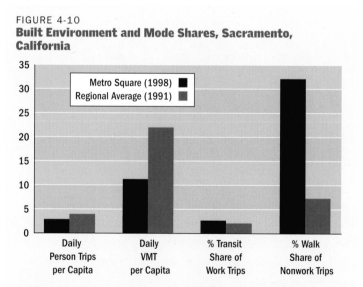

FIGURE 4-10
Built Environment and Mode Shares, Sacramento, California

SOURCE: Natural Resources Defense Council (NRDC). *Environmental Characteristics of Smart Growth Neighborhoods: An Exploratory Case Study.* Washington, D.C., October 2000, www.nrdc.org/cities/smartGrowth/char/charinx.asp.

FIGURE 4-11
Effects of Density and Mixed Use on Choice of Transit for Commutes*

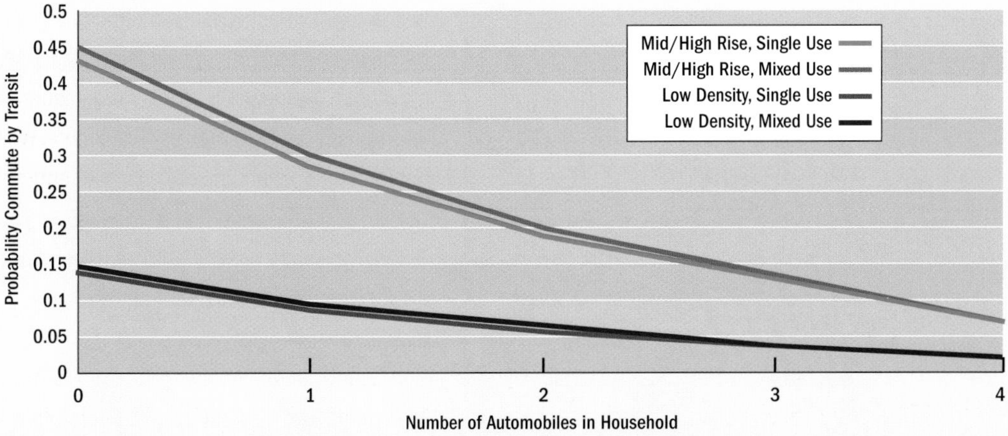

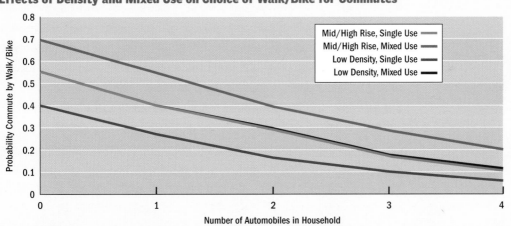

*Data for more than 45,000 U.S. households showed transit use primarily dependent on density of development. At higher densities, the addition of retail uses in neighborhoods was associated with several percentage point higher levels of transit commuting across 11 U.S. metropolitan areas.

SOURCE: R. Cervero. "Mixed Land-Uses and Commuting: Evidence from the American Housing Survey." Transportation Research A, Vol. 30, 1996, pp. 361–377.

FIGURE 4-12
Effects of Density and Mixed Use on Choice of Walk/Bike for Commutes*

*Rates of walk and bicycle trips (for a one-mile home-to-work trip) are comparable for low-density, mixed-use neighborhoods as compared with high-density, single-use ones, controlling for vehicle ownership levels.

SOURCE: See Figure 4-11.

These studies indicate that transit use varies primarily with local densities and secondarily with the degree of land use mixing (see Figure 4-11). Some of the density effect is, no doubt, due to shorter distances to transit service. Walking varies as much with the degree of land use mixing as with local densities (see Figure 4-12). An unresolved issue is whether the relationship of density to travel behavior is due to density itself or to other variables with which density co-varies, such as limited parking and better walking conditions.

FIGURE 4-13
Values of the Urban Design Factor across the Portland Metropolitan Area

SOURCE: Portland Metro.

The third D—design—has a more ambiguous relationship to travel behavior than do the first two. Any effect is likely to be a collective one involving multiple design features. It also may be an interactive effect involving land use and transportation variables. This is the idea behind composite measures such as Portland, Oregon's "urban design factor" (see Figure 4-13). The urban design factor is a function of intersection density, residential density, and employment density.

For 14 carefully controlled travel studies, Ewing and Cervero (2001) synthesized the literature by computing elasticities of VMT and VT with respect to the first four Ds—density, diversity, design, and destination accessibility. These summary measures were incorporated into the EPA's Smart Growth Index (SGI) model, a widely used sketch planning tool for travel and air quality analysis. In the SGI model, density is measured in terms of residents plus jobs per square mile; diversity in terms of the ratio of jobs to residents relative to the regional average; and design in terms of street network density, sidewalk coverage, and route directness (two of three measures relating to street network design). These are just a few of the many ways in which the 3Ds have been operationalized at the neighborhood level (see literature review, Ewing and Cervero 2001).

Figure 4-14 presents elasticities of VT and VMT with respect to the four Ds. From the elasticities presented in Figure 4-14, we would expect a doubling of neighborhood density to result in approximately a 5 percent reduction in both VT and VMT, all other things being equal. The effects of the four Ds captured in this table are additive.

FIGURE 4-14
Typical Elasticities of Travel with Respect to the Four Ds

	Vehicle Trips (VT)	Vehicle Miles Traveled (VMT)
Local density	–0.05	–0.05
Local diversity (mix)	–0.03	–0.05
Local design	–0.05	–0.03
Regional accessibility	0.0	–0.20

SOURCE: R. Ewing and R. Cervero. "Travel and the Built Environment." *Transportation Research Record,* Vol. 1780, 2001, pp. 87–114.

Doubling all four Ds would be expected to reduce VMT by about one-third. Note that the elasticity of VMT with respect to destination accessibility is as large as the other three combined, suggesting that areas of high accessibility—such as center cities—may produce substantially lower VMT than dense mixed-use developments in the exurbs.

Meta-Analysis of Disaggregate Travel Studies

Since Ewing and Cervero's 2001 literature review, the published literature on the built environment and travel has mushroomed. A more recent review identified 40 published studies of the built environment and travel, and selected 17 that met minimum methodological and statistical criteria (Leck 2006). While the analysis stopped short of estimating average effect sizes, it did evaluate the statistical significance of relationships between the built environment and travel. Residential density, employment density, and land use mix were found to be inversely related to VMT at the $p < 0.001$ significance level.

The number of rigorous studies now exceeds 100, including studies examining four or five D variables at once, studies comparing travel behavior outside the United States, studies focusing on children, and studies accounting for residential preferences that may confound results. The EPA is funding a full-blown meta-study of this ever-expanding literature, which will summarize the most pertinent literature qualitatively and, using standard methods of meta-analysis, will combine individual study results into average elasticities or percentage point adjustments of VMT, VT, and transit use and walking with respect to the D variables. Confidence intervals will be computed for the average values. These summary measures will become available for sketch planning applications.

Regional Growth Simulations

In the "old days," metropolitan planning organizations (MPOs) developed their plans by testing different transportation alternatives against a single future land use forecast. One alternative might have more transit, another a new beltway or more arterial street improvements. But future land use patterns were always assumed to be fixed.

Future land use projections typically were extrapolations of recent trends, assumed to be unaffected by additions to urban infrastructure, most importantly by transportation improvements. In other words, future land use patterns were treated as fixed inputs into the analysis, not as variables or possible outcomes.

All that changed in the early 1990s with the advent of regional scenario planning, which matches alternative land use plans with alternative transportation plans. These plans are run through simulation models to project impacts on VMT, land consumption rates, air pollutant emission levels, housing affordability indices, and other outcome measures. In theory, the most cost-effective plan is adopted.

FIGURE 4-15
The LUTRAQ Plan for the Western Portland Metro

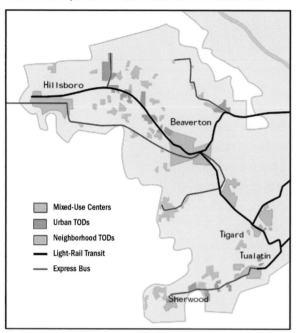

SOURCE: 1000 Friends of Oregon. *Making the Connections: A Summary of the LUTRAQ Project.* Portland, Oregon, 1997.

FIGURE 4-16
Number of Scenario Planning Projects by Completion Date

SOURCE: K. Bartholomew. "Land Use-Transportation Scenario Planning: Promise & Reality." Transportation, Vol. 34, Issue 4, 2007, pp. 397–412.

The Rise of Scenario Planning

Scenario planning got a major boost from the well-publicized success of Portland, Oregon's Land Use, Transportation, Air Quality (LUTRAQ) study, which called for combining light-rail investments with transit-oriented development and travel demand management policies (1000 Friends of Oregon 1997). Portland Metro, the regional government, turned down a proposed western bypass beltway in favor of the LUTRAQ plan when regional travel forecasts showed the LUTRAQ alternative would produce significantly less VMT and lower levels of congestion than would trend development with the new freeway (see Figure 4-15).

The number of scenario planning studies undertaken in the United States has grown dramatically since LUTRAQ (see Figure 4-16). Regional scenario planning has transitioned from state-of-the-art to state-of-the-practice at MPOs (Ewing 2007). Such studies also have become common outside the United States (Johnston 2006). In fact, many advances in integrated land use/transportation modeling have come from outside the United States.

The Scenario Planning Process

The typical scenario planning process compares a "trend" scenario to one or more alternative future "planning" scenarios. In the trend scenario, urban development and transportation investment patterns of the recent past are assumed to continue through the planning horizon (20 to 50 years in the future). The trend scenario—usually some version of urban sprawl—is assessed for its impacts on VMT and other regional outcomes.

This is followed by the formulation of one or more alternative futures that vary with respect to land use and transportation. Compared to the trend scenario, the planning alternatives usually have higher gross densities, mix land uses to a greater extent, and/or channel more development into urban centers. They may incorporate a variety of transportation infrastructure investments and pricing policies, usually matched to land use alternatives. A transit-oriented plan would feature transit-oriented development and transit investments, while a highway-oriented plan might feature development with multiple centers and toll roads or high-occupancy-vehicle (HOV) lanes.

These alternative scenarios are then assessed for their impacts using the same travel forecasting models and same set of outcome measures as with the trend scenario. Vehicle miles traveled is almost always among the outcomes forecasted. The resulting comparison of scenarios can provide the basis for rational urban policy development.

CASE STUDY: The Sacramento Region Blueprint Study

A leading example of scenario planning comes from the Sacramento region. Concerned about dispersed future growth patterns, housing, transportation, and air quality, the Sacramento Area Council of Governments (SACOG) launched the Sacramento Region Blueprint Transportation–Land Use Study to craft a future growth strategy for the region (SACOG undated). Scenarios were constructed through a bottom-up process, starting at the neighborhood level. At a series of 25 neighborhood workshops, residents were shown future "business as usual" development scenarios for their neighborhoods. Then they were asked to develop a series of smart growth alternative scenarios, which were fed into a geographic information systems (GIS) modeling program that provided real-time assessments of each scenario's land use and transportation impacts.

Based on the neighborhood scenarios, four countywide scenarios were crafted for each of the region's six counties—a trend scenario plus three alternatives that assumed different growth rates, land use mixes, housing types, densities, and infill/redevelopment proportions. These scenarios were analyzed for their land use and transportation impacts, and results presented at countywide workshops. Preferred scenarios from the countywide workshops formed the basis for four regional scenarios. These scenarios then were discussed and revised at regional-level workshops, and SACOG ultimately adopted a preferred regional scenario. The preferred scenario from the blueprint project is now being implemented through amendments to local government land use plans and through the region's long-range transportation plan.

FIGURE 4-17
Urban Footprints of Base Case and Preferred Scenarios for the Sacramento, California, Region

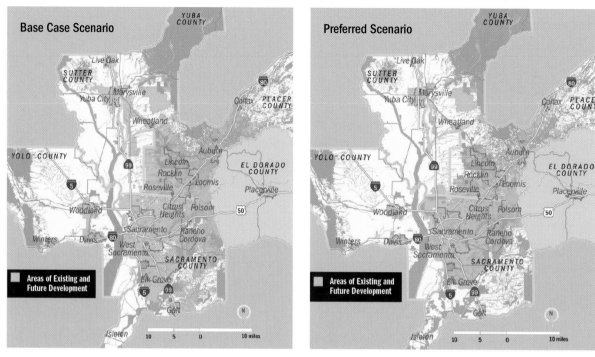

SOURCE: Sacramento Area Council of Governments (SACOG), TALL Order Regional Forum, April 30, 2004.

FIGURE 4-18
Selected Data for Scenarios from the Sacramento Region Blueprint Study

Scenarios	Single-Family: Multifamily Housing	% Housing Growth through Infill	% Auto Trips	% Transit	% Walk/ Bike	Daily VMT per Household
A: Business as usual (trend)	75:25	27.0	93.7	0.8	5.5	47.2
B: Higher housing densities than A, with growth focused at the urban fringe	67:33	39.0	83.2	4.0	12.7	37.6
C: Higher housing densities than A, with growth focused on central infill sites	65:35	38.3	81.8	4.8	13.4	36.7
D: Higher housing and employment densities, with growth focused on central infill sites	64:36	44.0	79.9	4.8	15.3	35.7
Preferred Scenario	65:35	41.0	83.9	3.3	12.9	34.9

SOURCE: SACOG, TALL Order Regional Forum, April 30, 2004; SACOG Preferred Blueprint Alternative, Special Report, January 2005.

The preferred regional scenario has a substantially smaller urban footprint than the so-called base case or trend (see Figure 4-17). Vehicle miles traveled is projected to be 26 percent lower with the preferred scenario than it would have been with the base case. How realistic is the preferred scenario? In 2006, two-thirds of the region's growth was in attached or small-lot detached housing. This represents a dramatic rise in density compared to five years earlier, and actually exceeds the goal of 60 percent attached or small-lot detached housing by 2050.

A Sample of Regional Scenario Studies

An open-ended survey was conducted in 2003/2004 to gather information on current and past scenario planning practices (Bartholomew 2007). The survey initially was sent to the planning directors of 658 member organizations in the National Association of Regional Councils (NARC). Additional surveys were sent to members of the Association of Metropolitan Planning Organizations that were not also NARC members. Responses to the two surveys were supplemented by hundreds of e-mails, telephone calls, and Internet searches, resulting in an initial data pool of 153 studies.

This initial pool was subjected to a threshold analysis to determine whether the studies actually used land use/transportation scenario planning techniques. The primary screening factor was whether future land use inputs—such as the density, diversity, design, and destination accessibility of growth—varied across scenarios. Those that held land use patterns static were excluded from the data set. This left a total of 80 studies, spread geographically across the country. Large and fast-growing regions are overrepresented in the sample.

Most studies test three or four scenarios (including a trend scenario) that vary in density, mix, and arrangement of future land uses. Half of the studies also test alternative transportation infrastructure investments. Twelve incorporate a transportation pricing element. Three-quarters of the studies evaluate scenarios for transportation impacts, more than half for impacts on open space and resource lands, 33 for impacts on criterion air pollutants, 18 for impacts on fuel use, and ten for GHG emissions (Bartholomew 2005).

A subset of 23 studies was selected for this publication, based on three criteria: simulations conducted at the regional scale, consistent population and employment totals across the scenarios, and availability of data for all scenarios on density, population growth, and VMT. Together, these studies tested a total of 85 regional development scenarios—one trend scenario per study, plus 62 planning scenarios that could be compared to trend.

Differences across Scenarios

The percentage difference in regional VMT for each planning scenario, relative to its respective trend scenario, is shown in Figure 4-19. Each bar represents a different planning scenario; the value shown is the percentage difference between that sce-

FIGURE 4-19
VMT Differences for 62 Planning Scenarios Relative to the Trend Scenario*

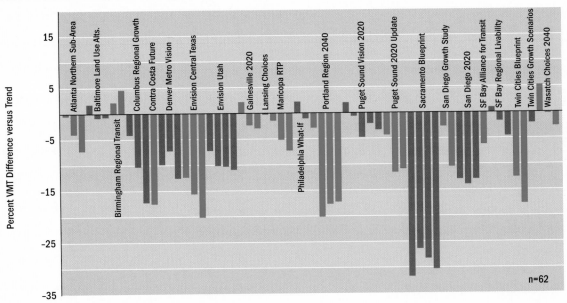

*Additional information about most of these projects is available through a digital library on scenario planning maintained by the University of Utah (http://www.lib.utah.edu/digital/collections/highways/).

SOURCE: Source: K. Bartholomew. "Integrating Land Use Issues into Transportation Planning: Scenario Planning—Summary Report," 2005, http://content.lib.utah.edu/cgi-bin/showfile.exe?CISOROOT=/ir-main&CISOPTR=99&filename=189.pdf.

FIGURE 4-20
Scenario Densities for 62 Planning Scenarios Relative to the Trend Scenario

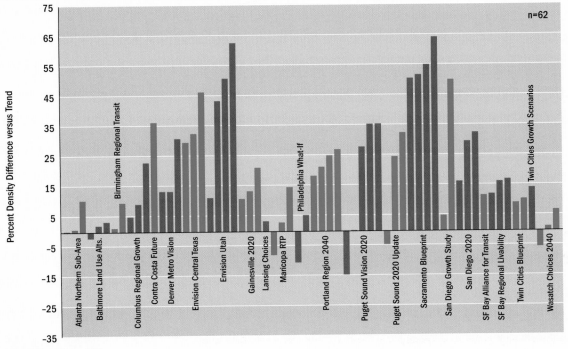

SOURCE: See Figure 4-19.

FIGURE 4-21
VMT versus Density

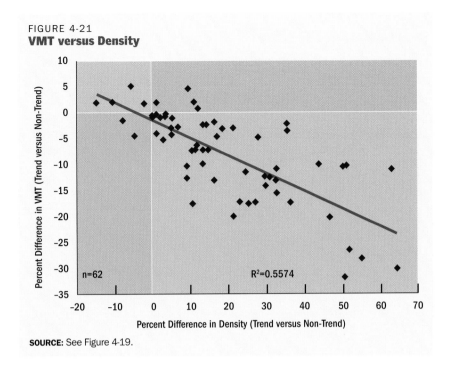

SOURCE: See Figure 4-19.

nario and the study's trend scenario. Across studies, the median reduction in regional VMT is 5.7 percent, none too impressive. However, there is wide variation in values across scenarios, from + 5 percent to –32 percent, which suggests that regional growth patterns may have a substantial impact in the best-case scenario.

Why is there so much variation in VMT across scenarios? Bartholomew identifies many of the potential sources of variation that could be considered in a meta-analysis. These, with their presumed impact on VMT, include the following:

- nature of the scenarios (denser, more mixed, and more centered ones result in bigger VMT reductions);
- planning time horizon (longer horizons result in bigger VMT reductions);
- rate of growth (more growth that can be redirected results in bigger VMT reductions);
- reallocation of transportation dollars (higher transit investments result in bigger VMT reductions); and
- addition of travel demand management strategies (higher costs of automobile travel result in bigger VMT reductions).

While a few planning scenarios are more dispersed than trend, the great majority are more compact (see Figure 4-20). The median increase in regional density of planning scenarios over trend is 13.8 percent. Here, again, there is wide variation across scenarios, from a 15 percent lower density for the most dispersed scenario to a 64 percent higher density for the most compact scenario.

The two variables are plotted against one another in Figure 4-21. As anticipated, this simple scatter plot shows that higher scenario densities are associated with greater VMT reductions relative to trend. The relationship appears strong and linear.

FIGURE 4-22
VMT versus Population Growth

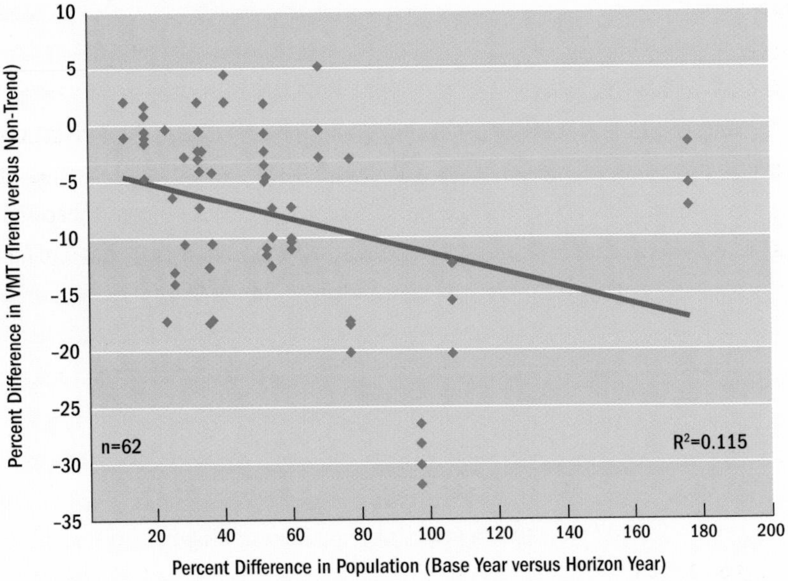

SOURCE: See Figure 4-19.

While a portion of the VMT reduction may be accounted for by higher densities, the scatter around the regression line in Figure 4-21 suggests that other factors also are at work. Figure 4-22 plots the percent difference in VMT for each planning scenario relative to trend against the percent population growth during the planning period for the metropolitan region as a whole (from base year to target year). Again, a correlation is apparent. The greater the increment of population growth that can be redirected in a planning scenario, the greater the difference in VMT. The growth increment is a function of both planning horizon (the further out, the more growth can be reallocated) and growth rate (the higher the growth rate, the more growth can be reallocated).

Other variables may contribute to VMT changes as well. Several were represented by dummy variables in this meta-analysis. A dummy variable is a variable that assumes a value of one or zero, depending upon whether a condition is met. Dummies are regularly used to represent categorical variables in analyses such as this.

Lacking numeric data on these variables, we relied on narrative descriptions of scenarios in study documents to create dummy variables. For example, one dummy variable was used to distinguish between scenarios that mix and balance residential and commercial land uses to a high degree (assigned a value of one), and scenarios that mix and balance land uses only to the same degree as trend development (assigned a value of zero). Some of the dummies were specific to scenarios; others were specific to regions and/or studies.

Meta-Analysis of Regional Simulation Studies

With so many independent variables, it becomes hard to discern relationships from simple scatter plots. This is a multivariate problem that requires a multivariate analysis to isolate the effect of each independent variable on the dependent variable, holding the other variables constant.

The analysis is further complicated by the multilevel nature of the data structure. Scenarios are "nested" within regions, with the typical region having two or three alternatives to the trend. Scenarios for the same region are not independent of each other, as they share the characteristics of their respective regions. Thus, standard (ordinary least squares) regression analysis cannot be used to analyze this multivariate data set. Rather, a hierarchical or multilevel modeling technique is required.[3]

A hierarchical linear model was estimated for the continuous outcome, percent difference in VMT relative to trend. Independent variables tested were at two levels, those specific to scenarios and those specific to studies (the latter common to all scenarios for a given region). Independent variables specific to scenarios were as follows:

- percent difference in gross density relative to trend development (–15 percent to +64 percent);
- development centralized/infill emphasized (1 if yes, 0 if no); and
- land uses highly mixed (1 if yes, 0 if no).

Independent variables common to scenarios for a given region but different across regions/studies were as follows:

- percent population growth increment relative base population (10 percent to 176 percent);
- auto use priced higher (1 if yes, 0 if no); and
- transportation investments coordinated with land uses (1 if yes, 0 if no).

The best-fit model is presented in Figure 4-23. For theoretical reasons, the model was estimated with no constant term (as a regression through the origin). If nothing changes from trend, there should be no reduction in regional VMT. There are three significant influences on VMT: the population growth increment, centralized

FIGURE 4-23
Best-Fit Model of Percent VMT Reduction
Relative to Trend (with Robust Standard Errors)

	Coefficient	t	P
Difference in density (% above trend)	–0.074	–1.48	0.15
Development centralized	–1.50	–2.13	0.037
Land uses mixed	–4.64	–2.15	0.036
Population growth increment (% above base)	–0.068	–2.02	0.056
Transportation coordinated	–2.12	–1.01	0.33

development, and mixed land use. All three are associated with decreases in VMT relative to trend. The increase in density relative to trend has the expected sign but falls just short of significance. Coordinated transportation investment also has the expected sign but is not significant.

The elasticity of VMT with respect to the population growth is –0.068, meaning that there is a 0.068 percent decrease in VMT per capita for every 1 percent increase in population relative to the base year. This does not argue for population growth per se, but simply indicates that regions that are growing rapidly have more opportunity to evolve toward a compact urban form than regions that are growing slowly.

Centralization of regional development and mixing of land uses both are inversely related to VMT at the 0.05 probability level. From their coefficients, we would expect a 1.5 percent drop in regional VMT with centralized development, and a 4.6 percent drop in regional VMT with mixed-use development (after controlling for other variables).

While the regional density variable is not statistically significant, our best guess at the elasticity of VMT with respect to regional density is –0.075, meaning that there would be a 0.075 percent decrease in VMT for every 1 percent increase in population density. This is a little higher than the elasticity estimate from the disaggregate travel studies presented earlier in this chapter. The density variable likely is soaking up some of the effect of other D variables that are not adequately represented in the regional growth simulations.

The coordinated transportation investment variable also is not statistically significant. Again, our best estimate of the impact of coordinated transportation investments, controlling for other variables, is a 2.1 percent reduction in regional VMT.

When forced into the model, the imposition of transportation pricing policies has a positive coefficient, suggesting that it would lead to higher VMT. This counterintuitive result is discussed in the section labeled "Regional Growth and Transportation Pricing."

Plugging realistic numbers into the best-fit model in Figure 4-23, we can estimate the VMT reduction associated with a shift to compact development. If such a shift increases average regional density by 50 percent in 2050, emphasizes infill, mixes land uses to a high degree, and has coordinated transportation investments, it would be expected to reduce regional VMT by about 18 percent over 43 years at an average metropolitan growth rate of 1.3 percent annually.[4]

The Conservative Nature of Scenario Forecasts

This forecasted reduction in regional VMT with compact development is almost surely an underestimate due to limitations of the travel forecasting models used in these studies. It is widely known, and oft-stated, that conventional regional travel models of the type used in most regional scenario studies are not sensitive to the effects of the first three Ds—density, diversity, and design (Walters, Ewing, and Allen 2000; Johnston 2004; Cervero 2006; DKS Associates and University of California 2007; Beimborn,

Kennedy, and Schaefer undated). Conventional models can simulate land use and transportation system effects on travel at the gross scale of a region, but not at the fine scale of a neighborhood. In particular, they cannot account for the micromixing of land uses, interconnection of local streets, or human-scaled urban design. Most do not even consider walk or bike trips, adjust vehicle trip rates for car shedding at higher densities, or estimate internal trips within mixed-use developments.[5]

These failings and others have prompted:

- the U.S. Department of Transportation to spend millions of dollars developing a new generation of travel forecasting models under the Travel Model Improvement Program;
- the U.S. EPA to develop the Smart Growth Index model;
- leading MPOs such as Portland Metro and SACOG to enhance their conventional "four-step" models with additional steps and feedback loops; and
- other leading MPOs to post-process model outputs or develop direct transit ridership models.

How much additional VMT reduction might be achieved with compact development, beyond that forecasted in regional growth simulations? To a first approximation, we can think of conventional travel models as accounting for two of the D variables, destination accessibility and distance to transit. The effects of the other D variables, outlined above in "Disaggregate Travel Studies," are largely neglected. Were they factored into the analyses, one could easily reach VMT reductions of 20 percent or more.

Regional Growth and Vehicle Emissions

Our sample of regional growth studies is not large enough, and the studies themselves are not sophisticated enough, to support meta-analyses of impacts of smart growth on other outcomes (beyond VMT). At most, they support qualitative statements and inferences.

Vehicle emissions, including CO_2, are not merely a function of VMT, but also reflect the numbers of cold starts plus vehicle operating speeds (see "VMT and CO_2 Projections" in Chapter 3). Figure 4-24 shows that for many scenarios, an increase in density is associated with a drop in average peak-hour operating speeds—an outcome that could result in increased emissions because gasoline engines function more efficiently at higher speeds. From these data, the elasticity of average peak-hour speed with respect to density is –0.22.

Figure 4-25 plots nitrogen oxide (NOx) emissions versus density for 24 planning scenarios. The scatter plot shows a strong association between the two variables. The strength of the association appears equivalent to that between VMT and density. Because most or all of these studies use vehicle emission models that account for differences in vehicle operating speeds, we can reasonably conclude from these data that any effect of density on emissions through vehicle operating speeds is overwhelmed by the effect of density on emissions through VMT. As with the observations above on

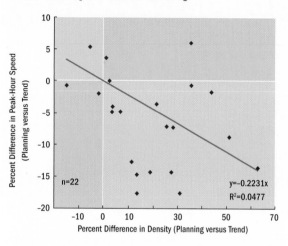

FIGURE 4-24
Peak-Hour Speed versus Density

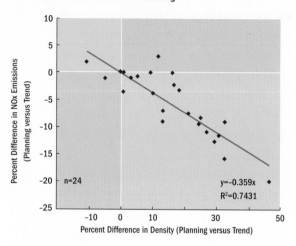

FIGURE 4-25
NOx Emissions versus Density

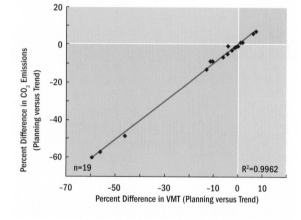

FIGURE 4-26
CO_2 Emissions versus VMT

gasoline consumption and speed (see Figure 4-4), compact development is associated with lower emissions, notwithstanding possible reductions in vehicle speeds.

Data on regional CO_2 emissions are more limited, illustrating an historic lack of focus on carbon emissions by metropolitan planning organizations. Figure 4-26 plots VMT versus CO_2 differences for 19 planning scenarios. The near-perfect correlation and the elasticity value close to 1.0 suggest the multiplication of VMT by a constant factor to arrive at CO_2 forecasts.

Regional Growth and Transportation Pricing

The meta-analysis presented above, in "Meta-Analysis of Regional Simulation Studies," produced one anomalous result. When forced into the model, the imposition of transportation pricing policies has a positive coefficient, suggesting that it would lead to higher VMT.

In theory, the impact of pricing schemes on land development patterns could be positive or negative, depending on the pricing scheme. Increasing the price of driving (roads or parking) in only one part of a metropolitan region or along only a limited number of corridors could shift future economic and development activity away from the priced area or corridors and toward areas that are unpriced (Deakin et al. 1996). This could lead to more sprawl and VMT. Adopting areawide pricing would have the opposite effect, concentrating future growth. This would occur as households and businesses seek to reduce or avoid the extra costs (Komanoff 1997). Some simulation-based evidence supports this conclusion (Gupta, Kalmanje, and Kockelman 2006).

FIGURE 4-27
Percentage Reduction in Transportation Outcomes with Transportation Pricing, and Pricing and Compact Development Combined

	Pricing/Subsidy	LUTRAQ with Pricing/Subsidy
Daily VMT	–2%	–7.9%
NOx emissions (kilograms/day)	–2.9%	–8.7%
CO$_2$ emissions (kilograms/day)	–2%	–7.9%

SOURCE: 1000 Friends of Oregon. Making the Land Use, Transportation, Air Quality Connection: Analysis of Alternatives. Vol. 5, Portland, Oregon, 1996, http://www.onethousandfriendsoforegon.org/resources/lut_vol5.html.

If transportation pricing is ultimately adopted as a strategy to reduce VMT and CO$_2$, compact development could prove useful in both cushioning the blow to household budgets and enhancing the travel reduction effects (see Cambridge Systematics 1994). The LUTRAQ study, which was not included in the meta-analysis because it was subregional, provides data that support this conclusion. The project compared three scenarios: 1) a trend scenario that assumed the continuation of recent development practices and transportation investments, including a new highway; 2) the same scenario with an areawide parking pricing/free transit pass policy added;[6] and 3) a transit-oriented development scenario (LUTRAQ) with two additional rail lines and the same parking/transit pass component. Adding the LUTRAQ land use/transit element to the pricing/subsidy package tripled reductions in NOx and nearly quadrupled reductions in VMT and CO$_2$ emissions (see Figure 4-27).

Project-Level Simulations

We also can assess the effects of the built environment through comparisons of VMT and vehicle emissions generated by individual land developments. These comparisons may be based on actual travel diaries or odometer readings for residents of existing developments. Or they may be based on simulations using conventional travel models calibrated and validated for the study region and, in some cases, enhanced to capture the effects of local variations in the D variables.

Unlike regional scenario studies, project-level simulations have the advantage of focusing on the subset of the regional population for whom the built environment actually varies. Site plans can vary in density, diversity, or design, without a change in regional location or transit access. Or regional location and transit access can vary, from transit-served brownfields to auto-dependent greenfields, without a change in site plans. Or both can vary. The amount of development (housing and employment) generally is held constant in project-level simulations, but acreage may differ across site plans.

CASE STUDY: Atlantic Station

The 1999 study of the Atlantic Steel project—now known as Atlantic Station—is a prominent example of project-level simulation with both types of variation. The redevelopment project is on a 138-acre former steel mill and brownfield site in Midtown Atlanta. A developer proposed converting the vacant site into a "new town in town." Its location—close to primary regional destinations and to rapid transit—and its dense, mixed-use design made the proposed Atlantic Steel redevelopment a classic smart growth infill project, favored by everyone from the city's mayor to the vice president of the United States (then, Al Gore).

The dilemma was that the redevelopment project required a bridge over Interstate 75/85 to connect to a rapid transit station and a neighborhood to the east, plus ramps for access to the interstate highways. At the time, the Atlanta region was out of compliance with federal transportation conformity requirements and, as a result, could not tap into federal funds to add to its highway system. It could not even construct certain highway improvements using nonfederal funds. The proposed bridge and ramps were included in this prohibition.

Under a program called Project XL (excellence and leadership), the EPA has the power to waive environmental regulations when a superior environmental outcome can be achieved by some otherwise prohibited action. Based on an analysis showing that redevelopment of the Atlantic Steel site would produce less VMT and vehicle emissions than development at likely alternative sites in outlying areas, the EPA ultimately waived the conformity requirement for this project.

For this analysis, a team of consultants evaluated the Atlantic Steel project from two standpoints:

Regional Location. The Midtown site was compared to three greenfield sites large enough to accommodate the proposed development. The sites were at increasing distances from the urban core: a perimeter beltway location, a suburban location, and an exurban location, each with a development density and site plan typical of its location. The map on the facing page shows the location of the Atlantic Steel site and the three greenfield sites relative to the urban core.

Site Plan. Three alternative plans for the Atlantic Steel site—incorporating different internal densities, land use mixes, street networks, and streetscape design elements—were compared. They were the Jacoby Development Corporation's original site plan, an "improved new urbanism case" developed through a charrette process by Duany Plater-Zyberk & Company (DPZ), and a final compromise plan incorporating key DPZ concepts.

The original Jacoby design mixed land uses primarily on the site's east side, nearest the MARTA rapid transit station. On the west side, the developer proposed a

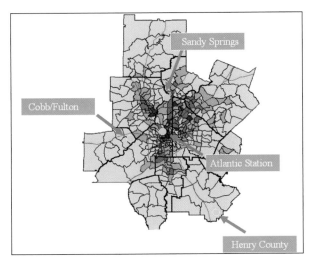

Alternative regional locations evaluated.

CREDIT: Based on Environmental Protection Agency (EPA). "Transportation and Environmental Analysis of the Atlantic Steel Development Proposal." EPA 231-R-99-004, September 1999, http://www.epa.gov/projctxl/atlantic/page1.htm.

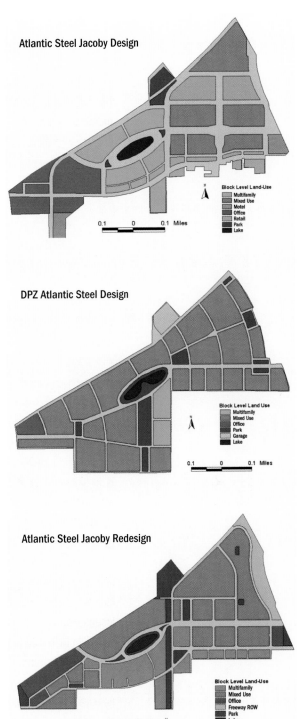

Alternative site plans evaluated.

CREDIT: Based on EPA. "Transportation and Environmental Analysis of the Atlantic Steel Development Proposal." EPA 231-R-99-004, September 1999, http://www.epa.gov/projctxl/atlantic/page1.htm.

single-use office park with buildings set back from the street and separated by stretches of undeveloped green area and parking. Residences were located between the office park and the retail/hotel district. The street network was an adaptation of the site's existing grid system, with some connections to neighborhood streets to the south.

With everything riding on EPA approval, the agency had the leverage to push for a more integrated site plan. The DPZ plan, generated at a design charrette, mixed land uses within the site to a great degree, while holding the amount of office, retail, and residential development constant. Only the far west side retained the single-use character of the original site plan, in an office district. The redesign featured shorter blocks, narrower streets, improved streetscapes, and clear pedestrian paths. Auto speeds were controlled to provide a better pedestrian environment. Densities were increased near transit stops. The street grid of the surrounding neighborhood was extended into the site, and land uses were moved to permit shared parking.

Jacoby's final site plan is a compromise between the two earlier plans. The land use mix is more fine-grained than the original plan's but not as fine-grained as the DPZ redesign. The street network is more fine-meshed than the original plan's but less so than the redesign. Other concepts

FIGURE 4-28
VMT Generated by Regional Location and Site Plan Alternatives

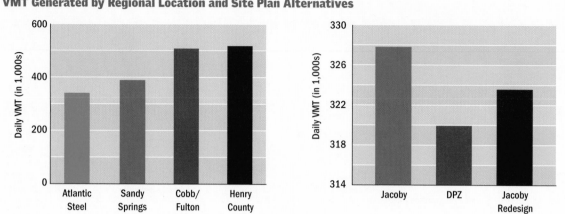

SOURCE: EPA. "Transportation and Environmental Analysis of the Atlantic Steel Development Proposal." EPA 231-R-99-004, September 1999, http://www.epa.gov/projctxl/atlantic/page1.htm.

from the DPZ charrette, and from the literature on the built environment and travel, have been retained.

First, the EPA consultant team performed an in-depth evaluation of travel forecasting methods used in the Atlanta region. The evaluation resulted in various refinements to the Atlanta Regional Commission's conventional travel forecasting model to better account for regional location and destination accessibility, and in the postprocessing of model outputs to better account for the first three Ds—density, diversity, and design (Walters, Ewing, and Allen 2000). Postprocessing employed an early version of the Smart Growth Index model with elasticities derived from a review of recent research on the built environment and household travel (as described earlier in this chapter in "Disaggregate Travel Studies").

Model results demonstrated that VMT and emissions would be about 34 percent lower at the Atlantic Steel infill site than at the remote greenfield locations, and an additional 2 percent lower with the revised site plans (see Figure 4-28). As a result, for the first time, the EPA designated a land development proposal as a regional transportation control measure, allowing for approval of the project and funding of transportation improvements.

Atlantic Station has become a highly successful, largely built and occupied, infill community (see the photographs on the facing page). An early evaluation of travel by residents and employees of Atlantic Station suggests even larger VMT reductions than projected originally. Based on a travel diary survey, residents were estimated to generate eight VMT per day and employees to generate 11 VMT per day (Center for Transportation and the Environment 2006). These estimates compare favorably with a regional average daily VMT of more than 32, among the highest in the nation. Despite a low response rate and high margin of error, the Atlantic Station travel diary survey points toward VMT reductions of more 50 percent relative to sprawl.

Atlantic Station today.

JACOBY DEVELOPMENT COMPANY

Site Plan Influences on VMT

The Atlantic Station study—and similar studies in San Diego, Wilmington, Portland, Oak Ridge, San Antonio, and Toronto—have projected the impacts of site design on vehicle trips, VMT, and/or CO_2 emissions (Hagler Bailly, Inc., and Criterion Planners/Engineers 1998; EPA 1999, 2001a, 2001b; IBI Group, Canada Mortgage, and Natural Resources Canada 2000). Figure 4-29 presents the findings of these studies. In each case, alternative development plans for the same site are compared to a baseline or trend plan.

Results suggest that VMT and CO_2 per capita decline as site density increases and the mix of jobs, housing, and retail uses becomes more balanced. However, the limited number of studies, differences in assumptions and methodologies from study to study, and the variability of results make it difficult to generalize.

FIGURE 4-29
Effect of Site Design Alone on VMT

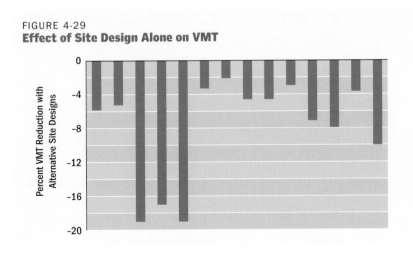

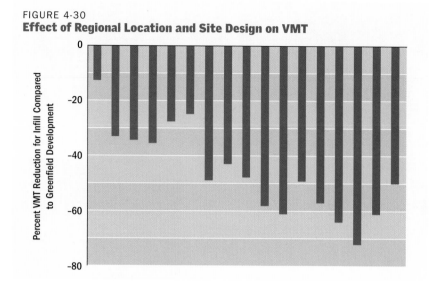

FIGURE 4-30
Effect of Regional Location and Site Design on VMT

Regional Location Influences on VMT

Approximately ten studies have considered the effects of regional location on travel and emissions generated by individual developments (EPA 1999, 2001a, 2001b, 2006; Hagler Bailly, Inc. 1998; Hagler Bailly, Inc., and Criterion Planners/Engineers 1999; IBI Group, Canada Mortgage, and Natural Resources Canada 2000; Allen and Benfield 2003; U.S. Conference of Mayors 2001; SACOG 2007). The studies differ in methodology and context, and in some cases include changes in site design. But they tend to yield the same conclusion: infill locations generate substantially lower VMT per capita than do greenfield locations, from 13 to 72 percent lower (see Figure 4-30).

In Figure 4-31, the distribution of data points indicates that, while higher density is associated with reduced VMT, other factors also are at work. We suspect

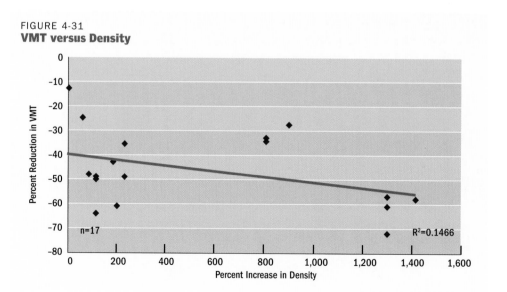

FIGURE 4-31
VMT versus Density

FIGURE 4-32
CO$_2$ Emissions versus VMT

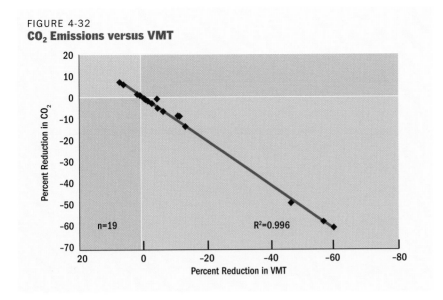

that regional location explains most of the scatter, and that the relationship between density and VMT is due in part to regional location as well. The highest densities are programmed for the most central locations.

VMT reductions cluster between about 30 and 60 percent. When compared with the results of the site design studies, which show VMT reductions of 2 to 19 percent, the effect of regional location appears much stronger than that of site design.

The Relationship between VMT Reduction and CO$_2$ Reduction

Dense infill developments also are credited with reduced CO$_2$ emissions (see Figure 4-32). On a percentage basis, CO$_2$ reductions are not quite as large as VMT reductions. The slope of the regression line suggests an elasticity of CO$_2$ emissions with respect to VMT of 0.96. This is likely due to emission penalties associated with reduced vehicle operating speeds at infill locations.

5

Environmental Determinism versus Self Selection

There is a long-running debate in urban planning about the degree to which the physical environment determines human behavior. The theory of environmental or architectural determinism ascribes great importance to the physical environment as a shaper of behavior. The counter view is that social and economic factors are the main or even exclusive determinants of behavior.

To outsiders, this debate may seem simplistic. Any extreme view would be. Yet, we all bring paradigms to the study of travel behavior, paradigms that affect our interpretation of the facts. Depending on one's point of view, the documented relationship between the built environment and travel might just as well be due to 1) individuals who want to walk or use transit selecting pedestrian- or transit-friendly environments (self selection) as it is to 2) pedestrian- and transit-friendly environments causing individuals to use these modes of travel more than they would otherwise (environmental determinism).

For many of the studies reviewed in Chapter 4, we can discount self selection because the geographic scale is the region or county. Travel preferences likely fall far down the list of factors—after job access, climate, cost-of-living, school quality, and family ties—that people consider when choosing a region or county in which to live. For those moving from one neighborhood to another, however, a desire to walk or use transit could be a factor in their decision, a possibility to which we now turn our attention.

The Empirical Literature on Self Selection

Does residential choice come first, and travel choice or some other outcome follow (environmental determinism)? Or do people's propensities for travel and physical activity determine their choice of residential environment (self selection)? Between environment and attitude, which drives behavior?

More than anything else recently, the possibility of self-selection bias has engendered doubt about the travel benefits of compact urban development patterns. According to a Transportation Research Board/Institute of Medicine report (2005), "If researchers do not properly account for the choice of neighborhood, their empirical results will be biased in the sense that features of the built environment may appear to influence activity more than they in fact do. (Indeed, this single potential source of statistical bias casts doubt on the majority of studies on the topic to date.)"

Self selection occurs if the choice of residence depends in a significant way on attitudes about, or preferences for, one mode of transportation over another. In the language of research, such attitudes will confound the relationship between residential environment and travel choices.

Many studies have cited associations between attitudes and travel choices as evidence of self selection. Favorable attitudes about walking correlate with walking; favorable attitudes about the environment correlate with transit use. It would be surprising, indeed, if travelers who are favorably disposed toward a given mode did not use that mode more frequently than others, regardless of where they live. But this does not mean that attitudes account for the observed relationship between the built environment and travel. For self selection to occur, attitudes must also influence residential choices.

Planning researchers frequently ask new residents whether transit accessibility, walkability, or access to specific destinations were factors in their location decisions. Access considerations usually fall well down the list of location factors, after housing price and quality, neighborhood amenities, and school quality.

Typical of such surveys is one by Dill (2004). Fairview Village is a mixed-use, new urbanist neighborhood in suburban Portland, Oregon, with interconnected streets and attractive streetscapes (see the photograph and site plan on the facing page). Residents were asked to rate the importance of location factors in choosing their new home. The highest-rated factors were neighborhood safety, neighborhood style, and house price. Among access variables, "quick access to the freeway" was ranked highest at number eight. Pedestrian access ranked lower. "Having stores within walking distance" was 12th in importance, and "having a library within walking distance" was 14th. Still, pedestrian access was rated as more important in Fairview Village than in two nearby subdivisions matched for income, home value, home size, and year built. Apparently, self selection is present but weak. Whatever the underlying cause—attitude or environment—walk trips are much more frequent in Fairview Village, and VMT per adult is 20 percent lower than in otherwise comparable suburban subdivisions (see Figure 5-1).

The strongest survey-based evidence of self selection is Lund's (2006) study of residents who had recently moved to transit-oriented developments (TODs) on rail lines in California. For TOD residents, transit access ranked third among location

Fairview Village City Hall and nearby housing (above) and Fairview Village site plan (left).

PLAN CREDIT: M. Rose. "Neighborhood Design & Mode Choice," Portland State University, Field Area Paper, Masters of Urban and Regional Planning, 2004.

FIGURE 5-1
Trip Frequency by Mode and by Neighborhood

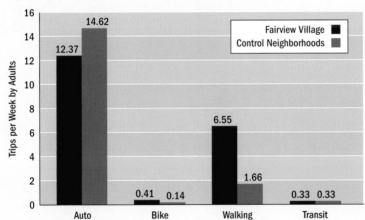

SOURCE: Based on data in J. Dill. "Travel Behavior and Attitudes: New Urbanist vs. Traditional Suburban Neighborhoods," presented at the 2004 Annual Meeting of the Transportation Research Board, Washington, D.C.

factors in San Francisco and fifth in Los Angeles and San Diego (where, amazingly, it ranked lower than highway access). One-third of all respondents mentioned transit access as one of the top three reasons for locating in a TOD. These residents were much more likely to use transit than those not citing transit access as a location factor. Yet, because the survey did not collect comparable data on prior travel mode, we cannot draw any inference regarding the strength of attitudes versus environment or on the effect of transit-oriented development on net regional transit use.

The strongest survey-based evidence of environmental determinism is Frank et al.'s (forthcoming) in-depth study of 8,000 households in Atlanta, which indicates

FIGURE 5-2
Average VMT by Neighborhood Type and Residential Preference

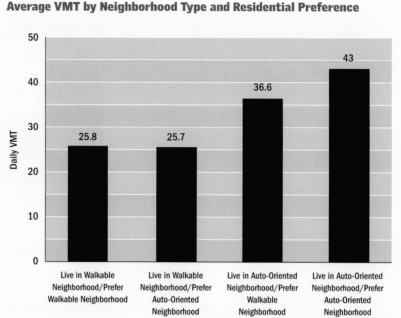

SOURCE: L. Frank, B. Saelens, K.E. Powell, and J.E. Chapman. "Stepping Towards Causation: Do Built Environments or Neighborhood and Travel Preferences Explain Physical Activity, Driving, and Obesity?" *Social Science & Medicine*, forthcoming.

that the built environment and availability of alternatives can lead anyone, regardless of preference, to drive less. Just comparing those who stated a preference for walkable environments, VMT was 30 percent lower among those who actually lived in a walkable neighborhood than among those who lived in an auto-oriented neighborhood (see Figure 5-2). Roughly one in three current residents of automobile-oriented neighborhoods would prefer to live in a walkable environment but were unable to find one, given current development patterns. This alone indicates a ready-made market for compact development.

At least 28 studies using different research designs have attempted to test and control for residential self selection (Mokhtarian and Cao forthcoming; Cao, Mokhtarian, and Handy 2006). Nearly all of them found "resounding" evidence of statistically significant associations between the built environment and travel behavior, independent of self-selection influences: "Virtually every quantitative study reviewed for this work, after controlling for self-selection through one of the various ways discussed above, found a statistically significant influence of one or more built environment measures on the travel behavior variable of interest" (Cao, Mokhtarian, and Handy 2006).

Mokhtarian and colleagues find research designs used in studies to date all wanting in some respect. Still to be determined through future research are the absolute and relative magnitudes of self-selection effects.

FIGURE 5-3

Mechanisms by which Attitudes and Preferences Might Affect Travel Choices and VMT

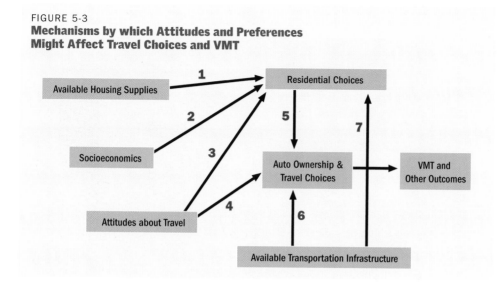

The Built Environment May Matter in Any Case

The fact that people to some extent "self select" into neighborhoods matching their attitudes is itself a demonstration of the importance of the built environment in travel behavior. If there were no such influence, people who prefer to travel by transit or non-motorized modes might as well settle in sprawling areas, where they have no alternative to the automobile.

Whether the association between the built environment and travel is due to environmental determinism or self selection may have little practical import. Where people live ultimately depends on housing supply and demand. As Lund, Willson, and Cervero (forthcoming) note, ". . . if people are simply moving from one transit-accessible location to another (and they use transit regularly at both locations), then there is theoretically no overall increase in ridership levels. If, however, the resident was unable to take advantage of transit service at their prior residence, then moves to a TOD (transit-oriented development) and begins to use the transit service, the TOD is fulfilling a latent demand for transit accessibility and the net effect on ridership is positive."

The conceptual model presented in Figure 5-3 indicates why self selection may be less important than the recent focus in the literature suggests. Attitudes about travel have direct effects on travel choices (link 4). Attitudes also may have indirect effects through the mediator, residential choice (link 3). This is the theory of self selection. If link 3 is strong relative to link 4, self selection may be the main mechanism through which the built environment affects travel and health outcomes. If link 3 is weak, residential choices may still affect travel directly through link 5. This is the theory of environmental determinism.

Note that strong self selection may actually enhance the effect of the built environment on travel, not render it insignificant, as some of the literature implies. Whether

FIGURE 5-4

Effect of New Walkable, Transit-Oriented Developments on Regional VMT

	Self Selection Dominates	Environmental Determinism Dominates
Walkable, transit-oriented places undersupplied at present	VMT decreases	VMT decreases
Walkable, transit-oriented place adequately supplied at present	VMT stays the same	VMT decreases

it does or not depends on housing supply (link 1) relative to demand (links 2 and 3). Housing supply may affect travel regionally if certain types of residential environments are undersupplied. We will refer to this as the theory of latent demand. As shown in Figure 5-3, the ability to self select (link 3) is moderated by housing supplies.

Think of travel outcomes in two dimensions (as in Figure 5-4). One dimension relates to the relative strength of self selection versus environmental determinism. The other depends on the supply of walkable or transit-served places relative to demand across a region. Of course, these dichotomies are false. Both dimensions are continuous, and reality almost certainly lies somewhere along a continuum.

But for three of the four extreme scenarios, the development of new walkable, transit-oriented places should lead to net increases in walking and transit use across the region. Even if self selection is the dominant mechanism through which the built environment influences travel, developers meeting latent demand for walkable, transit-oriented environments will be contributing to reduced VMT. Indeed, the only way that these developers will not have a positive impact is if such places already are adequately supplied.

This does not appear to be the case. There is ample evidence that the demand for walkable, transit-oriented environments far exceeds the current supply. In a study of residential preferences in Boston and Atlanta, Levine, Inam, and Tong (2005) find a huge unmet demand for pedestrian- and transit-friendly environments, particularly among Atlanta residents (see Figure 5-5). It causes these researchers to conclude:

> . . . given the gap depicted in Figure [5.5], it seems unlikely that new transit-oriented housing in Atlanta would fill up with average Atlantans; rather, it would tend to be occupied by people with distinct preferences for such housing who previously lacked the ability to satisfy those preferences in the Atlanta environment. Self-selection in this case would be a real effect, but it would hardly negate the impact of urban form on travel behavior. This is because in the absence of such development, those households would be unlikely to reside in a pedestrian neighborhood and would have little choice but to adopt auto-oriented travel patterns.

FIGURE 5-5

Relationship of Transit-Pedestrian Preference to Residence in Transit- and Pedestrian-Friendly Zones

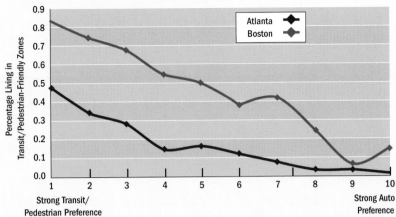

SOURCE: J. Levine, A.Inam, G. Tong. "A Choice-Based Rationale for Land Use and Transportation Alternatives—Evidence from Boston and Atlanta." *Journal of Planning Education and Research*, Vol. 24, Issue 3, 2005, pp. 317–330.

For more data on the unmet and growing demand for compact development, see Belden Russonello & Stewart (2003), Myers and Gearin (2001), Center for Transit-Oriented Development (2004), Levine and Frank (2007), Logan (2007), and Nelson (2006).

Thus, it is clear that both self selection and environmental determinism may account for VMT reductions with compact development. A recent study in the San Francisco Bay Area suggests that more than 40 percent of the ridership bonus associated with TOD is a product of residential self selection (Cervero and Duncan 2003). Whatever the source, regional transit ridership is higher than it would be otherwise, and regional VMT is lower.

6

Induced Traffic and Induced Development

Some have claimed that the climate crisis could be eased by building new highways and expanding existing ones (AASHTO 2007). The logic is simple: additional highway capacity would lessen congestion and move urban areas toward the sweet spot on the CO_2 emission rate curve, where vehicle efficiency is at its peak (see Figure 3-9, page 45). This might be a viable strategy but for two links in Figure 5-3 (see page 95). Link 6 represents induced traffic, link 7 induced development. Both could boost regional VMT, undoing any short-term advantage of highway capacity expansion.

Tony Downs of the Brookings Institution first explained the phenomenon of induced traffic in his 1962 "Law of Peak-Hour Traffic Congestion." As he explained more recently:

> ... traffic flows in any region's overall transportation networks form almost automatically self-adjusting relationships among different routes, times, and modes. For example, a major commuting expressway might be so heavily congested each morning that traffic crawls for at least thirty minutes. If that expressway's capacity were doubled overnight, the next day's traffic would flow rapidly because the same number of drivers would have twice as much road space. But soon word would spread that this particular highway was no longer congested. Drivers who had once used that road before and after the peak hour to avoid congestion would shift back into the peak period. Other drivers who had been using alternative routes would shift onto this more convenient expressway. Even some commuters who had been using the subway or trains would start driving on

CHICKEN OR EGG, PART 2?

Controversy exists over whether and to what extent the addition of highway capacity induces new traffic and promotes urban development in proximity to the added highway capacity. The concept of induced traffic challenges the view that the expansion of existing roads or the building of new roads will necessarily relieve highway congestion. The concept of induced development challenges the notion that highway investments are a response to growth and development, as opposed to a cause of them.

this road during peak periods. Within a short time, this triple convergence onto the expanded road during peak hours would make the road as congested as it was before its expansion (Downs 2004).

Controversy exists over whether and to what extent the addition of highway capacity induces new traffic and promotes urban development in proximity to the added highway capacity. The concept of induced traffic challenges the view that the expansion of existing roads or the building of new roads will necessarily relieve highway congestion. The concept of induced development challenges the notion that highway investments are a response to growth and development, as opposed to a cause of them. In the highway "wars" that ensue between environmental and development interests, opposing sides have very different positions on the nature and magnitude of induced traffic and induced development. In this brief review, we will attempt to sort out facts from debating points.

CASE STUDY: Interstate 270

Interstate 270, which angles to the northwest from the Washington, D.C., beltway in Montgomery County, Maryland, was widened in the late 1980s and early 1990s. In 1999, the *Washington Post* ran a story comparing actual traffic volumes on I-270 to pre-construction projections (*Washington Post* 1999). The article declared the widening a failure based on the amount of induced traffic, which effectively used up the added capacity. By the year 2000, traffic volume for certain sections of I-270 already exceeded forecasts for 2010.

This was a time of growing interest in the phenomena of induced traffic and induced development. The Maryland-National Capital Park and Planning Commission and the Metropolitan Washington Council of Governments responded with a study that suggested that highway-induced development was mainly responsible for the high and premature levels of congestion on I-270 (NCRTPB/MWCOG 2001). Also blamed was the failure to build all transportation facilities in the adopted regional transportation plan. Some projects had been delayed and others dropped.

On the subject of induced development, the study concluded that "higher observed traffic volumes relative to the 1984 forecast appear to be due in large part to shifts in population, employment, and travel to the I-270 corridor from other areas in the region, rather than to entirely new travel." For the region as a whole, population growth was 5 percent lower than had been forecasted in 1984, while employment growth was 9 percent higher. The two together suggested small (if any) net impacts of I-270 on regional growth.

However, population and employment had clearly shifted to the I-270 corridor, at the expense of other areas. Specifically, population and employment in the I-270 corridor were, respectively, 23 and 45 percent higher than forecasted in 1984. For all of Montgomery County, they were 7 and 21 percent higher than forecasted. Meanwhile,

FIGURE 6-1
Difference between Actual and Forecasted Households by Subarea, 2000

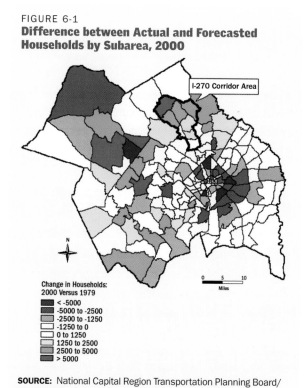

Change in Households:
2000 Versus 1979
- < -5000
- -5000 to -2500
- -2500 to -1250
- -1250 to 0
- 0 to 1250
- 1250 to 2500
- 2500 to 5000
- > 5000

SOURCE: National Capital Region Transportation Planning Board/ Metropolitan Washington Council of Governments (NCRTPB/ MWCOG). "Induced Travel: Definition, Forecasting Process, and a Case Study in the Metropolitan Washington Region." Washington, D.C., Sept. 19, 2001.

FIGURE 6-2
Difference between Actual and Forecasted Employment by Subarea, 2000

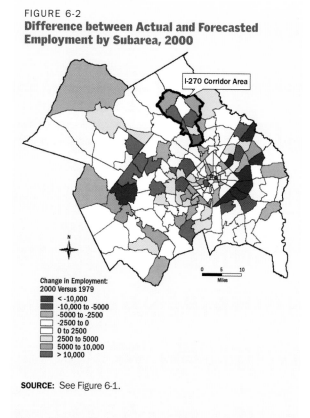

Change in Employment:
2000 Versus 1979
- < -10,000
- -10,000 to -5000
- -5000 to -2500
- -2500 to 0
- 0 to 2500
- 2500 to 5000
- 5000 to 10,000
- > 10,000

SOURCE: See Figure 6-1.

population and employment were 9 and 23 percent lower than forecasted in Prince George's County, and 29 and 3 percent lower than forecasted in the District of Columbia. These shifts in development are illustrated in Figures 6-1 and 6-2.

The experience with the I-270 widening mirrors the literature on highway-induced traffic and highway-induced development.

The Magnitude of Induced Traffic

Cervero (2002) compares elasticity values across studies in a meta-analysis. Again, an elasticity is the percentage change in one variable that accompanies a 1 percent change in another variable. An elasticity of VMT with respect to lane miles of 0.5 implies that every 1 percent increase in lane miles is accompanied by a 0.5 percent increase in VMT. At the facility level, a 100 percent increase in lane miles is what we would get if a facility were widened from two to four lanes.

In his meta-analysis, Cervero (2002) derives the average elasticities shown in Figure 6-3. Based on the meta-analysis, Cervero (2002) concludes that "... the preponderance of research suggests that induced-demand effects are significant, with an appreciable share of added capacity being absorbed by increases in traffic, with a few

FIGURE 6-3
Elasticities of VMT with Respect to Capacity

	Facility-Specific Studies	Areawide Studies
Short-term	0	0.4
Medium-term	0.265	NA
Long-term	0.63	0.73

SOURCE: R. Cervero. "Induced Travel Demand: Research Design, Empirical Evidence, and Normative Policies." *Journal of Planning Literature*, Vol. 17, Issue 1, 2002, pp. 3–20.

notable exceptions." The average long-term elasticity of 0.73 suggests that for every 1 percent increase in areawide highway capacity, VMT increases by 0.73. The actual increase in a given corridor or metropolitan area depends on the level of congestion. Adding capacity in an area with no congestion has no effect; adding capacity in an area with severe congestion has huge effects. This is apparent from Figure 6-4, which shows the VMT increase per lane-mile of capacity added in California metropolitan areas. The induced traffic effect is greatest in the congested San Francisco, Los Angeles, and San Diego metropolitan areas.

FIGURE 6-4
Estimated Additional VMT from an Additional Lane-Mile, California Metropolitan Areas

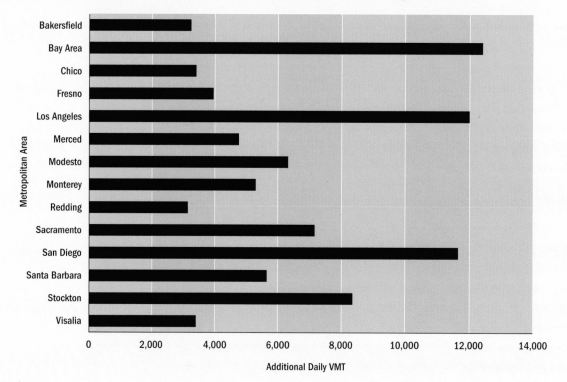

SOURCE: M. Hansen and Y. Huang. "Road Supply and Traffic in California Urban Areas." *Transportation Research A*, Vol. 31, Issue 3, 1997, pp. 205–218.

The Role of Induced Development

Induced traffic and induced development are related. One can think of induced development as a cause of induced traffic, not immediately but over the longer term. To better understand induced traffic and its connection to induced development, it is necessary to explore the behavioral consequences of additions to roadway infrastructure capacity.

In the short term, a variety of behavioral changes can contribute to increased traffic without any induced development. These include route switches, mode switches, and changes in destination. In addition, new trips may be taken that would not have occurred without the additional highway capacity.

In the longer run, increases in highway capacity may lower travel times so that new residents and businesses are drawn to locate near the highway. The question is always whether this new development was induced to locate there by the highway expansion or whether it would have occurred anyway, regardless of the highway. Indeed, the highway investment may be a response to new or anticipated development, rather than vice versa. If the development itself would not have occurred otherwise, the development and the traffic it generates can be considered induced.

Definitionally, a gray area exists if the development that occurs near a highway would have occurred somewhere else in the region in the absence of the investment. Some would call this induced development, others redistributed development. We use the term induced development liberally, to mean any development that would not have occurred at a given location without a highway investment.

The Complexity of Induced Development

Induced development is a complex phenomenon, which helps explain the divergent viewpoints regarding its magnitude and even its existence. One source of complexity is the two distinct roles of highway infrastructure. On the one hand, highways allow movement, communication, and market exchange. Highway investments may affect household location decisions by lowering travel costs. Household location decisions may, in turn, influence the location decisions of firms and industries, and vice versa.

On the other hand, highways also are a factor in the production of private goods and services. Lower transportation costs may boost private sector productivity and output generally across the region. In this case, highways will affect the economic landscape in ways that no simple location model can capture.

Because of these two distinct roles, the interjurisdictional effects of highway investments may be either positive or negative. Development and other economic activity may flow from jurisdictions that have not made highway investments to those that have. Alternatively, positive spillovers from jurisdictions with highway investments may spur economic growth in neighboring jurisdictions without highway investments. Metaphorically, highway investments may create a rising tide that lifts all boats, or this tide may lift some as it capsizes others. Which effect dominates is an empirical question, hence the need to review the empirical literature.

The Historical Role of Induced Development

Clearly, the impacts of highway investments are less today than they once were. Construction of the Interstate Highway System, in particular, has tied virtually every place in the country to everywhere else. Most studies finding sizable highway impacts (for example, Mohring 1961 and Czamanski 1966) date back to the first round of interstate highway construction, which created huge positive externalities for areas gaining access to the network. By the early 1970s, the Interstate Highway System was largely complete. Incremental additions or improvements to the network have since produced comparatively small improvements in interregional accessibility.

How great are highway impacts on economic and land development in the post-interstate era? This is a subject of great debate. In a well-known point-counterpoint, Giuliano (1995) minimized the importance of highway investments for three reasons: "The transportation system in most U.S. metropolitan areas is highly developed, and therefore the relative impact of even major investments will be minor. The built environment has a very long life…. Even in rapidly growing metropolitan areas, the vast proportion of buildings that will exist 10 to 20 years from now are already built…. Transport costs make up a relatively small proportion of household expenditures."

Cervero and Landis (1995) countered that "although new transportation investments no longer shape urban form by themselves, they still play an important role in channeling growth and determining the spatial extent of metropolitan regions by acting in combination with policies such as supportive zoning and government-assisted land assembly." They then challenged Giuliano's empirical evidence, and presented evidence of their own.

What Is Known about Induced Development

Who is right? Giuliano probably is right about aggregate impacts, while Cervero and Landis probably are right about localized impacts. The induced development literature has been reviewed by Huang (1994), Boarnet (1997), Boarnet and Haughwout (2000), Ryan (1999), and Bhatta and Drennan (2003). Recent reviews by Ewing (2007, 2008) conclude:

- Major highway investments have small net effects on economic growth and development within metropolitan areas. Instead, they mostly move development around the region to take advantage of improved accessibility. Induced development is very close to a zero-sum game.
- Highway investment patterns tend to favor suburbs over central cities, and thereby contribute to decentralization and low-density development.

- Major highway investments may actually hurt regional productivity, if they induce inefficient (read "low-density") development patterns.

- Corridors receiving major highway investments experience land appreciation, and therefore are likely to be developed at higher densities than developable lands outside the corridors.

- Highways may be necessary to induce development, but they are not sufficient to do so. To the extent that current planning and zoning limits hold, impacts within a corridor will be moderated.

- Counties receiving major highway investments attract population and employment growth to a greater degree than they would otherwise.

- Nearby counties may experience more or less growth than they would otherwise, depending on the strength of spillover effects.

- Nonresidential development is more strongly attracted to major highways than is residential development, particularly in the immediate vicinity of facilities.

- The induced development impacts of interstate-quality highways are wider and deeper than those of lesser highways and streets.

- It takes many years after construction for development to adjust to a new land use/transportation equilibrium.

- The induced development impacts of major highways extend out at least one mile, and probably farther.

- The relationship between highway capacity and growth is a two-way relationship, in that growth induces highway expansion as well as the reverse.

7

The Residential Sector

When it comes to urban energy use and related emissions, the transportation sector has gotten all the attention (Kessler and Schroeer 1995; Burchell et al. 1998; Bento et al. 2003; EPA 2003; Frank and Engelke 2005; Frank et al. 2006; Stone et al. 2007; Stone in press). This is understandable. The transportation sector is the second-biggest energy user in the United States, and is catching up with the industrial sector (see Figure 7-1). It is the sector that is most reliant on oil as an energy source. The geopolitics of oil are headline grabbing.

However, as a long-term threat to the planet, energy use by the residential sector also is significant. In 2006, the U.S. residential sector accounted for more than one-fifth of the nation's total energy use and produced more than one-fifth of the total CO_2 emissions, approximately 1,254 million metric tons per year (EIA 2007).

FIGURE 7-1
Total U.S. Energy Use by End-Use Sector, 1949 to 2005

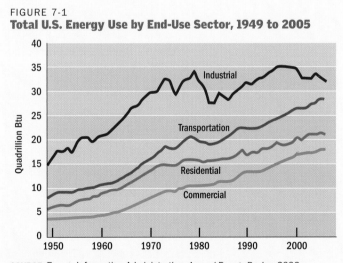

SOURCE: Energy Information Administration, *Annual Energy Review 2006*, Washington, D.C., 2007.

Causal Pathways

As in the transportation sector, causal pathways between urban form and energy use may exist in the residential sector. Urban form may affect residential energy consump-

FIGURE 7-2
Causal Paths between Urban Development Patterns and Residential Energy Consumption

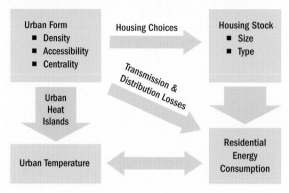

SOURCE: R. Ewing and F. Rong. "Impact of Urban Form on U.S. Residential Energy Use," *Housing Policy Debate*, in press.

tion through changes in housing stock, urban heat differentials (urban heat island effects), and transmission and distribution losses (see Figure 7-2).

The first two effects have been explored by Ewing and Rong (in press) using a county sprawl index initially calculated for 448 metropolitan counties (Ewing et al. 2003) and now available for 954 metropolitan counties or county equivalents representing 82 percent of the nation's population (Ewing, Brownson, and Berrigan 2006). The county sprawl index, and analogous metropolitan sprawl indices described in Chapter 4, have been validated in a host of sprawl-related studies (Ewing et al. 2003; Kelly-Schwartz et al. 2004; Sturm and Cohen 2004; Cho et al. 2006; Doyle et al. 2006; Kahn 2006; Plantinga and Bernell 2007; Stone 2007; Joshu et al. in press; Trowbridge and McDonald in press).

The county sprawl index is a linear combination of the following six variables:

- gross population density (persons per square mile);
- percentage of the county population living at low suburban densities (less than 1,500 persons per square mile);
- percentage of the county population living at moderate or high urban densities (greater than 12,500 persons per square mile);
- population density in urban areas (persons per developed square mile);
- average block size (in square miles); and
- percentage of blocks with areas less than 1/100 of a square mile (the size of a typical traditional urban block).

The six variables were combined via principal components analysis into one factor that represents the degree of sprawl within the county. The factor was normalized such that the mean value for the 448 counties is 100, and the standard deviation is 25. The higher the value of the index, the more compact the county. The smaller the value of the index, the more sprawling the county. At the very compact end of the scale are four New York City boroughs, Manhattan (New York County), Brooklyn, the Bronx, and Queens; San Francisco County; Hudson County (Jersey City); Philadelphia County; and Suffolk County (Boston). At the very sprawling end of the scale are outlying counties of metropolitan areas in the Southeast and Midwest such as Goochland County in the Richmond, Virginia, metropolitan area and Geauga County in the Cleveland, Ohio, metropolitan area. The county sprawl index is positively skewed, with most coun-

WWW.MAPS.GOOGLE.COM

Satellite photographs show the nation's most compact county—New York County, also known as Manhattan—at left and its most sprawling county—Geauga County, Ohio—at right. Photographs are at the same scale.

ties clustering around intermediate levels of sprawl but with a few counties such as New York and San Francisco having very high index values.

Urban Form, Housing Stock, and Residential Energy Use

The effect of urban form on the housing stock is complex. Housing consumption is constrained by housing market conditions such as the availability and cost of residential land, construction cost, and other metropolitan area–specific characteristics (Cheshire and Sheppard 1998; Wassmer and Baass 2005). On the supply side, constrained land supplies and higher land prices, often found in compact areas, may favor multifamily and single-family attached housing so as to conserve an expensive factor of production (Nelson et al. 2002). Or higher land prices may simply lead to larger houses on smaller lots (Staley and Mildner 1999). On the demand side, because of higher prices (Glaeser and Kahn 2003), households in compact areas may have less disposable income and thus reduce the quantity of housing demanded, an "income effect" (Katz and Rosen 1998). Or they may consume more housing because they have more money to spend because of lower transportation costs (STPP 2000), a "substitution effect" (Katz and Rosen 1998). The net impact of urban form on households' demand on housing is ambiguous and calls for empirical analysis.

Housing mix varies across U.S. metropolitan counties. Among the counties in Ewing and Rong's sample, the highest share of multifamily housing is 99 percent in New York County (with a sprawl index of 352), while the lowest is 0.6 percent in New Kent County, Virginia (with an index of 73). Recall that compact places have higher index values, while sprawling places have lower values. Some of the difference in housing mix is related to sociodemographics, and some is related to urban form.

Median house size also varies across U.S. metropolitan counties. Among the counties in the sample, the smallest median house size is about 1,000 square feet in San Francisco County (with a sprawl index of 209), and the largest is approximately 2,300 square feet in Waukesha County, Wisconsin (with an index of 90). Some of the difference in house size is related to sociodemographics, and some is related to urban form.

Controlling for sociodemographic variables, a household's choice of house type is strongly related to urban form (Ewing and Rong in press). The odds of a household living in multifamily housing are seven times greater for a compact county, one standard deviation above the mean index, than for a sprawling county, one standard deviation below the mean index (that is, a 50-point spread in the sprawl index).

A household's choice of house size also is related to urban form (Ewing and Rong in press). A comparable household consumes 21 percent more floor area in a sprawling county, one standard deviation below the mean index, than in a compact county, one standard deviation above the mean index.

Compared to those living in multifamily housing, otherwise comparable households living in single-family detached housing consume 35 percent more energy for space heating and 21 percent more energy for space cooling. Not surprisingly, energy for heating, cooling, and all other uses increases with house size. Compared to a household living in a 1,000-square-foot house, an otherwise comparable household living in a 2,000-square-foot house consumes 16 percent more energy for space heating and 13 percent more energy for space cooling.

These relationships, taken together, allow us to estimate the effects of urban form on residential energy use indirectly, through the mediators of house type and size. The average household living in a compact county, one standard deviation above the mean sprawl index, can be expected to consume 17.9 million fewer British thermal units (Btu) of primary energy annually than the same household living in a sprawling county, one standard deviation below the mean index.

Urban Form, Urban Heat Islands, and Residential Energy Use

Roads, buildings, and other constructed surfaces mostly absorb, rather than reflect, the sun's radiation. The displacement of trees, shrubs, and groundcover eliminates the natural cooling effects of shading and evapotranspiration. Urban activities such as motor vehicle travel and space heating and cooling produce waste heat. The resulting "urban heat island" (UHI) effect is estimated to raise air temperature in a typical city by 1° to 3°C relative to the surrounding rural area (Rosenfeld et al. 1995).

Development patterns affect the formation of urban heat islands in complex ways. Sprawling urban areas have less concentrated heat sources but also have more motor vehicle travel and resulting higher fossil fuel combustion. Large-lot housing has more pervious surface and tree canopy than does small-lot housing but, because of larger houses, longer driveways, and bigger yards, also has more impervious surface and uncanopied area. It is not clear whether large- or small-lot housing generates more radiant heat per housing unit. "On average, each ¼-acre increase in parcel area was found to be associated with an increase in net thermal emissions of 33%. This finding directly challenges the common assumption that higher residential densities are less thermally efficient than lower residential densities." (Stone and Rodgers 2001, p. 194). Like the impact of urban form on the housing stock, the impact on the formation of UHIs is ambiguous and calls for empirical analysis.

Ewing and Rong (in press) find that because of the UHI effect, temperatures are higher in compact counties than in sprawling ones. With each 10 percent increase in the county sprawl index—which reflects an increase in compactness—the number of observed heating degree-days decreases by 2.0 percent while the number of observed cooling degree-days increases by 4.7 percent.

Controlling for other influences, total delivered energy use for space heating and cooling per household per year increases with the number of heating and cooling degree-days, respectively. With 95 percent confidence, for example, ten extra heating degree days are associated with a 0.2 percent increase in energy use for heating, while ten extra cooling degree days are associated with a 0.5 to 0.6 percent increase in energy use for cooling.

These relationships, taken together, allow us to estimate the effects of urban form on residential energy use indirectly, through the mediating effect of UHIs. Nation-wide, as a result of UHIs, an average household in a compact county (one standard deviation above the mean sprawl index) would be expected to consume 1.4 million fewer Btu of primary energy annually than an average household in a sprawling county (one standard deviation below the mean index).

Throughout most of the nation, the two effects—housing and UHI—are in the same direction, although the housing effect is much stronger than the UHI effect. The total average savings of 19.3 million Btu amounts to 20 percent of the average primary energy use per U.S. household.

The Combined Effect of Compact Development, Transportation Investments, and Road Pricing[1]

The recently passed Energy Independence and Security Act of 2007 (U.S. Congress 2007) requires corporate average fuel economy for new passenger vehicles to rise to at least 35 miles per gallon by 2020. Such a rise will result in a 34 percent improvement in fleetwide fuel economy by 2030 (see Figure 1-2, page 3). The energy act also sets requirements for renewable fuels that coauthor Steve Winkelman estimates will reduce lifecycle GHG emissions by 10 percent in 2025.

Yet, even such dramatic technological advances are expected to be offset by the growth of VMT. In Chapter 3, we projected that CO_2 emissions from cars and light trucks will hold steady at 2005 levels through 2030. Holding these levels steady will leave the nation 26 percent above 1990 levels. The energy act calls for unspecified fuel economy improvements beyond 2020. Optimistically assuming that fuel economy for new passenger vehicles could rise as high as 45 mpg by 2030 and that the carbon content of fuels could be reduced by 15 percent, CO_2 emissions from cars and light trucks would remain 8 percent above 1990 levels.

These projections fall far short of what is needed for climate stabilization. To stay on course toward a CO_2 reduction of 60 to 80 percent by 2050, the U.S. transportation sector will have to lower CO_2 emissions to 33 percent below 1990 levels by 2030. Thus, for 2030, we project an excess of 59 percent (26 + 33 percent) in the amount of CO_2 emitted by cars and light trucks relative to a climate-stabilizing path. Worse, for 2050, without further improvements in vehicles and fuels, there would be an excess of at least 86 percent (26 + 60 percent) in the amount of CO_2 emitted by cars and light trucks relative to a climate-stabilizing level. And this estimate assumes no growth of VMT after 2030.

MORE QUESTIONS

What would it take to reach the 2030 CO_2 reduction target of 33 percent below 1990 levels? Will compact development with supportive transportation policies be enough? If not, how much VMT reduction must be achieved through pricing, and what price changes would be required? To answer these questions, we need a historical database that contains information on four key policy levers, plus VMT and socioeconomic data. We also need an analytical method that can capture the interactions among these four levers.

To what extent can this excess be addressed through reductions in VMT? The literature suggests that VMT can be reduced through compact development and/or through pricing of travel. In Chapter 2, we projected that compact development would reduce the *total* CO_2 emissions of the transportation sector in 2050 by 7 to 10 percent. While a 7- to 10-percent reduction in CO_2 is a healthy increment relative to other options on the table, it still leaves us far off the path toward climate stabilization.

The 7- to 10-percent estimate is the contribution of compact development alone, based on assumptions about expected market performance, without regard to complementary changes in transportation policies. Of course, in the real world, more compact development would be served by a different mix of transportation choices. How well would compact development perform if supported by policies such as the following:

- increasing investments in public transportation;
- directing highway funding first to the repair and proper maintenance of existing facilities; and/or
- expanding highway capacity only when the expansion meets climate, economic, and other performance and outcome-based measures?

All of this begs the question, "What would it take to reach the 2030 CO_2 reduction target of 33 percent below 1990 levels?" Would compact development with supportive transportation policies be enough? If not, how much VMT reduction would have to be achieved through pricing, and what price changes would be required? To answer these questions, we need an historical database that contains information on four key policy levers—land use, transit service levels, highway capacity, and road pricing—plus VMT and socioeconomic data. We also need an analytical method that can capture the interactions among these four levers. Fortunately, both the data and methodology exist and are well established. Our conclusion is that all four levers will be required to reach climate-stabilizing CO_2 levels.

The Data

Most of the data used in this analysis come from the Texas Transportation Institute's (TTI's) urban mobility database (Schrank and Lomax 2007). The TTI *Urban Mobility Report* is released annually amid much fanfare and media interest. It is widely accepted as the most complete assessment of congestion in the nation's urban areas. The report is based on data collected by the federal government from states and transit operators. In the last two years, it has undergone a substantial update and refinement. In sum, the TTI database is the best available.

What makes the TTI database so useful, for our purposes, is the fact that it provides data for many urbanized areas over many years. The annual series begins in 1982 and runs through 2005. It includes 85 urbanized areas ranging in size from the megaregion of New York and northern New Jersey to the subregion of Boulder, Colorado. Essential data not contained in the TTI database are available from other sources, specifically transit data from the Federal Transit Administration's National Transit Database and income data from the U.S. Census Bureau and the U.S. Bureau of Economic Analysis (BEA). Our final database includes 84 urbanized areas over a 21-year period. Lack of certain transit data forced us to exclude one urbanized area (Boulder) and the first three years of the series (1982 through 1984).

As detailed in the following section, two models were estimated with this combined dataset: a cross-sectional model for 2005 and a longitudinal model for the two ten-year periods between 1985 and 2005. The cross-sectional model was used to

FIGURE 8-1
Variables in the Cross-Sectional Model

Variable	Definition	Source	Mean	Standard Deviation
lnvmt	Natural log of freeway and arterial daily VMT in 2005 (in thousands)	TTI urban mobility database	9.927	0.981
lnpop	Natural log of population in 2005 (in thousands)	TTI urban mobility database	7.004	0.943
lnden	Natural log of gross population density in 2005 (in persons per square mile)	TTI urban mobility database	7.632	0.364
lnlm	Natural log of freeway and arterial lane miles in 2005	TTI urban mobility database	7.920	0.874
lninc	Natural log of annual per capita income in 2005 (in 1982 dollars)*	U.S. Census/BEA	9.497	0.196
lngas	Natural log of average fuel price in 2005 (in 1982 dollars)	TTI urban mobility database	0.261	0.054
lnrevmi	Natural log of transit vehicle revenue miles in 2005**	National Transit Database	9.506	1.326
lnpmt	Natural log of transit passenger miles in 2005***	TTI urban mobility database	4.527	1.659
lnhrt	Natural log of directional route miles of heavy-rail lines in 2005****	National Transit Database	0.599	1.587
lnlrt	Natural log of directional route miles of light-rail lines in 2005****	National Transit Database	1.049	1.694

*Per capita income for urbanized areas was estimated from BEA annual per capita income series for metropolitan areas and the U.S. Census decennial census per capita income data for urbanized areas in 1989 and 1999. The ratio of census income to BEA income for 1989 was applied to BEA per capita income for years 1985–1995, while the ratio of census income to BEA income for 1999 was applied to BEA income for years 1996–2005.

**Transit vehicle revenue miles is a measure of the miles traveled by transit vehicles when in revenue service (that is, when vehicles are available to carry passengers). Some clearly erroneous values in the National Transit Database were excluded or corrected.

***Transit passenger miles is a measure of passenger traffic calculated by multiplying the total number of revenue-paying passengers aboard transit vehicles by the distance traveled.

****Directional route miles is a measure of the distance in each direction over which transit vehicles travel while in revenue service. Directional route miles measures the length of a facility, not the service carried on the facility. The integer 1 was added to all values of these variables before taking natural logs, because many urbanized areas have no rail miles and the log of 0 is undefined. In the United States, the term "heavy rail" is applied to high-speed and high-capacity subway and elevated electric rail systems, also referred to as rapid transit systems. The term light rail is used for lower-speed and lower-capacity systems that use lightweight rail cars and often share rights-of-way with other traffic over some of their length. Light-rail vehicles typically are trolleylike, drawing power from overhead electric lines. Both types of rail transit are distinct from commuter rail systems, which cover longer distances, usually use diesel power locomotives, and may share tracks with freight trains.

FIGURE 8-2
Variables in the Longitudinal (Time-Step) Model

Variable	Definition	Source	Mean	Standard Deviation
chgvmt	Percent change in freeway and principal arterial VMT over ten years (1985–1995 and 1995–2005)	TTI urban mobility database	0.412	0.218
chgpop	Percent change in population over ten years	TTI urban mobility database	0.192	0.150
chgden	Percent change in gross population density over ten years	TTI urban mobility database	–0.010	0.123
chglm	Percent change in freeway and principal arterial lane miles per 1,000 people over ten years	TTI urban mobility database	0.213	0.136
chginc	Percent change in real annual per capita income over ten years (adjusted for CPI)	U.S. Census/BEA	0.124	0.091
chggas	Percent change in real average fuel price over ten years (adjusted for implicit price deflator)	TTI urban mobility database	0.146	0.467
chgrevmi	Percent change in transit revenue miles over ten years	National Transit Database	0.414	0.575
chgpmt	Percent change in transit passenger miles over ten years	TTI urban mobility database	0.309	0.876
chghrt	Percent change in directional route miles of heavy-rail lines over ten years*	National Transit Database	0.023	0.116
chglrt	Percent change in directional route miles of light-rail lines over ten years*	National Transit Database	0.134	0.344

*These percentage changes were computed relative to directional routes at the end of the time period since the starting values were 0 for new systems in the base years.

capture long-term relationships between transportation and land use. Each urbanized area has had decades to arrive at quasi equilibrium among density, road capacity, transit capacity, and VMT.

However, there is not enough spatial variation in fuel prices across the United States to detect effects on VMT in a cross-sectional sample. In 2005, the average price of gasoline (in the TTI dataset) varied by just 44 cents across the 85 urbanized areas. The average price of gasoline can fluctuate that much from year to year. So a longitudinal analysis was required to capture short- and medium-term responses to fuel price fluctuations.

The variables in our models are defined in Figures 8-1 and 8-2. All variables in the cross-sectional model were transformed by taking natural logarithms. The use of logarithms has two advantages in this case. First, it makes relationships among our variables more nearly linear and reduces the influence of extreme values (such as those for New York). Second, it allows us to interpret parameter estimates as elasticities, which summarize relationships in an understandable and transferable form. An elasticity is a percentage change in one variable with respect to a 1 percent change in another variable. (Much of the summary data on urban development and travel in Chapter 4 were presented in the form of elasticities.)

All variables in the longitudinal model were computed as percentage changes during a ten-year period relative to the base value (with the exceptions noted in Figure 8-2). Percentage changes also have the advantage of reducing the influence of extreme values and allowing parameter estimates to be interpreted as elasticities.

The Methodology

We are interested in the influences of various processes on vehicle usage because, ultimately, we want to be able to specify the conditions under which substantial VMT reductions might be achieved. The right methodology for this analysis is structural equation modeling (SEM), a statistical methodology for evaluating complex hypotheses involving multiple, interacting variables (Bollen 1989; Grace 2006).

Structural equation modeling is a "model-centered" methodology that seeks to evaluate theoretically justified models against data. The SEM approach is based on the modern statistical view that theoretically based models, when they can be justified on scientific grounds, provide more useful interpretations than conventional methods that simply seek to reject the "null hypothesis" of no effect.

There are several related and distinctive features of SEM. In SEM:

- Hypothesized path models are evaluated based on a priori knowledge about the processes under investigation using all available information.
- The investigator tests the degree to which the structure of one or more models is consistent with the structure inherent in the data. Many models that might be envisioned commonly are rejected because they are inconsistent with the data.
- Probability statements about the model are reversed from those associated with null hypotheses. Probability values (p-values) used in statistics are measures of the degree to which the data are unexpected, given the hypothesis being tested. In null hypothesis testing, a finding of a p-value <0.05 indicates that we can reject the null hypothesis because the data are very unlikely to come from a random process. In SEM, we seek a model that has a large p-value (>0.05) because that indicates that the data are not unlikely given that model (that is, the data are consistent with the model).
- Different processes operating in systems are distinguished by decomposing relationships into direct and indirect pathways. Pathways can, thus, be either simple or compound, depending on whether they pass through other variables or not. The total effect of one factor on another is the cumulative impact summed over all the pathways connecting the two factors.

The estimation of structural equation (SE) models involves solving a set of equations. There is an equation for each "response" or "endogenous" variable in the network. Variables that are solely predictors of other variables are termed "influences" or "exog-

FIGURE 8-3
Linear versus Log-Transformed Data*

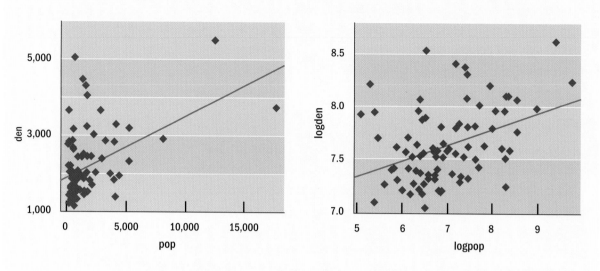

*The graph on the left presents a population size versus population density bivariate plot in raw units, while the one on the right presents population size versus population density in a log-log plot.

enous" variables. Typically, solution procedures for SE models focus on the observed versus model-implied correlations in the data. The unstandardized correlations or co-variances are the raw material for the analyses. Models are automatically compared to a "saturated" model (one that allows all variables to inter-correlate), and this comparison allows the analysis to discover missing pathways and, thereby, reject inconsistent models.

In this analysis, data first were examined for frequency distributions and simple bivariate relationships, especially for linearity. This suggested the need for data transformation in the cross-sectional model (see Figure 8-3). To equalize and stabilize variances, improve linearity, and still allow ready interpretations, all variables were log transformed. As already noted, the resulting coefficients from modeling data transformed in this way can be interpreted as elasticities.

Our first SE model presents a "snapshot" of conditions in different urbanized areas as they existed in the last year of the series, 2005 (see Figure 8-4). This year was chosen because it represents relatively current conditions and because it has the highest levels of transit service (rail in particular) in our time series. The structure of this model rests on a number of logical assumptions:

- that the size of an urbanized area, in terms of its total population, influences land use, road infrastructure, and transit infrastructure;
- that population density, while an imperfect measure of urban form, represents a key factor influencing driving conditions, demand for mass transit and, ultimately, vehicle usage;

FIGURE 8-4
Cross-Sectional Model Relating Land Use, Transportation, and Fuel Prices to VMT

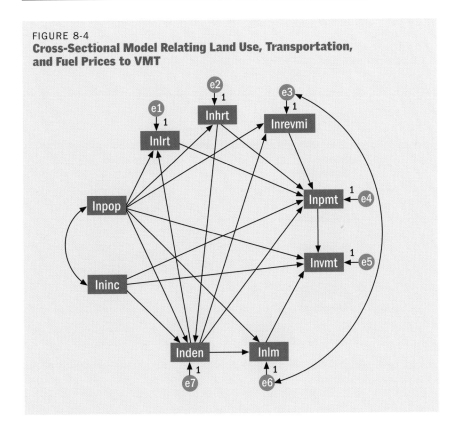

- that road and transit capacities affect the generalized cost of travel and hence vehicle usage; and
- that in a cross-sectional model such as this one, where only a single year is considered, effects of fuel price variations will not be discernable.

Based on its overall form, the cross-sectional model includes the indicated causal pathways among area population (lnpop), population density (lnden), per capita income (lninc), highway lane miles (lnlm), transit revenue miles (lnrevmi), transit passenger miles (lnpmt), route miles of heavy and light rail (lnhrt and lnlrt) and, ultimately, VMT (lnvmt). Note that population and income are allowed to be correlated in this model (positively, as it turns out), as are transit revenue miles and highway lane miles (negatively). By convention, circles e1 through e7 represent error terms in the model, of which there is one for each endogenous (response) variable.

A second SE model was specified to capture the short- and medium-term effects on VMT of fluctuations in fuel prices over time, as well as additions of highway and transit capacity (see Figure 8-5). This model focuses on *changes* in conditions over two ten-year periods, 1985 to 1995 and 1995 to 2005. These particular periods were selected because real fuel prices declined substantially during the first period, while prices rose sharply during the second period. The effect of fuel prices can be teased out through the differences between the two periods. Premises underlying this model are otherwise similar to those for the model in Figure 8-4.

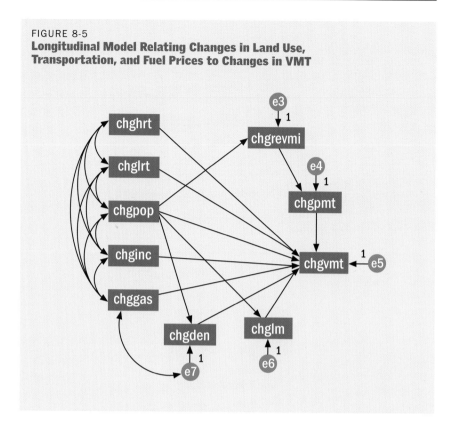

FIGURE 8-5
**Longitudinal Model Relating Changes in Land Use,
Transportation, and Fuel Prices to Changes in VMT**

Our two SE models were estimated with the software package Amos (version 7.0, SPSS 2007) and maximum likelihood procedures. Model evaluation was based on three factors: 1) chi-square tests of absolute model fit; 2) root-mean-square error of approximation (RMSEA), which is corrected for sample size; and 3) single-degree-of-freedom chi-square difference tests (Grace 2006, Chapter 5).[2]

The Results

The Cross-Sectional Model

The cross-sectional model in Figure 8-4 has a chi-square of 17.4, with 15 degrees of freedom and a p-value of 0.30. In SE models, a low chi-square relative to model degrees of freedom and a high (>0.05) p-value are indicators of good model fit and, thus, are desirable. The degrees of freedom are a function of the model, not the data (N was 84). The RMSEA for this model has a value of 0.044, a confidence interval of <0.00 to 0.12, and a p-value of 0.50. All of this indicates a very close fit between the structure of the data and the structure of the model.

Parameter estimates for this model are presented in Figure 8-6. For conceptual reasons, some paths were left in the model despite their lack of statistical significance, specifically, the paths from lnhrt to lnden (heavy-rail capacity to population density) and from lnden to lnlrt (population density to light-rail capacity). Explained

FIGURE 8-6
Path Coefficient Estimates (Regression Weights)
for the Cross-Sectional Model, with Associated Statistics

			Estimate	Standard Error	Critical Ratio	p-value
lnhrt	←	lnpop	1.093	0.141	7.770	< 0.001
lnden	←	lninc	–0.714	0.196	–3.647	<0.001
lnden	←	lnpop	0.188	0.051	3.668	<0.001
lnden	←	lnhrt	0.027	0.028	0.950	0.342
lnlrt	←	lnpop	0.953	0.168	5.658	<0.001
lnrevmi	←	lnpop	1.256	0.055	22.630	<0.001
lnrevmi	←	lnden	0.418	0.144	2.911	0.004
lnlrt	←	lnden	0.784	0.436	1.799	0.072
lnpmt	←	lnrevmi	1.097	0.035	31.381	<0.001
lnpmt	←	lnden	0.222	0.099	2.244	0.025
lnpmt	←	lninc	–0.358	0.176	–2.030	0.042
lnlm	←	lnpop	0.953	0.022	43.502	<0.001
lnpmt	←	lnlrt	0.047	0.021	2.208	0.027
lnpmt	←	lnhrt	0.111	0.024	4.701	<0.001
lnlm	←	lnden	–0.354	0.057	–6.250	<0.001
lnvmt	←	lninc	0.355	0.082	4.341	<0.001
lnvmt	←	lnpmt	–0.068	0.024	–2.841	0.004
lnvmt	←	lnpop	0.680	0.089	7.643	<0.001
lnvmt	←	lnlm	0.463	0.072	6.422	<0.001

variance is very high for most endogenous variables (variables with incoming arrows in Figure 8-6).

Note again that the path coefficient estimates (regression weights) are elasticities and can be interpreted as the proportional change in one variable expected to result from a proportional change in another. For example, "lnvmt ← lnlm = 0.463" means that if the number of highway lane miles were increased by 10 percent while other factors held constant, the amount of VMT would increase by 4.63 percent.

Of particular interest in this study are the total effects of different variables on VMT, accounting for both direct and indirect pathways. These are presented in Figure 8-7.

According to these cross-sectional results, the most important processes driving VMT growth involve population. Independent of other changes, the direct effect of population size on VMT is 0.68. In this cross-

FIGURE 8-7
Total, Direct, and Indirect Effects
of Variables on VMT in the
Cross-Sectional Model

	Total	Direct	Indirect
lnpop	0.97	0.68	0.29
lninc	0.531	0.355	0.177
lnden	–0.213	0	–0.213
lnlm	0.463	0.463	0
lnrevmi	–0.075	0	–0.075
lnpmt	–0.068	–0.068	0
lnhrt	–0.013	0	–0.013
lnlrt	–0.003	0	–0.003

sectional sample, a 10 percent increase in population is associated with a direct increase in VMT of 6.8 percent.

Indirect effects of population on VMT also are sizable. In SEM, we are able to trace the indirect effects of different variables through other variables. The most important indirect effect of population on VMT is through the number of lane miles, which increases with increasing population (the indirect effect on VMT is 0.95 x 0.46 = 0.44).[3] There are seven other potential indirect influences of population on VMT, all of which act to depress VMT as population increases. For example, greater population leads to higher density, which in turn leads to fewer lane miles, indirectly reducing VMT (indirect effect, 0.19 x –0.35 x 0.46 = –0.03). The effect of all negative influences related to population, summed over all paths, is –0.15. Thus, the net indirect effect of population on VMT is 0.29 (0.44 – 0.15). The total effect of population on VMT is just the sum of direct and indirect effects, or 0.97 (0.68 + 0.29). This is the overall elasticity of VMT with respect to population.

In addition to responses to population size and lane miles, VMT also has responded strongly to increases in real per capita income. The total income-related influence on VMT, or overall elasticity of VMT with respect to income, is 0.53. Most of income's influence on VMT is direct (0.36). The remaining influence is indirect, through the negative impact of income on transit use (the indirect effect of income on passenger miles and then VMT is –0.36 x –0.07 = 0.025) or the negative effect of income on density, density on lane miles, and lane miles on VMT (indirect effect, –0.71 x –0.35 x 0.46 = 0.11).

FIGURE 8-8
Path Coefficient Estimates (Regression Weights) for the Longitudinal Model, with Associated Statistics

			Estimate	Standard Error	Critical Ratio	p-value
pchgrevmi	←	pchgpop	2.218	0.242	9.176	<0.001
pchgpmt	←	pchgrevmi	0.753	0.103	7.322	<0.001
pchglm	←	pchgpop	0.435	0.061	7.087	<0.001
pchgden	←	pchgpop	0.242	0.061	3.991	<0.001
pchgvmt	←	pchglm	0.684	0.081	8.405	<0.001
pchgvmt	←	pchginc	0.538	0.111	4.859	<0.001
pchgvmt	←	pchgpmt	-0.030	0.012	-2.641	0.008
pchgvmt	←	pchgden	-0.152	0.084	-1.815	0.070
pchgvmt	←	pchghrt	-0.021	0.087	-0.237	0.813
pchgvmt	←	pchglrt	-0.002	0.030	-0.078	0.938
pchgvmt	←	pchgpop	0.663	0.079	8.422	<0.001
pchgvmt	←	pchggas	-0.171	0.022	-7.843	<0.001

The Longitudinal Model

The longitudinal or time-step model in Figure 8-5 has a chi-square of 16.2 with 22 degrees of freedom and a p-value of 0.805. The RMSEA for this model is 0.00, with a confidence interval of <0.00 to 0.042 and a p-value of 0.973, all indicating an extremely close fit between the data and model. Parameter estimates for this model are presented in Figure 8-8; direct, indirect, and total effects are presented in Figure 8-9.

Longitudinal study results lead to many of the same conclusions as the cross-sectional study results for 2005 (see Figure 8-7). The strongest influences on changes in VMT are changes in population, income, and lane miles. Density again has a moderate negative influence on VMT. Contained in the data series is an increase in transit service and use and, in our results, a significant but modest reduction in VMT (–0.03). In this analysis, we also see the negative effect of fuel prices on VMT (total effect = –0.17). It is likely that this value underestimates the impact of fuel prices on VMT, because the use of ten-year time steps blurs the dynamics and lag effects of shorter-term responses to fuel price fluctuations.

FIGURE 8-9
Total, Direct, and Indirect Effects of Variables on Percentage Change in VMT

	Total	Direct	Indirect
chgpop	0.874	0.663	0.21
chginc	0.538	0.538	0
hgden	-0.152	-0.152	0
chglm	0.684	0.684	0
chgrevmi	-0.023	0	-0.023
chgpmt	-0.03	-0.03	0
chghrt	-0.021	-0.021	0
chglrt	-0.002	-0.002	0
chggas	-0.171	-0.171	0

Implications for Climate Stabilization

Best-Estimate Elasticity Values

The cross-sectional and longitudinal models together give us a sound basis for deducing the elasticities of urban VMT with respect to different urban variables (see Figure 8-10). For most variables, we have split the difference between cross-sectional and longitudinal elasticity estimates, giving slightly more weight to cross-sectional values since our VMT forecast is for 2050, the long run in economic terms. Given the very different structures of the two models, elasticity values are remarkably similar for the

FIGURE 8-10
Elasticities of VMT with Respect to Urban Variables

	Cross Sectional	Longitudinal	Best Estimate
Population	0.97	0.874	0.95
Real per capita income	0.531	0.538	0.54
Population density	-0.213	-0.152	-0.30
Highway lane miles	0.463	0.684	0.55
Transit revenue miles	-0.075	-0.023	-0.06
Transit passenger miles	-0.068	-0.03	-0.06
Heavy-rail miles	-0.013	-0.021	-0.01
Light-rail miles	-0.003	-0.002	NA
Real fuel price	NA	-0.171	-0.17

two analyses. Our "best estimate" elasticity values are generally consistent with those in the literature, or possibly even a bit understated (Cervero 2002; Victoria Transport Policy Institute 2007; Bailey, Mokhtarian, and Little 2008).

For two variables, we have gone outside the range of modeled elasticity estimates. We will assume an elasticity of VMT with respect to the real price of fuel (or any other out-of-pocket cost of automobile use) of –0.17, its value in the longitudinal model. As explained above, there is not enough variation in our cross-sectional sample to estimate an elasticity.

The elasticity of VMT with respect to density has been bumped up to –0.30, from the cross-sectional and longitudinal values of –0.213 and –0.152, respectively. The bump up accounts for absence of compactness measures other than density. When land use mix, street accessibility, and other built environmental variables are missing from the analysis, density soaks up some of their effects, but not all of them. The assumed elasticity value is consistent with the literature reviewed in Chapter 4.

Historical and Projected Growth Rates

Figure 8-11 shows historical growth rates between 1985 and 2005 for all variables in our models. It also shows expected future growth rates under two scenarios, one a trend scenario and the other a low-carbon scenario. Using unweighted values, VMT grew at an average annual rate of 3.5 percent between 1985 and 2005, much faster than population or per capita income. Under the trend scenario, VMT will continue to grow as population and real income grow. Under the low-carbon scenario, VMT will have to decrease by an estimated 47 percent by 2030 to close the gap between CO_2 emissions under projected trends and CO_2 emissions on the path to climate stabilization. Vehicle miles traveled will have to drop even further by 2050 to achieve climate stabilization, the exact percentage depending on assumptions about the fuel economy of vehicles and carbon content of fuels after 2030.[4]

For these projections, the expected growth of key variables is as indicated in Figure 8-11. Population and income growth rates are assumed to be the same for the trend scenario—which is sprawling, auto oriented, and low priced for auto users—and the low-carbon scenario, which is compact, transit oriented, and higher priced for auto users. This assumption is consistent with the literature on regional development, which suggests that both variables are independent of land use and transportation decisions.

The Census Bureau's interim projections for 2030 and 2050 show U.S. population growth slowing down. Our expected value of urban population growth reflects this slowdown. We have adjusted census growth projections for countervailing trends: upward for the growing proportion of urban dwellers, and downward for the declining proportion of working age population.[5]

Between 1985 and 2005, real per capita income grew at an average annual rate of 1.2 percent. We assume that the average annual historical growth rate of real per capita income will continue through 2030.

FIGURE 8-11
Average Annual Growth Rates (Percent) of Key Variables for Urbanized Areas

	Historical (1985–2005)	Trend (2007–2030)	Low-Carbon Scenario (2007–2030)
VMT	3.5	Modeled outcome	Modeled outcome
Population	1.8	1.2	1.2
Real per capita income	1.2	1.2	1.2
Population density	0	0	1.0
Highway lane miles	2.0	1.5	0.5
Transit revenue miles	3.8	3.8	6.3
Real fuel price	0.4	-0.3	2.4

The remaining variables in our models assume different values for the two scenarios. Our 2030 trend scenario reflects recent trends in each of these variables for our sample of urbanized areas. Collectively, these areas had 153 million residents in 2005, 52 percent of the total U.S. population or almost two-thirds of the urban population. So they may be considered generally representative of urban America.

Between 1985 and 2005, population density increased in some urbanized areas and declined in others. On average, it was flat. Under the trend scenario, we will assume it remains flat through 2030. We already have argued that development between 2007 and 2050 will represent two-thirds of the development on the ground in 2050 and that, with smart growth, this new development would be 75 percent more compact than existing development (see Chapter 2). Hence average gross density of urbanized areas would rise about 50 percent between 2007 and 2050, which translates into an annual growth rate just under 1 percent. We have rounded up to 1 percent.

Lane miles grew at an average rate of 2 percent per year between 1985 and 2005, slightly faster than population growth. Under the trend scenario, adjusting for slower population growth, we project an increase in lane miles of 1.5 percent per year. Under the low-carbon scenario, our policy recommendations call for performance-based highway expansion projects that meet regional climate, economic, and other goals. Accordingly, under the low-carbon scenario, lane miles are assumed to expand at 0.5 percent per year.

Between 1985 and 2005, transit revenue miles grew at an average annual rate of 3.8 percent. Under the trend scenario, this growth rate will be assumed to hold steady. Under a low-carbon scenario, transit revenue miles would have to grow by an additional 1 percent per year, to an overall rate of 4.8 percent per year, just to keep pace with the rising density. We expect that the actual expansion of transit service will be faster than this rate as the nation commits itself to climate stabilization and energy independence. Among the sampled urbanized areas, the highest rate of growth in per capita revenue miles was about 5 percent per year between 1985 and 2005. This per capita growth rate, if applied to projected population growth through 2030, suggests an annual growth rate of transit revenue miles of 6.3 percent.

Finally, between 1985 and 2005, the real price of gasoline initially dropped and then rose to just above its 1985 price. Historical trends may have little predictive power for fuel prices. As discussed in Chapter 1, in "A Climate-Sparing Strategy with Multiple Payoffs," there is a real possibility that worldwide oil production will peak and begin to decline before 2020, which would lead to sharp price hikes. However, this "doomsday scenario" is not reflected in any of the official forecasts. Thus, for the trend scenario, we will assume a small reduction in the real price of gasoline and ethanol, per the Energy Information Administration's *Annual Energy Outlook* series for 2007 through 2030 (EIA 2008). For the low-carbon scenario, we will assume that through fuel tax hikes, tolls, pay-as-you-drive insurance, or other means, the real price of fuel (the operating cost of auto use) will rise at twice the rate of real per capita income.

Trend Projections

Projecting the growth of VMT is not a simple matter of multiplying the elasticities in Figure 8-10 by the annual growth rates in Figure 8-11, and then summing the effects over all determinants of VMT. The effects of endogenous variables are already incorporated into the total effects of exogenous variables (see Figure 8-5). We would be double counting effects if we treated all variables as independent in a scenario analysis.

Instead, we focus on the three exogenous variables—urban population, real per capita income, and real fuel prices—which in our models are independent of one another. Their effects are additive. Using elasticities and growth rates from Figures 8-10 and 8-11, urban population will grow by 32 percent between 2007 and 2030 which, given its elasticity (including indirect effects), translates into a 30 percent rise in VMT. Real per capita income also will grow by 32 percent, which corresponds to a 17 percent increase in VMT. Real fuel prices will decline by 7 percent, which would increase VMT by 1 percent. The total effect of this scenario is a VMT rise of 48 percent by 2030 and 102 percent by 2050.

This projected 48 percent rise in VMT is virtually identical to the VMT growth projection in the Energy Information Administration's *Annual Energy Outlook 2008 (Early Release)* of 49 percent for light-duty vehicles. It leaves a gap of almost 60 percent in 2030 between CO_2 emissions under projected trends and CO_2 emissions on the path to climate stabilization.

Low-Carbon Projections

With the elasticity values in Figure 8-10 and the low-carbon assumptions in Figure 8-11, it is possible to see how close we would come to the path toward climate stabilization by 2030. Figure 8-12 combines elasticities of VMT with respect to policy variables (from Figure 8-10) with changes in growth rates for policy variables with the low-carbon scenario relative to trend (from Figure 8-11). The combination of these

FIGURE 8-12
Urban VMT Reduction under a Low-Carbon Scenario (2030)

	Elasticities of VMT with Respect to Policy Variables	Change in Annual Growth Rates of Policy Variables (Percent above/below Trend)	Effect on Annual VMT Growth Rate (Percent below Trend)
Population density	–0.30	1	–7.7
Highway lane miles	0.55	–1	–11.4
Transit revenue miles	–0.06	2.5	–4.6
Real fuel price	–0.17	2.7	–14.4
Total effect	NA	NA	–38.1

measures (including higher road user fees) would reduce VMT by an estimated 38 percent relative to trend. This is still above the path toward climate stabilization, but much closer than with technology alone.

It is important to keep in mind that fundamental behavioral changes are not captured in our models, which are based on historical data. Various behavioral adaptations may occur as urban compactness, transit service quality, road user prices, and/or congestion increase to "tipping points." As the imperatives of climate change force nonincremental changes in public policies and programs, we will enter uncharted waters.

Still, based on these quantitative findings, it seems likely that climate stabilization will require more policy leverage than assumed in our low-carbon scenario: more compact development, less highway expansion, more transit investment, and/or higher road user fees. Alternatively, we may need to shore up the other two legs of the policy stool, demanding more of vehicle and fuel technology than is required by the new energy act. With an increase in new vehicle fuel economy to 45 mpg and 15 percent fuel switching, the United States could essentially reach a climate-stabilizing CO_2 target by 2030.

9

Policy and Program Recommendations

Climate stabilization will require the United States to reduce greenhouse gas (GHG) emissions by 60 to 80 percent below 1990 levels by 2050. To keep the nation moving along that critical path, our GHG emissions will need to be well below 1990 levels by 2030, and leading analysts believe we have less than ten years, and possibly less than five years, to get on track (Bierbaum 2006). In the transportation sector, progress will be required on all three legs of the policy stool: vehicle efficiency, fuel content, and vehicle miles traveled (VMT). The national policy discussion on vehicles and fuels is mature and active, and a variety of proposals would have the automobile and oil industries take responsibility for their contributions to GHG. Thus far, however, no one has been put in charge of reducing the GHG impacts of VMT growth.

In this chapter, we aim to identify the roles and responsibilities of different levels of government to meet the climate challenge. Civic leaders, consumers, businesses, and other stakeholders also can make substantial contributions to this effort.

The key to making substantial GHG reductions is to get *all policies and practices, funding and spending, incentives, and rules and regulations pointing in the same direction,* toward smart growth and away from sprawl. Currently, most of these instruments are pointed toward sprawl, creating conditions that lead to ever-increasing GHG emissions. One example is the link between federal transportation funding and VMT levels, which rewards states for VMT growth (FHWA 2006). Another example is the low-density zoning that keeps localities dependent on cars, undermining public expenditures on transit, pedestrian, and bicycling facilities.

A MIGHTY CHALLENGE

The current mismatch between what exists and what is necessary to achieve meaningful VMT and GHG reductions highlights the enormity of the challenge and focuses attention on the need for bold initiatives. Incremental policy changes will not suffice. Only profound, systemic change will do. "Make no little plans," Daniel Burnham admonished a century ago. "They have no magic to stir humanity's blood and probably themselves will not be realized" (Moore 1921). Burnham's advice could not be more appropriate to the task at hand.

Our recommendations draw on the analyses in earlier chapters, most notably Chapter 4. That chapter makes clear the priority order of development if GHG emissions are to be substantially reduced. From a climate perspective, the best development is highly accessible to existing urban centers, served by transit, and dense, diverse, and well-designed. Such development has all 5D variables (discussed in Chapter 4) going for it. The next most climate-friendly development is highly accessible to existing urban centers and transit, but lacks one or more of the other Ds.

With 120 million additional Americans projected for 2050, it is not realistic to expect all development and redevelopment to take one of these forms. Inevitably, greenfield development will continue in suburban settings. But this development need not take the form of suburban sprawl. It can be dense, diverse, and well designed. Even in the absence of transit, it can be walkable, and can render many automobile trips much shorter than those in suburbia today.

Federal Policy Recommendations

The federal government plays a powerful role in shaping growth patterns and travel choices through regulations, funding, tax credits, technical assistance, and other policies. To accomplish the emissions reductions discussed in this book, we recommend the implementation of the following major federal policies.

Adopt a "Green-TEA" Federal Transportation Act

Approximately every six years, Congress reauthorizes the nation's federal transportation planning and funding legislation. One advantage of having to reauthorize transportation statutes so frequently is that each reauthorization has the potential to match the needs of the nation at that time. Past transportation statutes have focused on linking the nation with interstate highways (1956), providing for mass transit (1964), facilitating metropolitan planning (1973), and promoting system efficiency (1991) (Weiner 1999).

In 1991, Congress began the process of policy change by adopting the Intermodal Surface Transportation Efficiency Act (ISTEA), altering the ways that transportation planning and funding would occur in this country. Although these changes were largely carried forward in subsequent legislation—1998's Transportation Equity Act for the 21st Century (TEA-21) and 2005's Safe, Accountable, Flexible, Efficient Transportation Equity Act: A Legacy for Users (SAFETEA-LU)—the latter statutes did not build on the foundation laid by ISTEA.

As outlined in this book, the most pressing current need is to stabilize the climate for the future economic and environmental well-being, not only of this country, but of the entire planet. With the reauthorization of SAFETEA-LU slated for 2009, the time has come for the next transformation in how we think about, plan for, and fund the nation's surface transportation system. The reauthorization will allocate approximately $300 billion, representing by far the largest category of federal infrastructure spending. How this spending is allocated, and what planning requirements accompany it, will have a profound impact on the nation's future VMT and GHG emissions. In a very real sense, transportation policy *is* climate policy. To meet the current need for VMT and GHG reductions, we suggest that the next surface transportation act build on the acronyms of the previous two statutes and be dubbed "Green-TEA" (Center for Clean Air Policy 2007). We further suggest that this new statute incorporate the following changes in law.

Establish National Goals for Transportation. Traditionally, federal transportation legislation has parceled out federal dollars to the states. Planning came late to the system, with the first mandates for long-range planning in metropolitan areas appearing in 1962; parallel requirements for states did not exist until 1991 (Weiner 1999). Even then, the emphasis was, and remains, on planning procedures, not outcomes. States and metropolitan planning organizations (MPOs) are required to incorporate certain "planning factors" into analyses used to develop long-range plans, but the requirement is couched in permissive language: states/MPOs must *consider* the specified factors. No particular result must be achieved or standard attained. The reality—that these planning factors are mere suggestions—is further cemented by language barring anyone from suing a state or MPO for failing to consider the factors (23 U.S.C. §§ 134(h), 135(d)). States and MPOs must certify to the U.S. Department of Transportation (USDOT) that they considered the planning factors, but oversight and enforcement of even this modest requirement are weak.

Given that most other federal programs that allocate funds to state or local governments—including those for education, public housing, and welfare—contain performance-based requirements, it is rather remarkable that transportation funding (with some exceptions) is more or less a blank check. It is time for transportation to incorporate performance standards as well. Performance- or goal-based planning is not new. Land use planning statutes in many states contain substantive standards that local plans must meet. In one of the better-known examples, the state of Oregon has articulated 19 goals that cities and counties must advance through their comprehensive land use plans (Oregon Department of Land Conservation and Development 2007).

A similar structure should be included in Green-TEA. The statute should articulate a national vision for transportation—one based on climate stability—and define a set of national goals and objectives. To ensure attainment of these goals and objectives, Green-TEA should require that all planning documents—including state and MPO long-range plans and transportation improvement programs, project-level environmental impact statements, and MPO certifications—demonstrate compliance with these goals and objectives. The U.S. Environmental Protection Agency (EPA), in consultation with the USDOT, should be put in charge of reviewing planning documents for compliance and should be given the enforcement tools necessary to guarantee compliance.

There are many goals that could be incorporated into a performance-based transportation planning system. Naturally, a planning system that has climate stability as its main goal should give highest priority to reductions in GHG emissions and VMT. Additional goals would prioritize repair and rehabilitation over new construction ("fix-it-first"), ensure seamless intermodal transfers, and provide for "complete streets" (see "Adopt a Statewide Complete Streets Policy and Funding Program" later in this chapter). Further goals are suggested by current metropolitan and state planning factors: economic vitality, safety, security, accessibility, mobility, environmental enhancement, energy conservation, operation and management efficiency, and system preservation (23 U.S.C. §§ 134(h), 135(d)).

Use Funding Formulas that Provide Incentives for VMT Reduction. Discussions of transportation policy frequently focus on the need for additional revenues to meet growing needs. Rarely is the alternative of balancing resources and needs by reducing demand seriously considered. This alternative can and should be pursued through Green-TEA.

For many decades, transportation funds have been allocated to states based, in large part, on VMT, fuel use, and lane miles (Federal Highway Administration 2006). The more of each factor a state can demonstrate, the more funding the state will receive, thereby allowing the state to build more lane miles, which in turn encourages more VMT (see Chapter 6). More VMT results in increased state gas tax revenues, further exacerbating the perverse spiral of revenue generation, facility expansion, and VMT growth. Obviously, one of the results is ever-increasing GHG emissions.

Funding allocation systems need to stop rewarding VMT growth and start rewarding measures that reduce travel demand and emissions. The original ISTEA legislation, as passed by the Senate in 1991—far ahead of its time—offers a model of how federal funding could be transformed to a performance-based system (S. 1204 § 106(b), June 19, 1991). This legislation would have created an Energy Conservation, Congestion Mitigation, and Clean Air Act Bonus program. A state's funding allocation would have been reduced if it showed a 10 percent or greater increase in VMT per person over an established base year. The withheld funds would have been pooled to provide bonuses to states achieving a 10 percent or greater decrease in VMT per person. Such a program could be administered either through state allocations and metropolitan suballocations or, better still, through direct allocations to MPOs (as described below).

Level the Playing Field for Transportation Choices. Prior to the passage of ISTEA, funding and planning processes essentially tipped the decision-making scales in favor of new road projects. Faced with a given transportation need, state and metropolitan decision makers could choose to address that need with new or expanded roads, which would receive 80 or 90 percent funding from the federal government, or they could address the need with transit, which would receive far less federal funding, often as little as 50 percent. Although ISTEA allowed for the equalizing of federal funding between highway and transit projects, it did not mandate it. The actual practice of the USDOT has largely maintained conditions as they existed prior to ISTEA. Transit projects rarely receive more than 50 percent federal funding, while highway projects frequently receive 80 percent (Beimborn & Puentes 2003).

Moreover, a series of procedural hurdles gives highways an additional edge. Virtually all major (and many minor) transit capital projects must go through a "new starts" application process that requires them to meet standards for cost effectiveness, operational efficiency, mobility improvement, environmental benefit, and supportive land uses—criteria that highways do not have to meet. In addition, funds are allocated to project applicants in very different ways under highway and transit programs. Highway capital funds are distributed to state DOTs via entitlement formulas, while transit capital funds are distributed through a highly competitive discretionary grant program. Finally, unlike highway projects, transit projects are subject to intense federal oversight and postcompletion evaluation.

Of course, there are at least two ways to level the transit/highway playing field: either make transit funding conform to highway procedures or vice versa. While most commentators suggest equalizing federal funding shares at 80 percent, many point to the project selection process and criteria currently used for transit as the basis for good transportation decision making. In other words, rather than "dumbing down" transit to highway funding procedures, we could make highways "smarten up" by applying the same rigorous qualification standards and evaluation processes to highways as we do to transit (Beimborn and Puentes 2003; Katz, Puentes, and Bernstein 2003). This would not only give transit a fair shake, but would ensure that road projects meet basic efficiency and effectiveness standards.

Provide Funding Directly to MPOs. ISTEA gave MPOs new planning authority and responsibilities. It also required state DOTs to provide MPOs for large metropolitan areas with a minimum suballocation of project funds. Under the current transportation law, SAFETEA-LU, that amount is approximately 5 percent of a state's federal highway allocation (Wolf et al. 2007). As important as these changes were, they have hardly made a dent in what is an increasingly inequitable distribution of transportation dollars. Metropolitan areas contain more than 80 percent of the nation's population and 85 percent of its economic output (Puentes and Bailey 2005). Investment by state DOTs in metropolitan areas lags far behind these percentages (Hill et al. 2005).

The issue, however, is not just the *amount* of funding; it is also the authority to decide *how* the money is spent. More than one-third of the states that receive funds from the federal Congestion Mitigation Air Quality Program—funds that by definition are to be used in MPO areas—do not suballocate those funds to their respective MPOs. Only 12 states suballocate federal Transportation Enhancement Program dollars to

MPOs. The other states decide how these funds are to be spent. Even among the 5 percent of funds that are required to be suballocated to MPOs, many MPO staff members report that state DOTs wield substantial influence (Puentes and Bailey 2005).

What is necessary to remedy the long history of structural and institutional inequities is a new system of allocating federal transportation funds directly to metropolitan areas. Instead of sending federal allocations to the states and expecting the states to "do the right thing" for metropolitan areas, future federal legislation should provide for the direct allocation of project funds to MPOs, without filtering these funds through state DOTs. Moreover, the amount of the allocation should be closely linked to the proportion of an MPO's population and economic activity compared to other MPOs and non-MPO areas in the same state. Because different states have different needs for rural and interstate facilities, this formula could be adjusted on a state-by-state basis.

Direct MPO funding likely would require significant institutional changes within many MPOs, so that boards and staff will be equipped to deal with new authority and responsibility, and will be held accountable for system performance and new GHG reduction requirements. California's MPOs, such as those in the Sacramento and Bay Area regions, have significant decision-making authority and are developing GHG reduction plans to comply with state GHG mandates. They will provide important lessons for other MPOs around the country.

Require Land Use/Transportation Scenario Planning. Good planning is critical to land use and transportation reforms at the regional level. The metropolitan planning sections of Green-TEA should require integrated land use/transportation scenario analyses (as described in "Regional Growth Simulations" in Chapter 4) for all regional transportation plans. Current law requires alternatives analyses for specific large projects. However, it does not require alternatives analyses for long-range plans or improvement programs. More importantly, current law does not require consideration of alternative land use patterns or plans.

As emphasized throughout this book, land use and transportation define each other; neither can be fully understood or rationalized in isolation. The costs and benefits of alternative land use patterns and transportation investments cannot be fully appreciated on a project-by-project basis. Because both sectors—land use and transportation—function in an integrated fashion at a regional level, intelligent analysis and policymaking must occur at that level. More detailed alternatives analyses still would occur at the project level, but would be tiered, to account for plan and program analyses of regional-scale impacts. Both levels of analysis would incorporate the performance goals described above. Recognizing that this level of analysis would require more resources than most states and MPOs currently invest in planning processes, Green-TEA should substantially increase funding for regional and state planning. Funding emphasis should be given to enhancements of land use and travel data, transportation models, scenario planning tools, visioning processes, and public engagement.

Establish a National Transportation System Administration. A half-century ago, Congress adopted the Federal-Aid Highway Act of 1956, launching the Interstate Highway System, an unprecedented engineering project that quickly changed everything about the way Americans traveled and built communities. During the same period, the nation developed and implemented a national aviation system, stitching together state and municipally owned airports into a seamless, efficient network. The nation's freight systems already were largely in place. Notably absent from the nation's transportation system is high-quality intercity passenger rail.

Passenger rail, once the exclusive purview of private railroad companies, is now the responsibility of Amtrak, the semipublic national rail agency. Aside from the northeast corridor—which extends from Washington, D.C., to Boston—Amtrak does not own the tracks on which it runs, but must purchase track rights from freight railroads. This effectively forecloses the possibility of significant upgrades to passenger rail service, especially in the critically important area of increased operating speeds. As the nation's airports become ever more congested, the price of oil continues to rise, and the climate impacts of airline travel become more apparent, it is time to get serious about a national high-speed passenger rail network.

To carry out this task, Green-TEA should create a new federal agency within the USDOT and charge it with building and operating a national passenger rail system. Ideally, the new agency would be in charge of all nationally operated passenger systems—aviation as well as rail—to ensure intermodal integration and policy consistency. Creating an effective high-speed passenger rail system would reinforce the other land use and transportation initiatives outlined in this book. It would strengthen central cities and subregional centers, further encouraging compact, infill development and discouraging sprawl. Directly and indirectly, such a system would increase transit usage and bicycle and pedestrian travel, further reducing GHG emissions.

Require Transportation Conformity for GHGs

In *Massachusetts* v. *EPA,* the U.S. Supreme Court affirmed the EPA's authority to regulate GHG emissions under the current federal Clean Air Act, and its duty to do so unless it found that such emissions were not harmful to public health and welfare—an impossibility, given the scientific evidence reviewed in Chapter 3. The obvious and best way for the EPA to respond is to extend transportation conformity requirements from criteria pollutants to GHGs (see "What is Conformity?" on the following page).

Under such a system, state and local governments would be required to adopt mobile source GHG emission reduction budgets (like the emissions budgets for other pollutants) that demonstrate reasonable progress in limiting emissions. Currently, regions that fail to develop transportation plans consistent with "reasonable further

WHAT IS CONFORMITY?

Under Section 110 of the Clean Air Act (42 U.S.C. § 7506(c)), states develop and implement air pollution control plans called state implementation plans (SIPs) to demonstrate attainment with national ambient air quality standards (NAAQS) set by the EPA at levels deemed necessary to protect public health and welfare. The Clean Air Act Amendments of 1990, along with subsequent transportation legislation, required air quality and transportation officials to work together through a process known as conformity. A metropolitan region that has exceeded the emission standards for one or more pollutants must show that the region's transportation plan will conform to applicable SIPs and contribute to timely attainment of the NAAQS. According to the regulations, a proposed project or program must not produce new air quality violations, worsen existing violations, or delay timely attainment of the NAAQS (62 Fed. Reg. 43780). Metropolitan planning organizations must demonstrate this conformity through their long-range transportation plans and transportation improvement programs (TIPs). Projects that do not conform cannot be approved, funded, or advanced through the planning process, nor can they be implemented unless the emissions budget in the SIP is revised.

Under such circumstances, if an MPO fails to adopt a new TIP that stays within the motor vehicle emissions budget in the SIP, the area faces what is known as a conformity lapse. During this period, the MPO cannot approve funding for new transportation projects or new phases of previously funded transportation projects except for those projects that are adopted as transportation control measures in the SIP or are otherwise exempt from conformity as air quality–neutral activities.

If an area fails to submit a required SIP by a deadline, it may face a "conformity freeze," in which it cannot approve any new projects until this deficiency is remedied. If this failure is prolonged, the area can face the ultimate sanction of losing federal transportation funding. For some metropolitan areas, this potential loss of transportation funds could amount to more than $100 million per year. While 63 U.S. areas have suffered conformity lapses, no state or region has ever lost federal transportation funds as a result of a conformity lapse, freeze, or sanctions (Center for Clean Air Policy 2004b).

progress" goals risk curbs on federal transportation funds. Withheld funds could be used to reward states and MPOs that effectively reduce per capita VMT.

Although we acknowledge that, to date, land use and transportation demand management (TDM) policies generally have not played a significant role in meeting regional conformity requirements,[1] we believe that comprehensive strategies aimed at GHG reductions would be more successful and less easily circumvented. Responsibility should be "nested" so that the federal government is responsible for the GHG impacts of federal transportation spending and state and local governments bear responsibility for the GHG impacts of their transportation spending.

Use a Cap-and-Trade System to Promote Smart Growth

Many Congressional proposals for climate stabilization would authorize a national cap-and-trade market system similar to those in Europe and under development in several states. By placing a price on GHG emissions, a cap-and-trade system can send the right signal for reducing the emissions associated with vehicle travel (Winkelman, Hargrave, and Vanderlan 2000). Moreover, regulated parties such as oil companies will have an incentive to support policies that slow VMT growth, because actions that increase VMT will make carbon emission allowances more costly.

Investment of Cap-and-Trade Revenues. Under recent Congressional cap-and-trade proposals, carbon allowances will be worth an estimated $50 billion to $300 billion per year by 2020. A portion of these revenues could be used to support smart growth. We identify a few worthwhile uses of such funds:

- **Technical Assistance for Smart Growth Planning.** Most state and local governments have very limited capacity to implement smart growth. A portion of carbon allowance revenue could support technical assistance to MPOs and to state and local governments for improvements in planning data, models, and scenario planning tools.

- **Smart Location Tax Credits.** The federal government and many state governments currently provide tax credits for hybrid vehicles, solar technology, and other technologies that reduce energy use. The same could be done for smart growth projects that will reduce regional VMT. The federal government could direct states and MPOs to identify smart locations based on the "five D" performance criteria—density, diversity, design, destination accessibility, and distance to transit—discussed in this book. Developers of new for-sale or rental units within the most efficient locations could qualify for a federal smart location tax credit. A portion of the incentive could be used to finance affordable housing units.

- **Increased Support for Travel Alternatives.** Efficient land use patterns and rich transportation choices go hand in hand. A portion of carbon allowance value could support transit, cycling, and pedestrian infrastructure that complement compact development.

- **National Infrastructure Bank.** Infill development and redevelopment in already built-up areas is one of the most effective strategies for reducing VMT and GHG emissions. The infrastructure in many central cities and older suburbs, however, is obsolete and in need of expensive upgrades and rehabilitation. Because many of these cities lack the tax base to adequately fund such projects, national resources are needed. Senator Christopher Dodd (D, Connecticut) has introduced legislation that would provide such funding through a national infrastructure bank, which would help fund improvements in transit systems, public housing, roads, bridges, drinking water systems, and wastewater systems (S.1926, 2007).

Smart Growth Offset Projects. In a cap-and-trade system, regulated industries—like electric power generation—would be subject to emission limits and could sell any unused emission capacity below those limits to other emitters. Although land development is unlikely to become a regulated activity, it might have a role to play in offset markets.

Offsets are projects that can demonstrate quantifiable emission reductions compared to some "business as usual" baseline. Purchasers of offsets might be regulated industries that need offsets to help them meet their emission obligations, or other interested parties, acting voluntarily, who wish to help reduce GHG emissions. Examples of this latter group include companies such as HSBC, an international banking and financial services organization, that want to become carbon-neutral for business and product-differentiation reasons; airline passengers who want to offset the carbon emitted by their travel; and organizations such as FIFA, the international soccer federation, that want to offset the carbon emissions associated with specific events such as the 2010 World Cup (Bayon, Hawn, and Hamilton 2007).

As this book documents, smart growth can substantially reduce GHG emissions compared to business as usual. As such, it should be considered as a project category in offset markets. Land development projects might be assumed to generate a certain level of GHGs under normal circumstances, but emit substantially less because of their higher density, better land use mix, or more central location. Developers could sell the difference in emissions as an offset.

One of the hurdles that will need to be overcome for this to work is the issue of bundling. Given the prevailing price per ton of carbon on most of the world's carbon exchanges, the emission reductions associated with the typical land development project are probably too small to justify the associated market transaction costs. Several projects bundled together, however, could make such a deal worth the effort. This is, after all, what happens with individual home mortgages—they are bundled into larger packages that can be bought and sold in secondary markets. The metropolitan region is probably the most appropriate scale for bundling. If a region were to outperform its GHG conformity target, it could sell its excess reductions as an offset to another region.

The rules governing cap-and-trade systems are very specific about how regulated entities can demonstrate compliance, including what types of offsets can be counted toward compliance. While those voluntarily seeking to reduce their carbon emissions are not affected by such restrictions, the effective elimination of the compliance-bound entities would substantially undercut the marketability of a particular offset type. Granted, the smart growth offset market is untested, but so are many of the other components of cap-and-trade systems. As Congress and various states consider adopting cap-and-trade systems, they should avoid restrictions that would preclude the use of smart growth projects as offsets.

Place More Housing within Reach

In general, the cost of housing declines with distance from job centers and other desired destinations. When the cost of gasoline was low, this led many households to seek housing far away from where they ideally would have lived, driving until they qualified for mortgages. With rising gasoline costs, however, the financial tradeoff between a longer commute and cheaper housing is changing (Lipman 2006). Living in a convenient location with transportation choices is becoming a more important aspect of affordability (Bernstein, Makarewicz, and McCarty 2005). Much of the need for housing during the next 30 years can be met within walking distance of the nation's 4,000 transit stations (Center for Transit-Oriented Development 2004). The challenge is to match affordable housing with transit availability.

Federal housing programs need to be better targeted. Take the Low Income Housing Tax Credit (LIHTC), the country's largest rental housing assistance program (U.S. Department of Housing and Urban Development 2008). The criteria governing the location for LIHTC-supported projects do not include access to transit (Gustafson and Walker 2002). In Washington, D.C., for example, only 6 percent of LIHTC housing units are located within walking distance of Metrorail stations (Rube 2008). With transportation costs now consuming more than 40 percent of income for households in the lowest-income quintile (Bureau of Labor Statistics 2001), proximity to high-quality transit needs to become a major factor in LIHTC allocations.

State Policy Recommendations

Traditionally, major U.S. public policy initiatives have originated at the federal level, with states and local governments providing implementation muscle and expertise. This has been especially true in the areas of environmental protection and public health. With respect to climate change, however, the federal government has chosen not to take a leadership role, effectively ceding that role to states and localities. More than half of the states—29 at last count—are filling this vacuum by creating their own plans to reduce GHG emissions. One-third of the states have set GHG reduction targets, and many more are in the process of doing so. Some states have taken the additional step of banding together in multistate compacts to create cap-and-trade programs (Regional Greenhouse Gas Initiative 2005; Western Climate Initiative 2008).

State climate control plans in New York, Connecticut, and Massachusetts include comprehensive VMT-reduction recommendations, although their experiences in implementing these plans have been mixed (Center for Clean Air Policy 2003, 2004a). The state of New York requires MPOs to report the GHG impacts of federally required transportation improvement programs and long-range transportation plans (ICF Consulting 2005). Connecticut created an Office of Responsible Growth to promote transit-oriented development, provide transit alternatives, encourage walkable communities, and target state funding to support development in designated "responsible growth" areas (Rell 2006). In California, a working group created by the state energy commission has established a set of policy recommendations on land use and climate change based on a comprehensive review of state and local efforts (California Energy Commission 2007).

Our recommendations for state policies build on many of these programs, focusing on land use strategies to reduce VMT and GHG emissions. As formulated, they can either stand alone or be integrated with future federal climate policies, such as those outlined in the preceding section. We recommend that states pursue all of the following policy changes.

Establish GHG Plans that Include Targets for VMT Reductions

Regardless of whether the federal government acts to reduce GHG emissions, states can and should develop GHG reduction plans that include targets for reducing vehicular travel (VMT). To be effective, these VMT targets need to be suballocated among regions and localities within the state. Metropolitan planning organizations and local governments then would develop plans to achieve the targets, using strategies that best fit their communities. The state would review and rate the regional and local plans for compliance with overall state goals and suballocated targets.

The Washington State Commute Trip Reduction program provides an example of how this system might work. The program, which is focused on reducing single-occupant vehicle commutes and GHG emissions, sets targets for reductions in single-occupant vehicle commutes and VMT per commuter. Local jurisdictions then must set goals that are at least equal to the state goals and create plans for achieving the target measures (Washington Administrative Code 468-63-030). Another example is New Mexico's recent requirement that state-funded comprehensive plans include an analysis of and a reduction plan for GHG emissions related to land use, economic development, housing, and transportation patterns.

Align State Spending with Climate Goals and Plans

Once local and regional VMT reduction plans are approved, states should align spending programs to support plans and reward successful local implementation efforts. All discretionary spending programs, whether funded directly by the state or through federal grants, would be considered in this realignment. Particularly important are programs with direct ties to land development, including those in housing, economic development, infrastructure, water and sewer systems, schools, transportation, and recreation.

Once identified and pooled, these discretionary funds could provide a significant incentive for counties and municipalities. When Massachusetts adopted this approach for its Commonwealth Capital funding program, discretionary funds totaled roughly $500 million within an annual state budget of $27 billion. To allocate these funds, Massachusetts uses a scorecard system to assess the consistency of local policies and implementation actions with state sustainable development goals. This incentive has led to hundreds of changes in local plans and zoning ordinances statewide.

In addition to its capital funding program, Massachusetts provides financial incentives for the establishment of smart growth zoning districts. To qualify, an area must meet certain minimum density, affordability, and location requirements. The program tightly links spending with results: communities get some funding when they make initial zoning changes, and additional funding when smart new development projects are built. A companion statute guarantees that the state will cover any additional costs incurred by a local school system as a result of housing construction in a smart growth zoning district.

The California Infrastructure and Economic Development Bank's Infrastructure State Revolving Fund Program uses a similar state scorecard system. This program rates applications on a 200-point scale. Preference is given to projects that are in or adjacent to already developed areas or areas with high unemployment, and to projects that contribute to public transit use and downtown revitalization.

One of the most comprehensive structures for aligning state spending with smart growth goals is Maryland's Smart Growth Funding Areas system. Enacted in 1997, the system restricts development-related state expenditures to designated priority funding areas (PFAs), which were defined to include all municipalities as well as unincorporated areas served by water and sewer services. Areas outside the PFAs are ineligible for state funding of infrastructure or economic development. A recent report by the National Center for Smart Growth suggests the need to carefully track spending under such as system, and illustrates the implementation failures that can occur if this is not done (Knaap and Lewis 2007).

In Illinois, the Business Location Efficiency Incentive Act, passed in 2005, gives companies a small additional corporate income tax credit if a new job site is accessible by public transportation or located near affordable workforce housing. Companies seeking the credit at sites that do not initially qualify can qualify later with a site remediation plan that provides employer-assisted housing, shuttle services, pre-tax transit passes, or carpooling assistance.

Reduce "Fiscalization of Land Uses"

Local governments rely upon a variety of development-related revenue streams to fund public services. However, not all types of development generate the same amount of revenue or the same degree of service demands. There is a fiscal incentive to limit low-revenue/high-demand land uses, such as workforce housing, in favor of high-revenue/low-demand uses, such as big-box retail. Competition among localities for high-revenue/low-demand uses is fierce, often leading jurisdictions to offer large economic inducements to commercial developers. Local governments that succeed at this competition frequently fail to provide sufficient land for low-revenue/high-demand uses, effectively exporting them to neighboring jurisdictions. The result is that people must travel longer distances between affordable workforce housing and job centers, shopping, and other important services (Thomas 2006).

Local governments in a few metropolitan areas—including Minneapolis/St. Paul; Charlottesville and Albemarle County, Virginia; Davis and Yolo County, California; and the New Jersey Meadowlands—have developed pacts to dampen these fiscal incentives and deter intraregional competition by sharing tax bases. Such arrangements often require state authorizing legislation. In California, authorization was provided recently through a ballot initiative.

There are other ways states can reduce perverse local fiscal incentives. In parts of the West where property tax caps are more common, sales taxes can be a driver of land use decisions, and reform efforts must focus on this dynamic. In Arizona, local government retail incentive packages became so large and so common that the state passed a law prohibiting them in the Phoenix metropolitan area. In many New England states, property taxes are the dominant funding source, and property tax reform is seen as a potential solution. Massachusetts now provides towns with a hold-harmless guarantee: if education costs rise because certain smart growth zoning regulations lead to an influx of families with school-age children, the state makes up the difference.

Adopt a Statewide Complete Streets Policy and Funding Program

With approximately 50 percent of trips in the United States less than three miles in length (USDOT 2001), walking and bicycling can and should provide alternatives to the automobile for many daily trips. Even for more distant destinations, walking and bicycling have a role to play as the first and last segments of transit trips. Yet, streets and highways all across America lack basic facilities for pedestrians and bicyclists. Many lack sidewalks, have lanes that are too narrow for bicycles, are dangerous to cross, lack comfortable transit stops, and are inaccessible to people with disabilities. According to a national survey of pedestrians and bicyclists, 25 percent of walking trips occur on roads without sidewalks or shoulders; only 5 percent of bike trips occur on roads with bike lanes (National Highway Traffic Safety Administration and Bureau of Transportation Statistics 2003). In short, public streets and roads are hostile environments for travelers who are not inside cars. To make other modes of transportation viable, a network of complete streets and highways is needed.

A complete streets policy would require that pedestrian and bicycle facilities be provided on all new and reconstructed streets and highways, and that pedestrians' and bicyclists' needs be considered in routine roadway operation and maintenance. For more than 35 years, the Oregon Bike Bill has done just that, requiring state and local governments to provide "[f]ootpaths and bicycle trails . . . wherever a highway, road or street is being constructed, reconstructed or relocated" (Oregon Revised Statute (ORS) 316.514(1)). Instead of using permissive language that would allow the inclusion of pedestrian and bicycle facilities, the Oregon bill mandates that inclusion, with narrowly defined exceptions. More than 50 jurisdictions at all levels of government have adopted complete streets policies in the last few years. The National Complete Streets Coalition (2005) has developed a nine-point program for complete streets, which should be the minimum standard in all states.

To create "complete communities," a complete streets policy could mandate that new streets be interconnected and culs-de-sac be discouraged so that travel distances for pedestrians and bicyclists are minimized. Again, Oregon provides useful examples. The state's Transportation Planning Rule requires all local and regional governments to adopt standards for the layout of local streets (Oregon Administrative Rule 660-12-0020(2) (b)). These standards must provide "reasonably direct routes for bicycle and pedestrian travel." Portland Metro, the Portland-area regional government, has interpreted this state provision as requiring local street plans that limit the use of cul-de-sacs and dead ends, create direct travel routes, and provide full intersections at least every 530 feet and pedestrian/bicycle accessways every 330 feet (Metro 2004, pp. 6-15–6-17). The state of Virginia is considering a similar requirement for all subdivision streets under its jurisdiction, but with specific performance standards for street connectivity.

The third component of a complete streets policy is adequate state-level funding. Oregon's Bike Bill requires both state and local governments to set aside at least 1 percent of state highway funds for pedestrian and bicycle facilities (ORS 366.514(3)). While this is a commendable base, it would be better to set funding levels commensurate with actual or desired mode shares. Approximately 10 percent of trips currently are made by bicycling or walking (USDOT 2001). A reasonable objective for 2030 is to double that percentage. To stand a chance of meeting this objective, state funding levels for pedestrian and bicycle facilities will have to be commensurate. Funding should be provided to retrofit all existing "incomplete" streets that present barriers to bicycling, walking, and transit use.

Require Analysis of GHG Emissions as Part of Planning Approvals

Following Congress's adoption of the National Environmental Policy Act (NEPA) in 1969, 13 states and the District of Columbia passed state-level "mini-NEPAs," requiring assessments of state and local actions in a manner similar to NEPA. The actions covered by these mini-NEPAs vary from state to state. In some states, such as Connecticut, the mini-NEPA affects only state agency activities. In others, such as New York, actions by local governments, including land use permitting, are covered. Although the specifics vary, all of the mini-NEPAs mandate some level of analysis and, in some cases, mitigation of actions that have significant impacts on the environment. The attorney general of California has interpreted that state's mini-NEPA—the California Environmental Quality Act (CEQA)—as applicable to GHG emissions. In a celebrated lawsuit against San Bernardino County, the attorney general asserted that CEQA required the county to assess and mitigate GHG emission impacts associated with an update of the county's general plan (see "Smart Growth and Climate Change Policy in California" on the following page).

In California, Assembly Bill 32 contains a legislative declaration that "[g]lobal warming poses a serious threat to . . . the environment of California." This declaration provides the basis for enforcement action under CEQA. Yet, even without similar

SMART GROWTH AND CLIMATE CHANGE POLICY IN CALIFORNIA

California must address VMT growth if the state is to meet its GHG reduction target pursuant to Assembly Bill 32 (AB 32), the Global Warming Solutions Act of 2006. California state agencies are working hard on a recipe for comprehensive policy changes to advance smart growth, cut VMT, and reduce GHG emissions. They have a rich set of ingredients with which to work, including a statewide climate target (AB 32), Blueprint Planning Grants to promote integrated regional transportation and land use planning, climate change impact assessment guidelines under the California Environmental Quality Act (CEQA), proposed legislation (SB 375) to provide incentives for smart growth planning and implementation, and some $40 billion in infrastructure bonds that could be "green-leveraged" to encourage climate-friendly development patterns. State, regional, and local officials, as well as environmental advocates and developers, are working out the details of policy design issues, including how to set and meet regional VMT/GHG targets, how to address GHGs in project and plan environmental impact reports (EIRs), and how to ensure that bond funds advance sustainable communities and GHG reduction goals.

In setting regional VMT or GHG targets, the twin challenges are to ensure that 1) regional VMT targets, in aggregate, are sufficient to help meet state GHG goals, and 2) targets are feasible in light of the unique conditions of each region, including population growth, demographic and economic trends, development patterns, and transportation infrastructure. There is an emerging sense—but no consensus—that it may be best to start with voluntary regional targets and support their implementation via technical assistance and planning support (for data and model improvements, and for scenario planning tools). As the regions' expertise and experience grows, these could evolve over time into mandatory targets, with incentives offered by attaching VMT/GHG performance conditions to allocation of transportation and other infrastructure funding.

The state already has established a precedent for requiring GHG reduction goals in regional and local plans. Last year, California Attorney General Jerry Brown, Jr., sued San Bernardino County on grounds that the county violated CEQA by not adequately addressing climate change impacts in its general plan update EIR. The parties subsequently reached a settlement wherein the county agreed to prepare a plan that will include a GHG emissions inventory and emissions reduction targets. Although it is temporarily barred from filing further lawsuits until the state provides more direction on climate change impact assessment in its CEQA guidelines (to become effective January 1, 2010), the attorney general's office continues to comment on general plan, regional plan, and development project EIRs, recommending further analysis and specific impact mitigations.

Today, all eyes are on California. Smart growth and climate change policy development in this state will offer important insights and models for other states and the federal government.

legislative pronouncements in other mini-NEPA states, the scientific evidence regarding GHG emissions and climate change—much of which is summarized in Chapter 3—argues for environmental assessments of GHG emissions.

While generally positive, mini-NEPA compliance can be costly. In states where a mini-NEPA covers private land development activities, the cost of compliance can negatively affect housing affordability. California is now considering legislation (Senate Bill 375) that would provide partial or full exemptions from CEQA compliance for compact development meeting specified standards. This combination of policies—generally requiring GHG assessments for development proposals, while exempting qualified compact developments—would give compact developments a significant edge in the real estate market. It is a model that could be duplicated in other mini-NEPA states.

Regional Policy Recommendations

Success in meeting our climate challenge will require cooperation across state and city boundaries. Minnesota's Twin Cities and their suburbs provide an example of regional coordination to tackle regional problems. When the state legislature created the Metropolitan Council in 1967, the region—which had 272 separate local units of government—was plagued by inadequately treated sewage, a deteriorating bus system, and rapid loss of open spaces. Making the situation worse, many communities lacked the funding to tackle these problems (Metropolitan Council 2004). Since its creation, the Metropolitan Council has contributed to the Twin Cities's reputation as a green, livable, vibrant region. This regional approach is now helping the Twin Cities reduce global warming pollution.

Although regional agencies like the Metropolitan Council are still rare in the United States, every medium and large metropolitan area has an MPO. Congress required the establishment of MPOs in the 1970s as a condition of federal transportation funding. These agencies often are also councils of governments (regional councils) that coordinate and assist their local cities and counties in addressing regional concerns. In some states, MPOs are now involved in land planning as well as transportation planning. MPOs are the logical entities to carry out many of the policies recommended in this section. They will need to be given enhanced powers and resources, consistent with the new duties assigned to them, and become more accountable for regional outcomes. Their governing bodies will need to be representative of the regions they serve, with cities and suburbs represented according to population. It would be best if MPOs operated as part of broad-based, multiservice regional councils.

Include Climate Goals in Regional Transportation Plans

Regional long-range transportation plans are the blueprints that guide investment in a region's transportation system. Including GHG and VMT reduction targets in these plans will help ensure that transportation investments contribute to climate protection. In California, MPOs, state agencies, and the state legislature currently are considering incorporating GHG reduction targets into long-range transportation plans to comply with AB 32, the California Global Warming Solutions Act of 2006.

Give Funding Priority to Compact, Transit-Served Areas

Metropolitan planning organizations could give funding priority to compact, transit-served areas where development will help reduce GHG emissions. In concert with local governments, MPOs would designate "priority funding areas" where local governments have planned for compact development.

In the Twin Cities, the Metropolitan Council's 2030 Regional Development Framework seeks to encourage infill of "developed communities," those in which more than 85 percent of the land is developed and infrastructure is well established. To advance this goal, the Metropolitan Council administers the Livable Communities Act (LCA), which underwrites grants for brownfields cleanup, affordable housing, and mixed-use projects, and is funded through a metro-area property tax (EPA 2003). This voluntary program has engaged more than 100 communities in the seven-county metropolitan area, leveraging billions of dollars in private investments as well as additional public investments.

The San Diego Association of Governments (SANDAG) has developed a smart growth concept map in concert with local governments. For a share of incentive funding, local governments have been willing to designate smart growth areas and accept more growth and density. Incentive funds will amount to $240 million through the year 2040. To be designated, an area must currently meet minimum density and transit service standards, or have planning and zoning in place that will lead to such densities. Because funds for the program come from a regional sales tax, qualifying areas can use the money for a wide range of improvements, not just those directly related to transportation. Areas that do not yet have the necessary planning and zoning in place can apply for planning grants to complete plan and code changes that would qualify them for infrastructure funding (SANDAG 2006).

Similar programs are in place in the San Francisco Bay Area, the Sacramento area, and Portland, Oregon. In these regions, however, because federal transportation funds are used (primarily CMAQ and enhancement funds), qualifying projects have to be transportation related.

Redirect Transportation Funds from Road Expansion to Transit and Bike/Pedestrian Facilities

Metropolitan planning organizations should redirect transportation resources in order to develop top-notch infrastructure for nonauto travel modes. Shifting investment away from road expansion toward transit, bicycling, and walking facilities can lead to better climate outcomes, not only by encouraging the use of alternative modes of transportation but by moderating induced traffic and induced development (see Chapter 6).

The Sacramento Area Council of Governments (SACOG), which is responsible for coordinating the planning of 22 cities and six counties in the Sacramento area, was dissatisfied with the projected outcomes of its 2025 Transportation Plan. Under the plan, it was projected that VMT would continue to outpace population growth, transit ridership would increase only marginally, and the nonmotorized (walking and bicycling) mode share would decline.

The SACOG 2035 Plan sought to reverse these trends. It focused on four performance indicators: VMT, congestion and delay, transit ridership, and nonmotorized travel mode share (SACOG 2007). Out of a total spending package of $41.7 billion, the 2035 Plan earmarks $14.3 billion for transit and $1.4 billion for bicycle and pedestrian projects. Projections show that VMT growth through 2035 will fall from its historic growth rate of 2.5 percent per year to 1.4 percent per year. The VMT growth rate is projected to be lower than the population growth rate of 1.6 percent (SACOG 2007, p. 4-4). This plan also will save money. A recent SACOG study found that infrastructure costs an average of $20,000 less per housing unit for compact development than for sprawl.

Use Land Use/Transportation Scenario Planning to Evaluate Growth Options

Land use/transportation scenario planning, once considered "state-of-the-art," should become state-of-the-practice everywhere. In regional scenario planning, one future scenario represents "business as usual" or a continuation of current growth trends, usually some variant of sprawl. Other scenarios usually represent more compact and transit-oriented development patterns. Scenarios are run through regional travel models and other performance assessments. Scenario planning helps clarify the costs and benefits of alternative development patterns. It helps identify options available to communities in the region, the different investments they will require, and the tradeoffs involved.

Scenario planning has been conducted all over the country (see "Regional Growth Simulations" in Chapter 4). One of the best examples is the Sacramento Region Blueprint Transportation–Land Use Study, which used an extensive public outreach process, cutting-edge Internet-accessible planning software, and a detailed business-as-usual baseline growth forecast to help participants explore alternative growth scenarios through 2050. The "preferred scenario," ultimately adopted, features infill development and transportation investments that will produce 12.3 fewer daily VMT per household by 2050, a 26 percent reduction below the baseline (SACOG 2005).

Other well-known scenario planning studies include Portland Metro's Region 2040, which began in 1992 and was the first large-scale scenario planning exercise in the nation (Metro 2000), and Louisiana Speaks (2007), which was launched to help coastal communities craft redevelopment plans after Hurricanes Katrina and

Rita. There are numerous examples of visioning and scenario planning that have not led to changes in development patterns (Bartholomew 2007). Those that have been successful were backed by political will and the resources required to continue the process after the initial public participation is complete.

Under a GHG conformity requirement (see "Require Transportation Conformity for GHGs" earlier in this chapter), regions such as Sacramento and Portland would be able to use their interactive transportation and land use models to develop land use and transportation scenarios that achieve VMT reduction targets, and limit investment to transportation projects that comply with the "constrained" plan. Coordination will be more difficult in the many regions without integrated land use and transportation models.

Establish a Regional Transfer of Development Rights Program

Transfer of development rights (TDR) programs enable landowners to sell their development rights to other landowners through a market-based system. Such programs have long been used to help protect farmland and open space by shifting development rights from such lands to areas designated for higher-density development. Effectively crafted, TDR programs can help reduce VMT by directing growth to compact, transit-served areas and away from low-density greenfield sites, thus reducing the need for long-distance travel.

Taxpayers benefit from TDR programs because they cost less than outright government purchase of open space or farmland. The programs also are generally popular with citizens in rural areas because they compensate rural landowners for the development potential of their land. While TDR programs typically are administered by local governments, a regional TDR program could have greater impact because it would encompass more rural and urban areas than a local program. Montgomery County, Maryland, located just north of Washington, D.C., has a large subregional TDR program that has protected nearly 51,000 acres of farmland in the past 25 years. Regional TDR programs exist in the New Jersey Pinelands and the Lake Tahoe area.

Create a Carbon Impact Fee for New Development

Cheap land and subsidized infrastructure make suburban and exurban development less expensive than urban infill. Regulatory reforms alone cannot overcome this advantage. For decades, governments have charged impact fees on new development to offset the costs of schools, libraries, sewers, parks, and transportation. Creating and implementing a regional CO_2 emissions impact fee would internalize carbon impacts into development costs, thereby rewarding best development practices and raising the price of carbon-inefficient development. Coupled with a TDR program as described above, an impact fee would require exurban landowners who developed their land to pay, while exurban landowners who stewarded their land would get paid. Fee revenues could be used to help fund transit, bicycling facilities, sidewalks and other pedestrian amenities, and other smart growth projects in compact areas.

Although novel, such a fee would not be the first instance of an emissions-based development impact fee. The San Joaquin Valley Air Pollution Control District in the Fresno, California, area imposes a fee on new development to fund mitigation of several transportation-related air pollutants and to encourage developers to build projects that minimize emissions. The program, which applies to all development above a minimum size, assesses fees for the estimated ten-year total emissions associated with the development. The fees, which in 2007 were $7,100 per ton for NOx and $5,594 per ton for PM10, are based on the cost of offsetting emission reduction strategies.

The incentive part of the San Joaquin program provides fee reductions for project features that will reduce transportation-related emission rates below base levels. These features include proximity to retail, a balance of jobs and housing, proximity to transit services, high intersection density, and the provision of sidewalks, bicycle lanes, and long-term bicycle parking. In 2006/2007, the district collected nearly $13 million in fees and spent more than $9.5 million on emission reduction projects. These projects resulted in emission reductions of 824 tons of NOx and 34 tons of PM10 (SJVAPCD 2007).

The San Joaquin program could be adapted for CO_2 emissions. Using the project-level simulation techniques outlined in Chapter 4 and borrowing elasticities from disaggregate travel studies discussed there, policy makers could craft a reasonable system for calculating project-level CO_2 emissions.

Enhance Regional Travel Models to Account for Land Use/Travel Interactions

Conventional regional travel models used in long-range transportation planning are unable to access the full impacts of the development patterns advocated in this book. They cannot account for the effects of density, diversity, or design on travel distance or mode choice. Most models disregard the possibility of walking or bicycle use on short trips, assuming instead that all trips are by motor vehicle. They predict travel between "traffic analysis zones," which usually are based on divisions of census tracts, leaving intrazonal travel poorly represented. As a consequence, these models underestimate the potential of smart growth to reduce VMT and GHG emissions.

Some MPOs have developed more advanced travel models that overcome these limitations. The Metropolitan Transportation Commission (MTC), the MPO for the San Francisco Bay Area, includes both walk and bicycle modes in its model, basing projections for these modes on such factors as travel time and employment density (for work trips). The MTC model also includes a wider variety of trip purposes than the typical travel model. Montgomery County, Maryland; Portland, Oregon; and Sacramento also are among the handful of regions with enhanced models. Planners in leading regions are beginning to use a new generation of activity-based travel models that simulate the travel of individual households. These microsimulation models overcome the limitations of travel analysis zones and also provide improved accounting of VMT and congestion.

Assist Local Governments with Land Development Reforms

Rewriting local land development codes to encourage more climate-friendly growth requires significant expertise and funding, which many communities lack. The EPA Smart Growth program, which runs a technical assistance program for localities, receives more than 60 applications a year for five or six grants. Regional governments as well as states should take the lead in helping communities bring their development regulations into the 21st century.

In the Bay Area, the MTC provides $7.5 million in Transportation for Livable Communities planning grants for local governments to plan and zone for transit-oriented development. The program provides grants of up to $750,000 to fund transit station area plans, zoning ordinances, and other land development guides designed to boost transit ridership and reduce VMT (MTC n.d.). The MTC also provides funding for capital improvements and may expand eligibility to include such unconventional projects as land banking for affordable housing. The Sacramento MPO, SACOG, has a similar program.

Local Policy Recommendations

More than 780 U.S. mayors are signatories to the U.S. Conference of Mayors Climate Protection Agreement (Mayors Climate Protection Center 2007), and about 600 have signed on as "Cool Mayors" with the Mayors for Climate Protection program (2008). Both programs commit cities to meeting the Kyoto target of emissions 7 percent lower than 1990 levels by the year 2012. Counties, too, are taking action under a "Cool Counties" campaign launched by the Sierra Club in partnership with King County, Washington; Fairfax County, Virginia; and Nassau County, New York. Concrete actions that localities can take are outlined in this section.

Develop a Local Climate Action Plan

To meet these commitments, many cities and counties are developing climate action plans. The best of these plans create a baseline inventory of GHG emissions from various sources, such as transportation, land use, energy use, and solid waste; identify actions and policies needed to reduce emissions from each source; set reduction targets, with benchmarks along the way to track progress; create a budget for what is needed to achieve the reductions; and identify potential funding sources to pay for improvements.

The Seattle Climate Action Plan (2007) has all these elements. With GHG emissions from transportation making up about 60 percent of the total, the city sees transportation as its biggest challenge. The city's plan incorporates transit service expansion,

PlaNYC: GREENING THE CITY

The average American is responsible for annual emissions of 24.5 metric tons of CO_2. Residents of New York City, however, are responsible for only 7.1 metric tons of CO_2 per year, less than one-third the national average. New York City is more energy efficient for two key reasons: a more efficient transportation system and more efficient buildings. Two-thirds of New Yorkers take transit or walk to work; fewer than 5 percent drive to work in the central business district. And almost no one drives to the store to pick up a quart of milk or to the gym to ride a stationary bicycle. The city's multifamily, mixed-use buildings share walls and use less energy than freestanding structures.

New York City's savings opportunities are not maxed out. Building upon an already efficient footprint, PlaNYC sets a goal of reducing citywide carbon emissions by 30 percent below 2005 levels. An annual GHG emissions inventory will track progress toward this goal. The city will address growing congestion on roadways and transit lines by expanding transit services, improving cycling and pedestrian infrastructure, and significantly increasing the availability of affordable housing near workplaces. The proposed revenue-raising mechanism, a congestion pricing program, would cut traffic and air pollution by more than 10 percent, while raising some $400 million to $500 million per year to be invested in transit. If this congestion pricing plan is approved by the city council and the state legislature, New York City will receive $350 million through an Urban Partnership Agreement with the U.S. Department of Transportation. Importantly, the city has attracted a dream team of experts and advisers from the private, public, and nonprofit sectors to develop, market, and implement the plan.

a complete streets ordinance, bicycle and pedestrian master plans, a commercial parking tax, a traffic calming program, and a "center city strategy" that promotes growth in the downtown and adjacent neighborhoods. The plan's well-defined benchmarks and reporting requirements help to hold city government accountable. Charlotte, North Carolina, has a Transportation Action Plan with essentially the same elements.

Change the Rules of Development

Some of the biggest impacts on VMT can be achieved through changes to local land development policies. Many communities have not overhauled their zoning and subdivision ordinances since they were created in the 1950s or 1960s, when they were designed to separate land uses, maintain low densities and large setbacks, ensure plentiful parking, keep streets wide, and save money by limiting sidewalks. Communities need to examine their development rules to determine if and how these rules should be changed to meet GHG reduction targets. They should include in their review the following items:

- zoning codes;
- subdivision regulations;
- street design standards;
- parking standards;

■ annexation rules; and

■ design guidelines.

Tools such as scorecards and zoning code audits are available to help in this review process (Smart Growth Leadership Institute 2006). New models such as form-based codes and smart codes are readily adaptable from other localities or from national models.

Favor Smart Growth Projects in the Approval Process

Once communities have reformed their codes to allow smart growth, they should make it easier for such projects to gain approval. Predictability in the approval process is valuable to everyone concerned, including local government, citizens, and developers, for whom time is money. Laying out the guidelines and rules for what local government seeks in the way of development makes the process more predictable and fair, as does defining the benefits developers will derive from meeting or exceeding a community's VMT reduction targets.

One way to favor compact development is to provide incentives. If development projects meet or exceed a community's targets, developers can be rewarded with, for example, density bonuses that allow them to build more or permitting fee waivers that allow them to pay less. Alternatively, local governments can calculate the traffic reduction benefits of compact development and reduce, accordingly, the amount of exactions or fees for which developers are responsible.

Another way to favor compact development is to offer streamlined permitting for projects that meet specified community targets. Of course, the process still must include opportunities for meaningful public input and ensure compliance with public safety and environmental safeguards. Nevertheless, because less time spent negotiating approval processes can translate into significant cost savings for developers, the promise of faster permitting can be an effective incentive for smart growth. Orlando, Florida, has provided all of these incentives for traditional urban development in the city's southeast sector.

Adopt Pedestrian-Friendly Site and Building Design Standards

Site and building design standards, especially for commercial and institutional uses, need to provide for a comfortable and attractive environment at the sidewalk. The regional transportation plan adopted by Portland Metro requires new retail, office, and institutional buildings at major transit stops to be located no farther than 20 feet from the stop or, alternatively, to provide a pedestrian plaza at the stop with a direct pedestrian connection to the building entrance (Metro 2004, p. 6-23). The city of Portland went a step further, requiring that all new multifamily residential, commercial, and institutional structures along transit-served streets be located within 20 feet of the sidewalk. The city also banned off-street parking from the front of buildings, requiring it to be located at the side or the back of a structure (Portland Code 33.266.130). Facilitating these changes in site design are off-street parking standards that reduce the minimum amount of parking required—in some cases eliminating it entirely—and establish a maximum amount that will be allowed (Metro Code 3.07.210–3.07.220).

The Local Government Commission (2003), a California-based nonprofit, has compiled a comprehensive catalog of additional design strategies, drawn in part from the Sacramento city code and recommendations from the U.S. Department of Housing and Urban Development (HUD).

Provide for Workforce Housing near Jobs

Two leading planning researchers recently asked, "which reduces vehicle travel more, jobs/housing balance or retail/housing mixing?" (Cervero and Duncan 2006). The answer—surprisingly, since work trips represent less than 20 percent of all trips—was jobs/housing balance. In most metropolitan areas, the cost of housing declines with distance from job centers and other desired destinations, while the cost of transportation increases. Without workforce housing, people have to drive until they qualify for a mortgage or else live in substandard housing. They also have to drive until they find decent schools for their kids. With rising gasoline prices, the financial tradeoff between a longer commute and less expensive housing is changing, and the potential savings from living in a convenient location with transportation choices is becoming a larger part of affordability.

Local governments have many options for promoting workforce housing (Haughey 2007):

- allowing accessory apartments on single-family house lots;
- enacting inclusionary zoning requirements that affordable homes be built along with market-rate housing;
- enacting linkage requirements that workforce housing be provided in return for approval of offices or industrial facilities;
- offering density bonuses in return for affordable units;
- donating or selling municipal lands with workforce housing requirements; and
- creating housing trust funds that earmark revenue from multiple sources for a community's housing needs.

Invest in Civic Engagement and Education

Successful planning requires the meaningful engagement of people who live and work in the affected community. Meaningful public engagement requires that planners and decision makers actively seek out public input early in the planning process, well before threshold questions are framed or alternatives crafted. When residents are engaged in the planning process from the beginning and know that their concerns and ideas are being considered, they are more likely to support new development. Visioning processes and design charrettes are two popular techniques that localities have used in recent years to engage citizens.

One example comes from Davidson, North Carolina, where the town's planning ordinance requires developers to hold design charrettes. Involving the public at this early stage can make the approval process smoother for developers, offsetting any added costs they may incur by involving the public.

Developing a Comprehensive Policy Package

Such a comprehensive overhaul of America's development processes will be a mighty challenge. But it is on the same ambitious scale as other proposals that are being considered in the climate change debate, including efforts to switch to renewable fuels, dramatically increase vehicle efficiency, end oil imports from hostile nations, and renew investments in nuclear power.

The fact is, no huge amount of reduction will come easily, and few strategies are likely to take advantage of consumer demand as well as those discussed in this book. Most communities that have adopted land development reforms have done so for self-interested reasons, such as traffic management or fiscal health, and not because they wished to reduce greenhouse gas emissions. We are confident that these improvements to the built environment can offer win-win benefits, for communities and the global climate.

10

Conclusion

With regard to urban development and travel demand management, this publication asks and answers three critical questions facing the urban planning profession, land development community, and federal, state, and local policy makers:

- What reduction in vehicle miles traveled (VMT) is possible in the United States with compact development rather than continuing urban sprawl?
- What reduction in CO_2 emissions will accompany such a reduction in VMT?
- What policy changes will be required to shift the dominant land development pattern from sprawl to compact development?

The answer to the first question is a 20 to 40 percent reduction in VMT for each increment of new development or redevelopment, depending on the degree to which best practices are adopted (see Chapter 4). The answer to the second question is a 7 to 10 percent reduction in total transportation CO_2 emissions by 2050 relative to continuing sprawl (see "The Effect of Compact Development on VMT and CO_2 Emissions" in Chapter 2). The answer to the third question is a set of dramatic policy changes at all levels of government (see Chapter 9).

Unlike other vehicle emissions, CO_2 emissions have never been regulated. Given the difficulty of changing longstanding policies, development patterns and, ultimately, lifestyles, is the 7 to 10 percent reduction in CO_2 emissions worth the effort? The answer, we believe, is "yes," for three primary reasons:

- The U.S. transportation sector cannot reach a sustainable level of CO_2 emissions through vehicle and fuel technology improvements alone. It also needs to reduce VMT, as the third leg supporting the policy stool (see Chapter 3).

WORTH THE EFFORT

Unlike other vehicle emissions, CO_2 emissions have never been regulated. Given the difficulty of changing longstanding policies, development patterns and, ultimately, lifestyles, is the 7 to 10 percent reduction in CO_2 emissions worth the effort? The answer, we believe, is "yes."

■ The shift from sprawl to compact development will have many other economic, environmental, and quality-of-life benefits, so any "costs" of this CO_2 reduction strategy will be offset by additional quantifiable benefits (see "Changing Consumer Demand" and "Changing Public Priorities" in Chapter 2).

■ Reductions in VMT and CO_2 emissions with compact development will be sizable and long lasting compared to reductions achievable with other available actions (see "The Effect of Compact Development on VMT and CO_2 Emissions" in Chapter 2, and Chapter 4).

Compact development provides an insurance policy against the worst effects of climate change and oil price spikes. Current or future residents of compact development will have a variety of viable transportation options, while the residents of sprawl will not. For this reason, as well as others outlined in this book, compact development has to become the nation's dominant urban pattern once again.

Notes

CHAPTER 1: Overview

[1] In this scenario, VMT growth increases by 2 percentage points (50 percent growth by 2030) due to the "rebound effect" whereby driving increases as fuel economy increases (10 percent short-run elasticity).

[2] These locations include Albuquerque, Atlanta, Boise, Charlotte, Chattanooga, Denver, Orlando, Phoenix, Provo, Savannah, and Tampa.

CHAPTER 2: Emerging Trends in Planning, Development, and Climate Change

[1] Between 1995 and 2001, total VMT in the United States increased by 34 percent, while average vehicle trip length increased by 11.5 percent (Hu and Reuscher 2004).

[2] The advent of "first-generation" catalytic converters in 1975 significantly reduced hydrocarbon and carbon monoxide (CO) emissions. Because lead inactivates the catalyst, 1975 also saw the widespread introduction of unleaded gasoline. The next milestone in vehicle emission control technology came in 1980 and 1981. Manufacturers equipped new cars with more sophisticated emission control systems that generally include a "three-way" catalyst (which converts CO and hydrocarbons to CO_2 and water, and also helps reduce nitrogen oxides to elemental nitrogen and oxygen). On-board computers and oxygen sensors help optimize the efficiency of the catalytic converters. Vehicle emissions are being further reduced under 1990 Clean Air Act amendments, which include even tighter tailpipe standards, improved control of evaporative emissions, and computerized diagnostic systems that identify malfunctioning emission controls.

[3] These surveys were conducted in Albuquerque, Atlanta, Boise, Charlotte, Chattanooga, Denver, Orlando, Phoenix, Provo, Savannah, and Tampa.

[4] Smart growth communities were described as follows: "Such communities have a town center that is surrounded by residential neighborhoods. The town center has small shops, restaurants, government buildings, churches, and public transit (bus, rail) stops. Residential neighborhoods are clustered around the town center, providing easy access to work and shopping. Each neighborhood has a variety of housing types (apartments, townhomes, single family homes) and houses are built on smaller lots and are closer to the street. Streets are designed to accommodate cars, pedestrians, and bicyclists. In residential areas streets are narrower, slower and quieter with sidewalks, trees and on-street parking. In commercial areas, sidewalks are wide and comfortable, streets are lined with trees, and parking lots are less conspicuous. The community includes a network of parks and trails for walking and biking. It also has a clearly defined boundary in order to preserve open space for parks, farmlands, and forests."

[5] The American Housing Survey reports about 124 million residential units in 2005 while the Census reports a population of about 296 million for the same year, for a ratio of 0.42 units per capita. As household size is not projected to change substantially over the next generation, the Census-projected population for 2050 is multiplied by the ratio of residential units to population in 2005 to estimate future residential demand (see http://www.census.gov/hhes/www/housing/ahs/ahs.html).

[6] The 1990 Census reports 102 million residential units while the 2000 Census reports that 96 million survived to 2000, indicating a loss rate of about 6 percent per decade (see www.census.gov).

[7] There is no consensus on the actual rate of loss of residential units through demolition and conversion to another land use. The one-third figure is conservative, based on Delphi consensus of experts (see Nelson 2006).

[8] The U.S. Department of Energy's Energy Information Administration conducts the Commercial Buildings Energy Consumption Survey (CBECS) about every five years. The 1992 survey reported 68 billion square feet of nonresidential space excluding industrial space. The 1999 survey (the most compatible in format) reported 58 billion nonresident square feet existing in 1992 surviving to 1999, or an imputed loss rate of slightly more than 20 percent per decade (see http://www.eia.doe.gov/emeu/cbecs/).

[9] This figure includes industrial space (see Nelson 2006).

[10] This figure assumes about 580 square feet of space per full- and part-time worker. It is the quotient of total nonresidential space (see Nelson 2006) and workers. The U.S. Department of Commerce's Bureau of Economic Analysis reported there were 173 million total full- and part-time workers in 2005 (see www.bea.gov.) In contrast, the CBECS for 2003 estimates 1,000 square feet per full-time worker. The more conservative figure is used.

CHAPTER 3: The VMT/CO₂/Climate Connection

[1] Carbon dioxide equivalent (CO_2e) is an internationally accepted measure of the amount of global warming of greenhouse gases (GHGs) in terms of the amount of carbon dioxide (CO_2) that would have the same global warming potential.

[2] NASA's Goddard Institute for Space Studies identifies the five warmest years for global temperatures as (in descending order): 2005, 1998, 2002, 2003, and 2006 (Goddard 2007). Five of the last nine years have been the warmest on record in the United States (in descending order: 1998, 2006, 1999, 2001, 2005) (National Climate Data Center 2007).

[3] In this scenario, VMT growth increases by 2 percentage points (61 percent growth by 2030) due to the "rebound effect" whereby driving increases as fuel economy increases (10 percent short-run elasticity).

[4] Authors' calculations based on data from EMFAC 2007, V2.3 Nov. 1, 2006, provided by Jeff Long, California Air Resources Board, July 24, 2007.

[5] Authors' calculations based on data from EMFAC 2007, V2.3 Nov. 1, 2006, provided by Jeff Long, California Air Resources Board, April 25, 2007.

[6] Authors' calculations based on data from EMFAC 2007, V2.3 Nov. 1, 2006, provided by Jeff Long, California Air Resources Board, July 9, 2007.

[7] 100% − (70% [VMT] x 102% [CO_2 per mile] x 96.7% [running emissions] + 3.3% [start emissions]).

CHAPTER 4: The Urban Environment/VMT Connection

[1] This is due to the so-called ecological fallacy. The ecological fallacy is a widely recognized error in the interpretation of statistical data, whereby inferences about individuals are based solely upon aggregate statistics for the group to which those individuals belong.

[2] "Residential density" was defined in terms of gross and net densities and proportions of the population living at different densities; seven variables made up the metropolitan density factor. "Land use mix" was defined in terms of the degree to which land uses are mixed and balanced within subareas of the region; six variables made up this factor. "Degree of centering" was defined as the extent to which development is focused on the region's core and regional subcenters; six variables made up this factor. "Street accessibility" was defined in terms of the length and size of blocks; three variables made up this factor.

[3] For region-level characteristics, ordinary least squares (OLS) regression analysis would underestimate standard errors of regression coefficients and would produce inefficient regression coefficient estimates. Hierarchical modeling overcomes these limitations, accounting for the dependence of scenarios for the same region and producing more accurate regression coefficient and standard error estimates (Raudenbush and Byrk 2002). Within a hierarchical model, each level in the data structure is represented by its own submodel. Each submodel captures the structural relations occurring at that level and the residual variability at that level. To represent such complex data structures, this study relied on HLM 6 (hierarchical linear and nonlinear modeling) software.

[4] Computed as −0.074 x 50 − 1.50 x 1 − 4.64 x 1 − 0.068 x 73 − 2.12 x 1. The 73 in the preceding formula represents a growth increment of 73 percent, or 43 years at an average growth rate of just over 1.28 percent per year.

[5] The following is true of nearly all conventional four-step models: 1) Only trips by vehicle are modeled, and trip rates are related only to characteristics of people, not characteristics of place. The possibility of households in urban settings making fewer vehicle trips—and instead using nonmotorized modes—is not considered. 2) Households, jobs, and other trip generators are assumed to be located at a single point, the zone centroid, and the entire local street network is reduced to one or more centroid connectors to the regional street network. This precludes the modeling of intrazonal travel in terms of the local built environment. 3) The choice between transit and auto modes is modeled solely in terms of characteristics of travelers and modes. The characteristics of origins and destinations—their transit-friendliness and walkability—are disregarded. 4) Trips are treated as unlinked, when a majority of trips nowadays are part of tours (trip chains) in which each trip depends on the trips preceding and following it, in a linked fashion. Destinations doubtless are chosen based not only on the attractions they contain, but also based on their accessibility to other trip attractions. 5) Trip attractions are summed for component land uses in a given zone, with each use treated as independent of the others. Yet mixed-use development is known to generate fewer vehicle trips than the component uses individually. 6) Daily travel is allocated to the peak hour based on fixed factors, disregarding the tendency for peak spreading when land uses become concentrated enough to produce serious peak-hour congestion. Peak spreading is the rescheduling of trips from the peak hour to the shoulders of the peak.

[6] The pricing policy assumed an areawide $3.00 per day parking charge for drive-alone work trips. The income was used to provide free transit passes to all commuters in the study area.

CHAPTER 8: The Combined Effect of Compact Development, Transportation Investments, and Road Pricing

[1] This chapter was coauthored by James B. Grace, a senior research ecologist with the U.S. Geological Survey in Lafayette, Louisiana, and an adjunct professor at the University of Louisiana at Lafayette. Grace has authored three books and more than 100 scientific papers. His current research focus emphasizes the relationship between statistical methodology and the advance of human knowledge, as well as numerous topics in environmental science.

[2] Since maximum likelihood procedures rely on the assumption of approximate normality of parameters, we sought to determine whether our results might be influenced by nonnormal distributions. To perform such an evaluation, we used a Bayesian approach (for example, Lee 2007) and the Markov chain Monte Carlo (MCMC) procedures available with Amos 7.0. The Bayesian approach examines the entire distribution of a parameter rather than simply parameter means and standard deviations. Thus the MCMC estimates are considered to be "exact" instead of based on distributional assumptions. Results were virtually identical for the two estimation methods. Therefore, we present only the maximum likelihood results.

[3] The number 0.95 is the direct effect of population on lane miles, which is not shown in Figure 8-7 to keep the figure simple.

[4] Any small effects of average vehicle operating speeds on emission rates will be disregarded.

[5] Urban VMT is projected to increase from two-thirds of the national total in 2007 to 80 percent in 2050. These values are weighted by CO_2 emission rates for light versus heavy vehicles, the former representing a larger share of urban traffic. The proportion of the working age population (25 to 64 years) is projected to decline from 60 percent in 2007 to 53 percent in 2050. The weighting of this variable reflects the higher person miles traveled by working age people, about 17 percent above the population average.

CHAPTER 9: Policy and Program Recommendations

[1] For example, in its 2002 SIP, the state of Maryland included smart growth policies that it expects to yield modest air quality benefits. Sacramento anticipates significant emissions savings from land use measures in its blueprint transportation plan. In Atlanta, a modeling exercise on the emissions benefits of infill development rescued the region from its conformity lapse and associated restrictions on funding new transportation projects, but the region lacked the political support or transit funding to implement the modeled smart growth scenario (see CCAP 2004).

References

CHAPTER 1: Overview

Bartholomew, K. "Integrating Land Use Issues into Transportation Planning: Scenario Planning—Summary Report," 2005, http://content.lib.utah.edu/cgi-bin/showfile.exe?CISOROOT=/ir-main&CISOPTR=99&filename=189.pdf.

——. "Land Use-Transportation Scenario Planning: Promise & Reality." *Transportation,* Vol. 34, Issue 4, 2007, pp. 397–412.

Campoli, J. and A. MacLean. *Visualizing Density.* Cambridge, Massachusetts: Lincoln Institute of Land Policy, 2007, www.lincolninst.edu/subcenters/VD/.

Energy Information Administration (EIA). *Annual Energy Outlook 2007.* Washington, D.C.: U.S. Department of Energy.

——. *Annual Energy Outlook 2008 (Early Release).* Washington, D.C.: U.S. Department of Energy, http://www.eia.doe.gov/oiaf/aeo/aeoref_tab.html.

Energy Watch Group. *Crude Oil: The Supply Outlook.* Ottobrunn, Germany: October 2007, http://www.energywatchgroup.org/fileadmin/global/pdf/EWG_Oilreport_10-2007.pdf.

Ewing, R., R. Pendall, and D. Chen. *Measuring Sprawl and Its Impact.* Washington, D.C.: Smart Growth America/U.S. Environmental Protection Agency, 2002.

——. "Measuring Sprawl and Its Transportation Impacts." *Journal of the Transportation Research Board,* Vol. 1832, 2003, pp. 175–183.

Federal Highway Administration (FHWA). "Vehicle Registrations, Fuel Consumption, and Vehicle Miles of Travel as Indices," *Highway Statistics 2005.* Washington, D.C.: U.S. Department of Transportation, 2006, http://www.fhwa.dot.gov/policy/ohim/hs05/htm/mvfvm.htm.

Frank, L.D., S. Kavage, and B. Appleyard. "The Urban Form and Climate Change Gamble." *Planning,* Vol. 73, No. 8, August/September 2007, pp. 18–23.

Hirsch, R.L., R. Bezdek, and R. Wendling. *Peaking of World Oil Production: Impacts, Mitigation, and Risk Management.* Washington, D.C.: U.S. Department of Energy, February 2005, http://www.projectcensored.org/newsflash/The_Hirsch_Report_Proj_Cens.pdf.

Intergovernmental Panel on Climate Change (IPCC). *Climate Change 2007: The Physical Science Basis, Summary for Policymakers.* Working Group I contribution of the Intergovernmental Panel on Climate Change: Fourth Assessment Report, 2007, www.ipcc.ch/.

International Energy Agency (IEA). *World Energy Outlook 2006*, Paris, 2007.

Moudon, A.V., P.M. Hess, M.C. Snyder, and K. Stanilov. "Effects of Site Design on Pedestrian Travel in Mixed-Use, Medium-Density Environments." *Transportation Research Record,* Vol. 1578, 1997, pp. 48–55.

National Association of Realtors and Smart Growth America. 2007 Growth and Transportation Survey, http://www.smartgrowthamerica.org/narsgareport2007.html.

Nelson, A.C. "Leadership in a New Era." *Journal of the American Planning Association,* Vol. 72, Issue 4, 2006, pp. 393–407.

Smart Growth Network. *This Is Smart Growth.* Washington, D.C.: International City/County Management Association (ICMA) and the U.S. Environmental Protection Agency (EPA), 2006, http://www.smartgrowth.org/library/articles.asp?art=2367.

U.S. Congress. H.R. 6, Renewable Fuels, Consumer Protection, and Energy Efficiency Act of 2007, http://frwebgate.access.gpo.gov/cgi-bin/getdoc.cgi?dbname=110_cong_bills&docid=f:h6enr.txt.pdf.

Walters, J., R. Ewing, and E. Allen. "Adjusting Computer Modeling Tools to Capture Effects of Smart Growth," *Transportation Research Record.* Vol. 1722, 2000, pp. 17–26.

CHAPTER 2: Emerging Trends in Planning, Development, and Climate Change

Air Resources Board (ARB). *Proposed Early Actions to Mitigate Climate Change in California.* Sacramento: California Department of Environmental Quality, April 30, 2007, www.climatechange.ca.gov/climate_action_team/reports/2007-04-20_ARB_early_action_report.pdf.

American Association of State Highway Transportation Officials (AASHTO). *A New Vision for the 21st Century*, July 2007, www.transportation1.org/tif5report/TIF5.pdf.

American Planning Association. *Planning for Smart Growth: 2002 State of the States.* Chicago, February 2002.

Anderson, L. "Baby Boomers: Play Down Age, Play Up Options." *Builder News,* December 2004, http://www.buildernewsmag.com/viewnews.pl?id=175.

Bayer, A. and L. Harper. *Fixing to Stay: A National Survey of Housing and Home Modification Issues.* Washington, D.C.: American Association of Retired Persons (AARP), May 2000.

Belden Russonello & Stewart. *National Survey on Growth and Land Development.* Washington, D.C.: Smart Growth America, September 2000, www.smartgrowthamerica.org/poll.pdf.

——. *Americans' Attitudes Toward Walking and Creating Better Walking Communities.* Washington, D.C.: Surface Transportation Policy Project, April 2003, www.transact.org/library/reports_pdfs/pedpoll.pdf.

——. *National Survey on Communities.* Washington, D.C.: National Association of Realtors and Smart Growth America, October 2004, www.brspoll.com/Reports/Smart%20Growth.pdf.

Burchell, R.W., G. Lowenstein, W.R. Dolphin et al. *Costs of Sprawl—2000.* Washington, D.C.: Transportation Research Board, National Academy Press, 2002.

Campoli, J. and A. MacLean. *Visualizing Density.* Cambridge, Massachusetts: Lincoln Institute of Land Policy, 2007, www.lincolninst.edu/subcenters/VD/.

Carruthers, J.I. and G.F. Ulfarsson. "Urban Sprawl and the Cost of Public Services." *Environment and Planning B*, Vol. 30, Issue 4, 2003, pp. 503–522.

Cervero, R., S. Murphy, C. Ferrell et al. *Transit-Oriented Development in the United States: Experiences, Challenges, and Prospects.* TRCP Report 102, Washington, D.C.: Transportation Research Board, 2004.

Climate Action Team. *Climate Action Team's Proposed Early Actions to Mitigate Climate Change in California—Draft for Public Review.* Sacramento: California Department of Environmental Quality, April 30, 2007, www.climatechange.ca.gov/climate_action_team/reports/2007-04-20_CAT_REPORT.PDF.

DeCicco, J. and F. Fung. *Global Warming on the Road: The Climate Impact of America's Automobiles.* Washington, D.C.: Environmental Defense, 2006.

Energy Information Administration (EIA). *Emissions of Greenhouse Gases in the United States 2005.* Washington, D.C.: U.S. Department of Energy, 2006.

——. *U.S. Carbon Dioxide Emissions from Energy Sources: 2006 Flash Estimate.* Washington, D.C.: U.S. Department of Energy, 2007a.

——. *International Energy Outlook 2007.* Washington, D.C.: U.S. Department of Energy, 2007b.

Environmental Protection Agency (EPA). "National Emissions Inventory (NEI) Air Pollutant Emissions Trends Data." Washington, D.C., undated, www.epa.gov/ttn/chief/trends/.

——. "Energy." *Inventory of U.S. Greenhouse Gas Emissions and Sinks: 1990–2005.* Washington, D.C., 2007, http://epa.gov/climatechange/emissions/usinventoryreport.html.

Envision Utah. *Quality Growth Strategy and Technical Review.* Salt Lake City, Utah, January 2000.

Eppli, M. and C. Tu. *Valuing the New Urbanism.* Washington, D.C.: ULI–the Urban Land Institute, 1999.

——. "Market Acceptance of Single-Family Housing in Smart Growth Communities." Washington, D.C.: Environmental Protection Agency, as reported in *On Common Ground,* Summer 2007, p. 55, http://www.realtor.org/smart_growth.nsf/docfiles/ocgsummer07.pdf/$FILE/ocgsummer07.pdf.

Ewing, R. "Is Los Angeles–Style Sprawl Desirable?" *Journal of the American Planning Association,* Vol. 63, 1997, pp. 107–126.

Ewing, R., S.J. Brown, and A. Hoyt. "Traffic Calming Revisited." *ITE Journal,* November 2005, pp. 22–28.

Ewing, R., R. Pendall, and D. Chen. *Measuring Sprawl and Its Impact.* Washington, D.C.: Smart Growth America/U.S. Environmental Protection Agency, 2002.

Federal Highway Administration (FHWA). "Vehicle Registrations, Fuel Consumption, and Vehicle Miles of Travel as Indices." *Highway Statistics 2005.* Washington, D.C.: U.S. Department of Transportation, 2006, http://www.fhwa.dot.gov/policy/ohim/hs05/htm/mvfvm.htm.

Fulton, W., R. Pendall, M. Nguyen, and A. Harrison. "Who Sprawls Most? How Growth Patterns Differ Across the U.S." Washington, D.C.: Brookings Center on Urban and Metropolitan Policy, 2001.

Goldberg, D. "The Pulse at the Polls." *On the Ground,* Summer 2007, pp. 6–13.

Gordon, P. and H. Richardson. "Are Compact Cities a Desirable Planning Goal?" *Journal of the American Planning Association,* Vol. 63, 1997, pp. 95–106.

Graham, D. and S. Glaister. *Review of Income and Price Elasticities of Demand for Road Traffic.* London: Centre for Transportation Studies, Imperial College, 2002, www.dft.gov.uk/pgr/economics/rdg/coll_reviewofincomeandpriceelast/reviewofincomeandpriceelasti3104.

Handy, S., J. F. Sallis, D. Weber, E. Maibach, and M. Hollander, "Is Support for Traditionally Designed Communities Growing? Evidence from Two National Surveys" *Journal of the American Planning Association*, in press.

He, W., M. Sengupta, V.A. Velkoff, and K.A. DeBarros. *65+ in the United States: 2005.* Washington, D.C.: U.S. Census Bureau, 2006, www.census.gov/prod/2006pubs/p23-209.pdf.

Hu, P.S. and T.R. Reuscher. *Summary of Travel Trends: 2001 National Household Travel Survey.* Washington, D.C.: Federal Highway Administration, 2004, http://nhts.ornl.gov/2001/pub/STT.pdf.

Intergovernmental Panel on Climate Change (IPCC). *Climate Change 2007: Mitigation of Climate Change, Summary for Policymakers.* Working Group III contribution of the Intergovernmental Panel on Climate Change: Fourth Assessment Report, 2007, http://www.ipcc.ch/.

Kimley-Horn and Associates et al. "Context Sensitive Solutions in Designing Major Urban Thoroughfares for Walkable Communities—Proposed Recommended Practice." Washington, D.C.: Institute of Transportation Engineers, 2006, www.ite.org/bookstore/RP036.pdf.

Kirby, S. and M. Hollander. *Consumer Preferences and Social Marketing Approaches to Physical Activity Behavior and Transportation Choices,* prepared as a resource paper for *Does the Built Environment Influence Physical Activity? Examining the Evidence— Special Report 282,* January 2005, http://trb.org/downloads/sr282papers/sr282KirbyHollander.pdf.

Leinberger, C. *Back to the Future: The Need for Patient Equity in Real Estate Development Finance.* Washington, D.C.: Brookings Institution, January 2007.

Logan, G. "The Market for Smart Growth," presented at the U.S. EPA High-Production Builder Conference, Robert Charles Lesser & Co., LLP, January 31, 2007.

Mathew Greenwald & Associates. *These Four Walls . . . Americans 45+ Talk About Home and Community.* Washington, D.C.: American Association of Retired Persons (AARP), May 2003.

Mui, S., J. Alson, B. Ellies, and D. Ganss. *A Wedge Analysis of the U.S. Transportation Sector.* Washington, D.C.: Transportation and Climate Division, U.S. Environmental Protection Agency, 2007.

Myers, D. and E. Gearin. "Current Preferences and Future Demand for Denser Residential Environments." *Housing Policy Debate,* 2001, pp. 633–659.

Myers, P. "Livability at the Ballot Box: State and Local Referenda on Parks, Conservation, and Smarter Growth, Election Day 1998." Washington, D.C.: Brookings Center on Urban and Metropolitan Policy, 1999.

Myers, P. and R. Puentes. "Growth at the Ballot Box: Electing the Shape of Communities in November 2000." Washington, D.C.: Brookings Center on Urban and Metropolitan Policy, 2001.

National Association of Homebuilders (NAHB). "Vanilla Not a Favorite Flavor of Generation X Home Buyers." *Nation's Building News*, July 19, 2004, http://www.nbnnews.com/NBN/issues/2004-07-19/Design/index.html.

Nelson, A.C. "Leadership in a New Era." *Journal of the American Planning Association*, Vol. 72, Issue 4, 2006, pp. 393–407.

"New Urban Projects on a Neighborhood Scale in the United States." *New Urban News*, December 2003.

Papas, M.A., A.J. Alberg, R. Ewing, K.J. Helzlsouer, T.L. Gary, and A.C. Klassen. "The Built Environment and Obesity: A Review of the Evidence." *Epidemiologic Reviews*, Vol. 29, Issue1, pp. 129–143, 2007.

Pickrell, D. *Fuel Options for Reducing Greenhouse Gas Emissions from Motor Vehicles*. Washington, D.C.: U.S. Department of Transportation, 2003, http://climate.dot.gov/docs/fuel.pdf.

Pisarski, A.E. *Travel Behavior Issues in the 90s*. Washington, D.C.: Federal Highway Administration, 1992, p. 10.

Robaton, A. "Lifestyle Centers Compete for Retailers." *Shopping Centers Today*, February 2005, http://www.icsc.org/srch/sct/sct0205/cover_3.php.

Schrank, D. and T. Lomax. *The 2007 Urban Mobility Report*. College Station: Texas Transportation Institute, 2007, http://mobility.tamu.edu/ums/.

Smart Growth Network. *This Is Smart Growth*. Washington, D.C.: International City/County Management Association (ICMA) and the U.S. Environmental Protection Agency (EPA), 2006, http://www.smartgrowth.org/library/articles.asp?art=2367.

Sobel, L. "Smart Growth: A Growing Real Estate Niche." Presentation at 5th Annual New Partners for Smart Growth Conference, January 27, 2006, Denver, Colorado, www.cmcgc.com/media/handouts/260126/FRI-PDF/210-Sobel.pdf.

Socolow, R. and S. Pacala. "A Plan to Keep Carbon in Check." *Scientific American*, September 2006, pp. 50–57.

Surface Transportation Policy Project (STPP). *Aging Americans: Stranded without Options*. Washington, D.C., April 2004.

ULI–the Urban Land Institute and PricewaterhouseCoopers LLP. *Emerging Trends in Real Estate 2005*. Washington, D.C.: ULI–the Urban Institute, 2005.

——. *Emerging Trends in Real Estate 2006*. Washington, D.C., 2006.

——. *Emerging Trends in Real Estate 2007*. Washington, D.C., 2007.

U.S. Census Bureau. "U.S. Interim Projections by Age, Sex, Race, and Hispanic Origin." Washington, D.C., 2004, www.census.gov/ipc/www/usinterimproj/.

U.S. Climate Action Partnership (USCAP). *A Call for Action*. Washington, D.C., January 2007, www.us-cap.org/USCAPCallForAction.pdf.

Victoria Transport Policy Institute. "Transportation Elasticities: How Prices and Other Factors Affect Travel Behavior." Victoria, British Columbia, March 7, 2007, www.vtpi.org/tdm/tdm11.htm.

CHAPTER 3: The VMT/CO_2/Climate Connection

Barnett, J. and W. Adger. "Climate Dangers and Atoll Countries." *Climatic Change*, Vol. 61, 2003, pp. 321–337.

California Energy Commission. *Alternative Fuels Commercialization*. Sacramento, 2005, http://www.energy.ca.gov/2005publications/CEC-600-2005-020/CEC-600-2005-020.PDF.

——. 2007 *Integrated Energy Policy Report*. Sacramento, 2007a, http://www.energy.ca.gov/2007publications/CEC-100-2007-008/CEC-100-2007-008-CTF.PDF.

——. *State Alternative Fuels Plan: Committee Report*. Sacramento, 2007b, http://www.energy.ca.gov/2007publications/CEC-600-2007-011/CEC-600-2007-011-CTF.PDF.

Canadell, J.G , C. Le Quéré, M. Raupach et al. "Contributions to Accelerating Atmospheric CO_2 Growth from Economic Activity, Carbon Intensity, and Efficiency of Natural Sinks." *Proceedings of the National Academies of Science, Early Edition, 2007*, www.pnas.org/cgi/reprint/0702737104v1.

Emanuel, K. "Increasing Destructiveness of Tropical Cyclones over the Past 30 Years." *Nature*, Vol. 436, 2005, pp. 686–688.

Energy Information Administration (EIA). *Annual Energy Outlook 2007*. Washington, D.C.: U.S. Department of Energy, 2007.

——. *Annual Energy Outlook 2008 (Early Release)*. Washington, D.C.: U.S. Department of Energy, http://www.eia.doe.gov/oiaf/aeo/aeoref_tab.html.

European Commission. "Limiting Global Climate Change to 2 degrees Celsius: The way ahead for 2020 and beyond, Impact Assessment." Memo/07/16, January 10, 2007, http://europa.eu/rapid/press ReleasesAction.do?reference=MEMO/07/16.

Ewing, R. and R. Cervero. "Travel and the Built Environment." *Transportation Research Record*, Vol. 1780, 2001, pp. 87–114.

Ewing, R., M. DeAnna, and S. Li. "Land Use Impacts on Trip Generation Rates." *Transportation Research Record*, Vol. 1518, 1996, pp. 1–7.

Farrell, A. E. and D. Sperling. *A Low-Carbon Fuel Standard for California, Part 1: Technical Analysis*. Davis, California: Institute of Transportation Studies, University of California at Davis, 2007, http://pubs.its.ucdavis.edu/publication_detail.php?id=1082.

Felderhoff, M., C. Weidenthaler, R. von Helmoltb, and U. Eberleb. "Hydrogen Storage: The Remaining Scientific and Technological Challenges." *Physical Chemistry Chemical Physics*, Vol. 9, 2007, pp. 2643–2653.

Goddard Institute for Space Studies. "2006 Was Earth's Fifth Warmest Year." February 8, 2007, http://www.nasa.gov/centers/goddard/news/topstory/2006/2006_warm.html.

Greenough, G., M. McGeehin, S. Bernard, J. Trtanj, J. Riad, and D. Engelberg. "The Potential Impacts of Climate Variability and Change on Health Impacts of Extreme Weather Events in the United States." *Environmental Health Perspectives*, Vol. 109, 2001, pp. 191–198.

Hegerl, G., T. Crowley, M. Allen, W. Hyde et al. "Detection of Human Influence on a New, Validated 1500-Year Temperature Reconstruction." *Journal of Climate*, Vol. 20, 2007, pp. 650–666.

Helme, N. and J. Schmidt. "Greenhouse Gas Stabilization Targets: Near-Term Implications for the U.S." 2007, http://www.ccap.org/domestic/documents/HelmeSchmidtTargetsPresentationCPI2.pdf.

Höhne, N., D. Phylipsen, and S. Moltmann. *Factors Underpinning Future Action: 2007 Update*. Ecofys, 2007, http://unfccc.int/resource/docs/2007/smsn/ngo/026c.pdf.

Höppe, P. and R. Pielke, Jr. (eds.). *Workshop on Climate Change and Disaster Losses: Understanding and Attributing Trends and Projections*. 2006. http://sciencepolicy.colorado.edu/sparc/research/projects/extreme_events/munich_workshop/index.html.

Intergovernmental Panel on Climate Change (IPCC). *Climate Change 2007: The Physical Science Basis, Summary for Policymakers*. Working Group I contribution of the Intergovernmental Panel on Climate Change: Fourth Assessment Report, 2007a, www.ipcc.ch/.

——. *Climate Change 2007: Impact, Adaptation and Vulnerability, Summary for Policymakers*. Working Group II contribution of the Intergovernmental Panel on Climate Change: Fourth Assessment Report, 2007b, www.ipcc.ch/.

——. *Climate Change 2007: Mitigation of Climate Change, Summary for Policymakers*. Working Group III contribution of the Intergovernmental Panel on Climate Change: Fourth Assessment Report, 2007c, http://www.ipcc.ch/.

Kintner-Meyer, M., K. Schneider, and R. Pratt. *Impacts Assessment of Plug-In Hybrid Vehicles on Electric Utilities and Regional U.S. Power Grids: Part 1: Technical Analysis*. Richland, Washington: Pacific Northwest National Laboratory, 2007, http://www.pnl.gov/energy/eed/etd/pdfs/phev_feasibility_analysis_combined.pdf.

Madsen, T. and E. Figdor, *When It Rains, It Pours: Global Warming and the Rising Frequency of Extreme Precipitation in the United States*. Boston: Environment America Research & Policy Center, December 2007, http://www.environmentamerica.org/uploads/oy/ws/oywshWAwZy-EXPsabQKd4A/When-It-Rains-It-Pours----US---WEB.pdf.

Meinshausen, M. "What does a 2°C target mean for greenhouse gas concentrations? A brief analysis based on multi-gas emission pathways and several climate sensitivity uncertainty estimates." In *Avoiding Dangerous Climate Change*. Cambridge, United Kingdom: Cambridge University Press, 2006, pp. 265–280.

Meinshausen, M. and M.G. J. den Elzen. *Meeting the EU 2°C Climate Target: Global and Regional Emission Implications*. Bilthoven: Netherlands Environmental Assessment Agency, 2005.

Melendez, M. and A. Milbrandt. *Hydrogen Infrastructure Transition Analysis: Milestone Report*. Golden, Colorado: National Renewable Energy Laboratory, 2006, http://www.eere.energy.gov/afdc/pdfs/hydrogen_infrastructure.pdf.

National Climate Data Center. *2006 Annual Climate Review: U.S. Summary*. Washington, D.C.: National Oceanic and Atmospheric Administration, June 21, 2007, http://www.ncdc.noaa.gov/oa/climate/research/2006/ann/us-summary.html#temp.

National Economic Council. *Advanced Energy Initiative*. Washington, D.C.: The White House, 2006, http://www.whitehouse.gov/stateofthe union/2006/energy/index.html.

Natural Resources Defense Council (NRDC). *Climate Facts: The Next Generation of Hybrid Cars*. San Francisco, 2007, http://www.nrdc.org/energy/plugin.pdf.

New England Governors/Eastern Canadian Premiers. "Climate Change Action Plan 2001," 2001, www.negc.org/documents/NEG-ECP%20 CCAP.PDF.

Pearce, F. "Fuels Gold." New Scientist, Vol. 191, 2006, p. 2570.

Pew Center on Global Climate Change. "What's Being Done in Congress." Washington, D.C., July 2007, www.pewclimate.com/what_s_being_done/in_the_congress/.

Pew Research Center. "47-Nation Pew Global Attitudes Survey." Global Attitudes Project, Washington, D.C., June 27, 2007, http://pewglobal.org/reports/pdf/256.pdf.

Pimentel, D. and T. Patzek. "Ethanol Production Using Corn, Switchgrass, and Wood; Biodiesel Production Using Soybean and Sunflower." Natural Resources Research, Vol. 14(1), 2005, pp. 65–76.

Polzin, S.E. *The Case for Moderate Growth in Vehicle Miles of Travel: A Critical Juncture in U.S. Travel Behavior Trends*. Washington, D.C.: U.S. Department of Transportation, 2006.

Schellnhuber, H.J., W. Cramer, N. Nakicenovich, T. Wigley, and G. Yohe (eds.). *Avoiding Dangerous Climate Change*. Cambridge, United Kingdom: Cambridge University Press, 2006, www.defra.gov.uk/environment/climatechange/research/dangerous-cc/index.htm.

Schipper, L. "Automobile Fuel; Economy and CO_2 Emissions in Industrialized Countries: Troubling Trends through 2005/6." Prepared for the 2007 Annual Meeting of the Transportation Research Board, World Resources Institute, Washington, D.C., August 2007.

Schwarzenegger, A. Executive Order S-3-05, 2005, www.governor.ca.gov/state/govsite/gov_htmldisplay.jsp?BV_SessionID=@@@@1148099 866.1187065401@@@@&BV_EngineID=cccdaddljehkekmcfngcfkmdffi dfng.0&iOID=69591&sTitle=Executive+Order+S-3-05&sFilePath=/govsite/executive_orders/20050601_S-3-05.html&sCatTitle= Exec+Order.

Scott, M., M. Kintner-Meyer, D. Elliott, and W. Warwick. *Impacts Assessment of Plug-In Hybrid Vehicles on Electric Utilities and Regional U.S. Power Grids: Part 2: Economic Assessment*. Richland, Washington: Pacific Northwest National Laboratory, 2007, http://www.pnl.gov/energy/eed/etd/pdfs/phev_feasibility_analysis_combined.pdf.

Stern, N. *The Economics of Climate Change: The Stern Review*. Cambridge, United Kingdom: Cambridge University Press, 2007, www.hm-treasury.gov.uk/independent_reviews/stern_review_economics_climate_change/stern_review_report.cfm.

TIAX. "Cost Analysis of Fuel Cell Systems for Transportation: Compressed Hydrogen and PEM Fuel Cell System." Presentation to Fuel Cell Tech Team, FreedomCar, Detroit, October 20, 2004, http://www1.eere.energy.gov/hydrogenandfuelcells/pdfs/tiax_cost_analysis_pres.pdf.

——. *Full Fuel Cycle Assessment: Well-to-Wheels Energy Inputs, Emissions, and Water Impacts*. Sacramento: California Energy Commission, 2007, http://www.energy.ca.gov/2007publications/CEC-600-2007-002/CEC-600-2007-002-D.PDF.

Trenberth, K. "Uncertainty in Hurricanes and Global Warming," *Science*, Vol. 308, 2005, pp. 1753–1754.

Union of Concerned Scientists. *Biofuels: An Important Part of a Low-Carbon Diet.* Cambridge, Massachusetts, 2007, http://www.ucsusa.org/assets/documents/clean_vehicles/ucs-biofuels-report.pdf.

U.S. Climate Action Partnership (USCAP). *A Call for Action.* Washington, D.C., January 2007, www.us-cap.org/USCAPCallForAction.pdf.

U.S. Conference of Mayors. *U.S. Conference of Mayors Climate Protection Agreement.* Washington, D.C., 2007, www.usmayors.org/climateprotection/agreement.htm.

U.S. Congress. H.R. 6, Energy Independence and Security Act of 2007, 2007a, http://frwebgate.access.gpo.gov/cgi-bin/getdoc.cgi?dbname=110_cong_bills&docid=f:h6enr.txt.pdf.

———. S2191, America's Climate Security Act of 2007, 2007b, http://frwebgate.access.gpo.gov/cgi-bin/getdoc.cgi?dbname=110_cong_bills&docid=f:s2191is.txt.pdf.

U.S. Department of Energy, DOE Hydrogen Program. *Hydrogen Storage.* Washington, D.C., 2006, http://www1.eere.energy.gov/hydrogen andfuelcells/pdfs/doe_h2_storage.pdf.

U.S. Department of Energy. Plug-In Hybrid Electric Vehicle R & D Plan (Working Draft). Washington, D.C., 2007, http://www1.eere.energy.gov/vehiclesandfuels/pdfs/program/phev_rd_plan_june_2007.pdf.

U.S. Department of Energy and Natural Resources Canada. *Study of North American Transportation Energy Futures.* Washington, D.C., 2003, www.nrel.gov/analysis/seminar/docs/2003/es_3-13-03.ppt.

Wang, M. "Energy and Greenhouse Gas Emissions Impacts of Fuel Ethanol." Presentation to the NGCA Renewable Fuels Forum, The National Press Club, August 23, 2005, http://www.transportation.anl.gov/pdfs/TA/349.pdf.

Westerling, A.L., H. G. Hidalgo, D. R. Cayan, and T. W. Swetnam. "Warming and Earlier Spring Increase Western U.S. Forest Wildfire Activity." *Science*, Vol. 313, August 18, 2006, pp. 940–943, http://www.sciencemag.org/cgi/rapidpdf/1128834.pdf.

CHAPTER 4: The Urban Environment/VMT Connection

1000 Friends of Oregon. *Making the Land Use, Transportation, Air Quality Connection: Analysis of Alternatives.* Vol. 5, Portland, Oregon, 1996, http://www.onethousandfriendsoforegon.org/resources/lut_vol5.html.

———. *Making the Connections: A Summary of the LUTRAQ Project.* Portland, Oregon, 1997.

Allen, E. and F.K. Benfield. *Environmental Characteristics of Smart Growth Neighborhoods, Phase II: Two Nashville Neighborhoods.* Washington, D.C.: Natural Resources Defense Council, February 2003.

Badland, H. and G. Schofield. "Transport, Urban Design, and Physical Activity: An Evidence-Based Update." *Transportation Research Part D*, Vol. 10, 2005, pp. 177–196.

Badoe, D.A. and E.J. Miller. "Transportation-Land-Use Interaction: Empirical Findings in North America, and Their Implications for Modeling." *Transportation Research Part D*, Vol. 5, 2000, pp. 235–263.

Bartholomew, K. "Integrating Land Use Issues into Transportation Planning: Scenario Planning—Summary Report," 2005, http://content.lib.utah.edu/cgi-bin/showfile.exe?CISOROOT=/ir-main&CISOPTR=99&filename=189.pdf.

———. "Land Use-Transportation Scenario Planning: Promise & Reality." *Transportation*, Vol. 34, Issue 4, 2007, pp. 397–412.

Beimborn, E., R. Kennedy, and W. Schaefer. *Inside the Blackbox: Making Transportation Models Work for Livable Communities.* Washington, D.C.: Citizens for a Better Environment and the Environmental Defense Fund, undated, http://ctr.utk.edu/TNMUG/misc/blackbox.pdf.

Boarnet, M.G., E.J. Kim, and E. Parkany. "Measuring Traffic Congestion." *Transportation Research Record*, Vol. 1634, 1998, pp. 93–99.

Burchfield, M., H. G. Overman, et al. "Causes of Sprawl: A Portrait From Space." *Quarterly Journal of Economics*, Vol. 121, Issue 2, 2005, pp. 587–633.

Cambridge Systematics. "The Effects of Land Use and Travel Demand Management Strategies on Commuting Behavior," Washington, D.C.: Travel Model Improvement Program, U.S. Department of Transportation, 1994.

Cameron, I., J.R. Kenworthy, and T.J. Lyons. "Understanding and Predicting Private Motorised Urban Mobility." *Transportation Research Part D: Transport and Environment*, Vol. 8, Issue 4, 2003, pp. 267–283.

Cameron, I., T.J. Lyons, J.R. Kenworthy, "Trends in Vehicle Kilometres in World Cities, 1960–1990: Underlying Drivers and Policy Responses." *Transport Policy*, Vol. 11, Issue 3, 2004, pp. 287–298.

Center for Transportation and the Environment. "Atlantic Station Monitoring and Evaluation Update: Year Two Assessment." Prepared for Atlantic Station LLC, November 2006.

Cervero, R. "Mixed Land-Uses and Commuting: Evidence from the American Housing Survey." *Transportation Research A*, Vol. 30, 1996, pp. 361–377.

———. "Alternative Approaches to Modeling the Travel–Demand Impacts of Smart Growth." *Journal of the American Planning Association*, Vol. 72, Issue 3, 2006, pp. 285–295.

Cervero, R. and K. Kockelman. "Travel Demand and the 3Ds: Density, Diversity, and Design." *Transportation Research Part D*, Vol. 2, 1997, pp. 199–219.

Crane, R. "The Influence of Urban Form on Travel: An Interpretive Review." *Journal of Planning Literature*, Vol. 15, Issue 1, August 2000.

Cutsinger, J. and G. Galster. "There Is No Sprawl Syndrome: A New Typology of Metropolitan Land Use Patterns." *Urban Geography*, Vol. 27, Issue 3, April–May 2006, pp. 228–252.

Cutsinger, J., G. Galster, H. Wolman, R. Hanson, and D. Towns. "Verifying the Multi-Dimensional Nature of Metropolitan Land Use: Advancing the Understanding and Measurement of Sprawl." *Journal of Urban Affairs*, Vol. 27, Issue 3, 2005, pp. 235–259.

Deakin, E., G. Harvey, R. Pozdena, G. Yarema et al. *Transportation Pricing Strategies for California: An Assessment of Congestion, Emissions, Energy and Equity Impacts.* Sacramento: California Air Resources Board, 1996.

DKS Associates and University of California. *Assessment of Local Models and Tools for Analyzing Smart-Growth Strategies.* Irvine, California: University of California, 2007, www.dot.ca.gov/hq/research/researchreports/reports/2007/local_models_tools.pdf.

Environmental Protection Agency (EPA). "Transportation and Environmental Analysis of the Atlantic Steel Development Proposal." EPA 231-R-99-004, September 1999, http://www.epa.gov/projctxl/atlantic/page1.htm.

——. "Comparing Methodologies to Assess Transportation and Air Quality," August 2001a (EPA 231-R-01-001).

——. "EPA's Smart Growth INDEX In 20 Pilot Communities: Using GIS Sketch Modeling to Advance Smart Growth," August 2001b (EPA 231-R-03-001).

——. "Environmental Benefits of Brownfield Redevelopment," unpublished draft, July 2006.

——. "Research You Can Use: Regional Scenario Plans and Meta-Analysis." *Planning*, March 2007, p. 38.

Ewing, R. and R. Cervero. "Travel and the Built Environment." *Transportation Research Record*, Vol. 1780, 2001, pp. 87–114.

Ewing, R., R. Pendall, and D. Chen. *Measuring Sprawl and Its Impact.* Washington, D.C.: Smart Growth America/U.S. Environmental Protection Agency, 2002.

——. "Measuring Sprawl and Its Transportation Impacts." *Journal of the Transportation Research Board*, Vol. 1832, 2003, pp. 175–183.

Ewing, R., T. Schmid, R. Killingsworth, A. Zlot, and S. Raudenbush. "Relationship Between Urban Sprawl and Physical Activity, Obesity, and Morbidity." *American Journal of Health Promotion*, Vol. 18, Issue 1, 2003, pp. 47–57.

Frank, L.D. "Land Use and Transportation Interaction: Implications on Public Health and Quality of Life." *Journal of Planning Education and Research*, Vol. 20, Issue 1, 2000, pp. 6–22.

Frank, L.D. and P. Engelke. "The Built Environment and Human Activity Patterns: Exploring the Impacts of Urban Form on Public Health." *Journal of Planning Literature*, Vol. 16, Issue 2, 2001, pp. 202–218.

——. "Multiple Impacts of the Built Environment on Public Health: Walkable Places and the Exposure to Air Pollution." *International Regional Science Review*, Vol. 28, Issue 2, 2005, pp. 193–216.

Fulton, W., R. Pendall, et al. *Who Sprawls Most? How Growth Patterns Differ across the U.S.* Washington, D.C.: Brookings Institution, 2001.

Galster, G., R. Hanson, M. Ratcliffe, H. Wolman, S. Coleman, and J. Freihage. "Wrestling Sprawl to the Ground: Defining and Measuring an Elusive Concept." *Housing Policy Debate*, Vol. 12, Issue 4, 2001.

Gomez-Ibanez, A. "A Global View of Automobile Dependence." *Journal of the American Planning Association*, Vol. 57, 1991, pp. 376–379.

Gordon, P., A. Kumar, and H.W. Richardson. "Congestion, Changing Metropolitan Structure, and City Size in the United States." *International Regional Science Review*, Vol. 12, Issue 1, 1989, pp. 45–56.

Gordon, P. and H.W. Richardson. "Gasoline Consumption and Cities— A Reply." *Journal of the American Planning Association.* Vol. 55, 1989, pp. 342–346.

Gupta, S., S. Kalmanje, and K.M. Kockelman. "Road Pricing Simulations: Traffic, Land Use and Welfare Impacts for Austin, Texas." *Transportation Planning & Technology*, Vol. 29, Issue 1, 2006, pp. 1–23.

Hagler Bailly, Inc. *Transportation and Environmental Analysis of the Atlantic Steel Development Proposal.* Washington, D.C.: U.S. Environmental Protection Agency, February 1998.

Hagler Bailly, Inc., and Criterion Planners/Engineers. *The Transportation and Environmental Impacts of Infill versus Greenfield Development: A Comparative Case Study Analysis*, EPA 231-R-99-005. Washington, D.C.: U.S. Environmental Protection Agency, October 1999.

Handy, S. "Critical Assessment of the Literature on the Relationships among Transportation, Land Use, and Physical Activity," prepared for the Transportation Research Board and Institute of Medicine Committee on Physical Activity, Health, Transportation, and Land Use, Washington, D.C., January 2006, http://trb.org/downloads/sr282papers/sr282Handy.pdf.

Heath, G.W., R.C. Brownson, J. Kruger, R. Miles, K.E. Powell, L.T. Ramsey, and the Task Force on Community Preventive Services. "The Effectiveness of Urban Design and Land Use and Transport Policies and Practices to Increase Physical Activity: A Systematic Review." *Journal of Physical Activity and Health*, Vol. 3, 2006, pp. S55–S76.

Holtzclaw, J. "Explaining Urban Density and Transit Impacts on Auto Use." San Francisco: Sierra Club, 1991.

——. "Using Residential Patterns and Transit to Decrease Auto Dependence and Costs." San Francisco: Natural Resources Defense Council, 1994.

Holtzclaw, J., R. Clear, H. Dittmar, D. Goldstein, and P. Haas. "Location Efficiency: Neighborhood and Socioeconomic Characteristics Determine Auto Ownership and Use—Studies in Chicago, Los Angeles and San Francisco." *Transportation Planning and Technology*, Vol. 25, 2002, pp. 1–27.

Hu, P.S. and T.R. Reuscher. *Summary of Travel Trends: 2001 National Household Travel Survey.* Washington, D.C.: Federal Highway Administration, 2004, http://nhts.ornl.gov/2001/pub/STT.pdf.

IBI Group, Canada Mortgage and Housing Corporation, and Natural Resources Canada. *Greenhouse Gas Emissions for Urban Travel: Tool for Evaluating Neighbourhood Sustainability*, February 2000.

Johnston, R. "The Urban Transportation Planning Process." In S. Hanson and G. Guiliano (eds.), *The Geography of Urban Transportation.* New York: Guilford Press, 2004, pp. 115–140.

——. "Review of U.S. and European Regional Modeling Studies of Policies Intended to Reduce Motorized Travel, Fuel Use, and Emissions." Victoria Transport Policy Institute, 2006, www.vtpi.org.

Journal of the American Planning Association. Special Issue on Health and Planning. M. Boarnet (ed.), Winter 2006.

Kahn, M.E. "The Quality of Life in Sprawled versus Compact Cities," prepared for the OECD ECMT Regional Round, Berkeley, California, March 2006, Table 137, pp.27–28.

Khattak, A.J. and D. Rodriquez. "Travel Behavior in Neo-Traditional Neighborhood Developments: A Case Study in USA." *Transportation Research Part A*, Vol. 39, 2005, pp. 481–500.

Komanoff, C. *Environmental Consequences of Road Pricing: A Scoping Paper for the Energy Foundation,*1997, www.tstc.org/reports/ckdraft6. pdf.

Leck, E. "The Impact of Urban Form on Travel Behavior: A Meta-Analysis." *Berkeley Planning Journal*, Vol. 19, 2006, pp. 37–58.

Lee, C. and A. V. Moudon. "Physical Activity and Environment Research in the Health Field: Implications for Urban and Transportation Planning Practice and Research." *Journal of Planning Literature*, Vol. 19, 2004, pp. 147–181.

Lopez, R. and H. P. Hynes. "Sprawl in The 1990s: Measurement, Distribution, and Trends." *Urban Affairs Review*, Vol. 38, Issue 3, 2003, pp. 325–355.

Malpezzi, S. and W. Guo. *Measuring "Sprawl": Alternative Measures of Urban Form in U.S. Metropolitan Areas.* Center for Urban Land Economics Research, University of Wisconsin, Madison, 2001.

Moudon, A.V., P.M. Hess, M.C. Snyder, and K. Stanilov et al. "Effects of Site Design on Pedestrian Travel in Mixed-Use, Medium-Density Environments." *Transportation Research Record*, Vol. 1578, 1997, pp. 48–55.

Nasser, H.E. and P. Overberg, "What You Don't Know about Sprawl: Controlling Development a Big Concern, but Analysis Has Unexpected Findings." *USA Today*, February 22, 2001.

Natural Resources Defense Council (NRDC). *Environmental Charac-teristics of Smart Growth Neighborhoods: An Exploratory Case Study.* Washington, D.C., October 2000, www.nrdc.org/cities/smartGrowth/char/charinx.asp.

Newman, P.W.G. "Transport Greenhouse Gases and Australian Suburbs." *Australian Planner*, Vol. 43, Issue 2, 2006, pp. 6–7.

Newman, P.W.G. and J.R. Kenworthy. "The Transport Energy Trade-Off: Fuel-Efficient Traffic versus Fuel-Efficient Cities." *Transportation Research A*, Vol. 22A, Issue 3, 1988, pp. 163–174.

——. *Cities and Automobile Dependence: An International Sourcebook.* Aldershot, United Kingdom: Gower Publishing, 1989a.

——. "Gasoline Consumption and Cities: A Comparison of U.S. Cities with a Global Survey." *Journal of the American Planning Association*, Vol. 55A, 1989b, pp. 24–37.

——. *Sustainability and Cities: Overcoming Automobile Dependence.* Washington, D.C.: Island Press, 1999.

——. "Urban Design to Reduce Automobile Dependence." *Opolis: An International Journal of Suburban and Metropolitan Studies,* Vol. 2, Issue 1, 2006, pp. 35–52.

——. "Greening Urban Transportation." In M. O'Meara (ed.), *State of the World 2007: Our Urban Future*, Washington, D.C.: Norton Publishers, 2007.

Owen, N., N. Humpel, E. Leslie, A. Bauman, and J.F. Sallis. "Under-standing Environmental Influences on Walking; Review and Research Agenda." *American Journal of Preventive Medicine*, Volume 27, Issue 1, 2004, pp. 67–76.

Raudenbush, S.W. and A.S. Byrk. *Hierarchical Linear Models: Appli-cations and Data Analysis Methods* (second edition). Thousand Oaks, California: Sage Publications, 2002.

Sacramento Area Council of Governments (SACOG), TALL Order Regional Forum, April 30, 2004.

——. Preferred Blueprint Alternative, Special Report, January 2005.

——. Comments on Placer Vineyards Specific Plan: Second Partially Recirculated Revised Draft EIR, May 15, 2007.

SACOG and Valley Vision. Sacramento Region Blueprint, undated, www.sacregionblueprint.org/sacregionblueprint/home.cfm.

Saelens, B.E., J.F. Sallis, and L.D. Frank. "Environmental Correlates of Walking and Cycling: Findings from the Transportation, Urban Design, and Planning Literatures." *Annals of Behavioral Medicine*, Vol. 25, Issue 2, 2003, pp. 80–91.

Sarzynski, A., H.L. Wolman, G. Galster, and R. Hanson. "Testing the Conventional Wisdom About Land Use and Traffic Congestion: The More We Sprawl, the Less We Move?" *Urban Studies*, Vol. 43, Issue 3, 2006, pp. 601–626.

Schrank, D. and T. Lomax. *The 2007 Urban Mobility Report.* College Station: Texas Transportation Institute, 2007, http://mobility.tamu.edu/ums/.

U.S. Conference of Mayors. Clean Air/Brownfields Report. Washington, D.C., December 2001.

van de Coevering, P. and T. Schwanen, "Re-evaluating the Impact of Urban Form on Travel Patterns in Europe and North-America." *Transport Policy*, Vol. 13, Issue 3, 2006, pp. 229–239.

Walters, J., R. Ewing, and E. Allen. "Adjusting Computer Modeling Tools to Capture Effects of Smart Growth." *Transportation Research Record*, Vol. 1722, 2000, pp. 17–26.

CHAPTER 5: **Environmental Determinism versus Self Selection**

Belden Russonello & Stewart. *Americans' Attitudes Toward Walking and Creating Better Walking Communities.* Washington, D.C.: Surface Transportation Policy Project, April 2003, www.transact.org/library/reports_pdfs/pedpoll.pdf.

Cao, X., P. Mokhtarian, and S. Handy. *Examining the Impacts of Residential Self-Selection on Travel Behavior: Methodologies and Empirical Findings.* Research Report UCD-ITS-RR-06-18, Institute of Transportation Studies, University of California, Davis, December 2006, http://pubs.its.ucdavis.edu/publication_detail.php?id=1057.

Center for Transit-Oriented Development. *Hidden in Plain Sight: Capturing the Demand for Housing Near Transit.* Washington, D.C., September 2004 (revised April 2005).

Cervero, R. and M. Duncan. Residential Self Selection and Rail Commuting: A Nested Logit Analysis. UCTC Working Paper 604, Berkeley, California: University of California Transportation Center, 2003, http://www.uctc.net/papers/604.pdf.

Dill, J. "Travel Behavior and Attitudes: New Urbanist vs. Traditional Suburban Neighborhoods." Presented at the 2004 Annual Meeting of the Transportation Research Board, Washington, D.C.

Frank, L., B. Saelens, K.E. Powell, and J.E. Chapman. "Stepping Towards Causation: Do Built Environments or Neighborhood and Travel Preferences Explain Physical Activity, Driving, and Obesity?" *Social Science & Medicine*, forthcoming.

Levine J., A. Inam, and G. Tong. "A Choice-Based Rationale for Land Use and Transportation Alternatives—Evidence from Boston and Atlanta." *Journal of Planning Education and Research*, Vol. 24, Issue 3, 2005, pp. 317–330.

Levine, J. and L.D. Frank. "Transportation and Land-Use Preferences and Residents' Neighborhood Choices: The Sufficiency of Compact Development in the Atlanta Region." *Transportation*, Vol. 34, 2007, pp. 255–274.

Logan, G. "The Market for Smart Growth," presented at the U.S. EPA High-Production Builder Conference, Robert Charles Lesser & Co., LLP, January 31, 2007.

Lund, H. "Reasons for Living in a Transit-Oriented Development, and Associated Transit Use." *Journal of the American Planning Association*, Vol. 72, Issue 3, 2006, pp. 357–366.

Lund, H., R. Willson, and R. Cervero. "A Re-Evaluation of Travel Behavior in California TODs." *Journal of Architectural and Planning Research*, forthcoming.

Mokhtarian, P. and X. Cao. "Examining the Impacts of Residential Self-Selection on Travel Behavior: A Focus on Methodologies." *Transportation Research Part B*, forthcoming.

Myers, D. and E. Gearin. "Current Preferences and Future Demand for Denser Residential Environments." *Housing Policy Debate*, Vol. 12, Issue 4, 2001, pp. 633–659.

Nelson, A.C. "Leadership in a New Era." *Journal of the American Planning Association*, Vol. 72, Issue 4, 2006, pp. 393–407.

Rose, M. "Neighborhood Design & Mode Choice." Portland State University, Field Area Paper, Masters of Urban and Regional Planning, 2004.

Transportation Research Board/Institute of Medicine. *Does the Built Environment Influence Physical Activity? Examining the Evidence.* Washington, D.C.: National Academy of Sciences, 2005.

CHAPTER 6: **Induced Traffic and Induced Development**

American Association of State Highway Transportation Officials (AASHTO). *A New Vision for the 21st Century*, July 2007, www.transportation1.org/tif5report/TIF5.pdf.

Bhatta, S.D. and M.P. Drennan. "The Economic Benefits of Public Investment in Transportation: A Review of Recent Literature." *Journal of Planning Education and Research*, Vol. 22, Issue 3, 2003, pp. 288–296.

Boarnet, M.G. "Highways and Economic Productivity: Interpreting Recent Evidence." *Journal of Planning Literature*, Vol. 11, Issue 4, 1997, pp. 476–486.

Boarnet, M.G. and A. Haughwout. "Do Highways Matter? Evidence and Policy Implications of Highways' Influence on Metropolitan Development." Washington, D.C.: Brookings Institution, 2000.

Cervero, R. "Induced Travel Demand: Research Design, Empirical Evidence, and Normative Policies." *Journal of Planning Literature*, Vol. 17, Issue 1, 2002, pp. 3–20.

Cervero, R. and J. Landis. "The Transportation-Land Use Connection Still Matters." *Access*, Vol. 7, 1995, pp. 2–10.

Czamanski, S. "Effects of Public Investments on Urban Land Values." *Journal of the American Institute of Planners*, Vol. 32, 1966, pp. 204–217.

Downs, A. "The Law of Peak-Hour Express Way Congestion." *Traffic Quarterly*, Vol. 16, July 1962, pp. 393–409.

——. "Traffic: Why It's Getting Worse, What Government Can Do." Policy Brief #128, Washington, D.C.: Brookings Institution, 2004, www.brookings.edu/printme.wbs?page=/comm/policybriefs/pb128.htm.

Ewing, R. "Induced Transportation Operating Costs." In R. Burchell et al., *Calculating the Transportation Cost Impacts of New Development: Literature Review Related to Procedures.* National Cooperative Highway Research Program Project 08-59, August 17, 2007 draft, pp. 83–104.

——. "Highway-Induced Development: What Research in Metropolitan Areas Tells Us." *Transportation Research Record*, forthcoming, 2008.

Giuliano, G. "The Weakening Transportation-Land Use Connection." *Access*, Vol. 6, 1995, pp. 3–11.

Hansen, M. and Y. Huang. "Road Supply and Traffic in California Urban Areas." *Transportation Research A*, Vol. 31, Issue 3, 1997, pp. 205–218.

Huang, W. "The Effects of Transportation Infrastructure on Nearby Property Values: A Review of the Literature." Working Paper #620, Berkeley, California: Institute of Urban and Regional Development, University of California, 1994.

Mohring, H. "Land Values and the Measurement of Highway Benefits." *Journal of Political Economy*, Vol. 79, 1961, pp. 236–249.

National Capital Region Transportation Planning Board/Metropolitan Washington Council of Governments (NCRTPB/MWCOG). "Induced Travel: Definition, Forecasting Process, and a Case Study in the Metropolitan Washington Region." Washington, D.C., Sept. 19, 2001.

Ryan, S. "Property Values and Transportation Facilities: Finding the Transportation-Land Use Connection." *Journal of Planning Literature*, Vol. 13, Issue 4, 1999, pp. 412–427.

Washington Post. "Widen the Roads, Drivers Will Come—MD's I-270 Offers a Lesson," January 4, 1999.

CHAPTER 7: **The Residential Sector**

Bento, A.M., M.L. Cropper, A. Mobarak, and K. Vinha. *The Impact of Urban Spatial Structure on Travel Demand in the United States.* Washington, D.C.: World Bank, 2003.

Burchell, R.W., N.A. Shad, D. Listokin et al. *The Costs of Sprawl—Revisited.* Washington, D.C.: Transportation Research Board, 1998.

Cheshire, P. and S. Sheppard. "Estimating the Demand for Housing, Land, and Neighborhood Characteristics." *Oxford Bulletin of Economics and Statistics*, Vol. 60, Issue 3, 1998, pp. 357–382.

Cho, S., Z. Chen, S.T. Yen, and D.B. Eastwood. "The Effects of Urban Sprawl on Body Mass Index: Where People Live Does Matter." Presented at the 52nd Annual ACCI Conference, Baltimore, Maryland, March 15–18, 2006.

Doyle, S., A. Kelly-Schwartz, M. Schlossberg, and J. Stockard. "Active Community Environments and Health: The Relationship of Walkable and Safe Communities to Individual Health." *Journal of the American Planning Association*, Vol. 72, Issue 1, 2006, pp. 19-31.

Energy Information Administration (EIA). *Annual Energy Review 2006*, Washington, D.C., 2007.

Environmental Protection Agency (EPA). *Characteristics and Performance of Regional Transportation Systems.* Washington, D.C., 2003.

Ewing, R., R. Brownson, and D. Berrigan. "Relationship between Urban Sprawl and Weight of U.S. Youth." *American Journal of Preventive Medicine*, Vol. 31, Issue 6, 2006, pp. 464–474.

Ewing, R. and F. Rong. "Impact of Urban Form on U.S. Residential Energy Use," *Housing Policy Debate*, in press.

Ewing, R., T. Schmid, R. Killingsworth, A. Zlot, and S. Raudenbush. "Relationship Between Urban Sprawl and Physical Activity, Obesity, and Morbidity." *American Journal of Health Promotion*, Vol. 18, Issue 1, 2003, pp. 47–57.

Frank, L.D. and P. Engelke. "Multiple Impacts of the Built Environment on Public Health: Walkable Places and the Exposure to Air Pollution." *International Regional Science Review*, Vol. 28, Issue 2, 2005, pp. 193–216.

Frank, L.D., J.F. Sallis, T.L. Conway, J.E. Chapman, B.E. Saelens, and W. Bachman. "Many Pathways from Land Use to Health." *Journal of the American Planning Association*, Vol. 72, Issue 1, 2006, pp. 75–87.

Glaeser, E.L. and M. E. Kahn. *Sprawl and Urban Growth*. Cambridge, Massachusetts: Harvard Institute of Economic Research, Discussion Paper No. 2004, 2003.

Joshu, C.E, T.K. Boehmer, R. Ewing, and R.C. Brownson. "Personal, Neighborhood, and Urban Factors Associated with Obesity in the United States." *Journal of Epidemiology and Community Health*, in press.

Kahn, M.E. "The Quality of Life in Sprawled versus Compact Cities," prepared for the OECD ECMT Regional Round, Berkeley, California, March 2006, Table 137, pp.27–28.

Katz, M. L. and H. S. Rosen. *Microeconomics*. Boston: Irwin McGraw-Hill, 1998.

Kelly-Schwartz, A., J. Stockard, S. Doyle, and M. Schlossberg. "Is Sprawl Unhealthy? A Multilevel Analysis of the Relationship of Metropolitan Sprawl to the Health of Individuals." *Journal of Planning Education and Research,* Vol. 24, 2004, pp. 184–196.

Kessler, J. and W. Schroeer. "Meeting Mobility and Air Quality Goals: Strategies that Work." *Transportation*, Vol. 22, Issue 3, 1995, pp. 241–272.

Nelson, A.C., R. Pendall, C.J.Dawkins, and G.J. Knaap. *The Link between Growth Management and Housing Affordability: The Academic Evidence.* Washington D.C.: Brookings Institution, 2002, http://www.brookings.edu/es/urban/publications/growthmang.pdf.

Plantinga, A. and S. Bernell. "The Association between Urban Sprawl and Obesity: Is It a Two-Way Street?" *Journal of Regional Science,* Vol. 47, Issue 5, 2007, pp. 857–879.

Rosenfeld, A., H.S. Akbari, S. Bretz et al. "Mitigation of Urban Heat Islands: Materials, Utility Programs, Updates." *Energy and Buildings*, Vol. 22, Issue 3, 1995, pp. 255–265.

Staley, S.R. and G.C.S. Mildner. *Urban Growth Boundaries and Housing Affordability: Lessons from Portland*. Los Angeles: Reason Public Policy Institute, Policy Brief, 1999.

Stone, B. "Urban Sprawl and Air Quality in Large U.S. Cities." *Journal of Environmental Management*, in press, doi: 10.1016/j.jenvman.2006.12.034.

Stone, B., A. C. Mednick, T. Holloway, and S.N. Spak. "Is Compact Growth Good for Air Quality?" *Journal of the American Planning Association*, Vol. 73, Issue 4, 2007, pp. 404–418.

Stone, B. and M. Rodgers. "Urban Form and Thermal Efficiency: How the Design of Cities Influences the Urban Heat Island Effect." *Journal of the American Planning Association*, Vol. 67, Issue 2, 2001, pp. 186–198.

Sturm, R. and D. Cohen. "Suburban Sprawl and Physical and Mental Health." *Public Health*, Vol. 118, Issue 7, 2004, pp. 488–496.

Surface Transportation Policy Project (STPP). Driven to Spend: The Impact of Sprawl on Household Transportation Expenditures. Washington, D.C., 2000, http://www.transact.org/report.asp?id=36.

Trowbridge, M. J. and N. C. McDonald. "Urban Sprawl and Miles Driven Daily by Teenagers in the United States." *American Journal of Preventive Medicine*, in press.

Wassmer, R.W. and M.C. Baass. "Does a More Centralized Urban Form Raise Housing Prices?" *Journal of Policy Analysis and Management*, Volume 25, Issue 2, 2006, pp. 439–462.

CHAPTER 8: The Combined Effect of Compact Development, Transportation Investments, and Road Pricing

Bailey, L., P. Mokhtarian, and A. Little. *Broadening the Connection between Public Transportation and Energy Conservation*. Fairfax, Virginia: ICF Consulting, 2008.

Bollen, K.A. *Structural Equations with Latent Variables*. New York: Wiley Interscience, 1989.

Cervero, R. "Induced Travel Demand: Research Design, Empirical Evidence, and Normative Policies." *Journal of Planning Literature*, Vol. 17, Issue 1, 2002, pp. 3–20.

Energy Information Administration (EIA). *Annual Energy Outlook 2008 (Early Release).* Washington, D.C.: U.S. Department of Energy, 2008, Tables 7 and 12, http://www.eia.doe.gov/oiaf/aeo/aeoref_tab.html.

Grace, J.B. *Structural Equation Modeling and Natural Systems.* Cambridge, United Kingdom: Cambridge University Press, 2006.

Lee, S.Y. *Structural Equation Modeling: A Bayesian Approach*. New York: Wiley Interscience, 2007.

Schrank, D. and T. Lomax. *The 2007 Urban Mobility Report.* College Station: Texas Transportation Institute, 2007, http://mobility.tamu.edu/ums/.

SPSS. Amos 7.0. Chicago: SPSS Inc., 2007.

U.S. Congress. H.R. 6, Energy Independence and Security Act of 2007, http://frwebgate.access.gpo.gov/cgi-bin/getdoc.cgi?dbname=110_cong_bills&docid=f:h6enr.txt.pdf.

Victoria Transport Policy Institute. "Transportation Elasticities: How Prices and Other Factors Affect Travel Behavior." Victoria, British Columbia, March 7, 2007, www.vtpi.org/tdm/tdm11.htm.

CHAPTER 9: **Policy and Program Recommendations**

Bartholomew, K. "Transportation-Land Use Scenario Planning: Promise and Reality." *Transportation*, Vol. 35, Issue 4, 2007, pp. 397–412.

Bayon, R., A. Hawn, and K. Hamilton. *Voluntary Carbon Markets: An International Business Guide to What They Are and How They Work.* London: Earthscan, 2007.

Beimborn, E. and R. Puentes. *Highways and Transit: Leveling the Playing Field in Federal Transportation Policy.* Washington, D.C.: Brookings Institution, 2003.

Bernstein, S., C. Makarewicz, and K. McCarty. *Driven to Spend.* Washington, D.C.: Surface Transportation Policy Partnership, 2005, www.transact.org.

Bierbaum, R. Presentation to Presidential Climate Action Program analyzing trends in IPCC analyses. Wingspread Conference Center, Racine, Wisconsin, June 2006.

Bureau of Labor Statistics. *Consumer Expenditure Survey.* Washington, D.C., 2001.

California Energy Commission. *The Role of Land Use in Meeting California's Energy and Climate Change Goals.* Sacramento, California, 2007, http://www.energy.ca.gov/2007publications/CEC-600-2007-008/CEC-600-2007-008-SF.PDF.

Center for Clean Air Policy. "Recommendations to Governor Pataki for Reducing New York State Greenhouse Gas Emissions." Washington, D.C., 2003, http://www.ccap.org/pdf/04-2003_NYGHG_Recommendations.pdf.

——. "Connecticut Climate Change Stakeholder Dialogue: Recommendations to the Governor's Steering Committee." Washington, D.C., 2004a, http://www.ccap.org/Connecticut.htm.

——. "Two for the Price of One: Clean Air and Smart Growth (Workshop Primer)." Washington, D.C., 2004b, http://www.ccap.org/transportation/smart_two.htm.

——. *Green-TEA: A Legacy for the Planet?* Washington, D.C., 2007, http://www.ccap.org/transportation/documents/Green-TEA.pdf.

Center for Transit-Oriented Development. *Hidden in Plain Sight: Meeting the Coming Demand for Housing Near Transit.* Washington, D.C., September 2004 (revised April 2005), www.reconnecting america.org.

Cervero, R. and M. Duncan. "Which Reduces Vehicle Travel More: Jobs-Housing Balance or Retail-Housing Mixing." *Journal of the American Planning Association*, Vol. 72, Issue 4, 2006, pp. 475–489.

Environmental Protection Agency (EPA). "National Award for Smart Growth Achievement 2003 Winners." Washington, D.C., 2003, http://www.epa.gov/piedpage/sg_awards_publication_final_10_17.htm#nat_award.

Federal Highway Administration (FHWA). *Highway Statistics 2005.* Washington, D.C.: U.S. Department of Transportation, 2006, Table FA-4A.

Gustafson, J. and J. C. Walker. *Qualified Allocation Plans for the Low-Income Tax Credit Program.* Washington, D.C.: the Urban Institute, 2002, http://www.huduser.org/Publications/pdf/AnalysisQAP.pdf.

Haughey R. *Developing Housing for the Workforce: A Tool Kit.* Washington, D.C.: ULI–the Urban Land Institute, 2007.

Hill, E., B. Geyer, R. Puentes et al. "Slanted Pavement: How Ohio's Highway Spending Shortchanges Cities and Suburbs," in B. Katz and R. Puentes (eds), *Taking the High Road: A Metropolitan Agenda for Transportation Reform.* Washington, D.C.: Brookings Institution, 2005, pp. 101–135.

ICF Consulting. "Estimating Transportation-Related Greenhouse Gas Emissions and Energy Use in New York State." Washington, D.C.: U.S. Department of Transportation, 2005, http://trb.org/news/blurb_detail.asp?id=5065.

Katz, B., R. Puentes, and S. Bernstein. *TEA-21 Reauthorization: Getting Transportation Right for Metropolitan America.* Washington D.C.: Brookings Institution, 2003.

Knapp, G. and R. Lewis. *State Agency Spending Under Maryland's Smart Growth Areas Act: Who's Tracking, Who's Spending, How Much, and Where?* College Park, Maryland: National Center for Smart Growth Research and Education, University of Maryland, September 30, 2007.

Lipman, B. *A Heavy Load: The Combined Housing and Transportation Burdens of Working Families.* Washington, D.C.: National Housing Conference, 2006, www.nhc.org.

Local Government Commission. *Creating Great Neighborhoods: Density in Your Community.* Sacramento, California: Local Government Commission, 2003.

Louisiana Speaks. *Louisiana Speaks Regional Plan, Executive Summary.* Baton Rouge: Louisiana Recovery Authority, 2007, http://www.louisianaspeaks.org/cache/documents/193/19311.pdf.

Mayors Climate Protection Center. "Participating Mayors." Washington, D.C.: The United States Conference of Mayors, 2007, http://usmayors.org/climateprotection/listofcities.asp.

Mayors for Climate Protection. "Cool Mayors." Oakland, California: ICLEI, 2008, http://www.coolmayors.com/common/news/reports/detail.cfm?Classification=report&QID=3473&ClientID=11061&TopicID=0&ThisPage=12&subsection=mayors.

Metro. *The Nature of 2040: The Region's 50-Year Plan for Managing Growth.* Portland, Oregon, 2000, http://www.metro-region.org/files/planning/natureof2040.pdf.

——. *2004 Regional Transportation Plan.* Portland, Oregon, 2004, http://www.metro-region.org/index.cfm/go/by.web/id=236.

Metropolitan Council. 2030 Regional Development Framework. Minneapolis, Minnesota, 2004, pp. 6–7, http://www.metrocouncil.org/planning/framework/Framework.pdf.

Metropolitan Transportation Commission (MTC). "Transportation for Livable Communities & Housing Incentive Program." Oakland, California, n.d., http://www.mtc.ca.gov/planning/smart_growth/#tlc.

Moore, C. *Daniel H. Burnham, Architect, Planner of Cities.* New York: Houghton Mifflin, 1921.

National Complete Streets Coalition. "Let's Complete America's Streets," 2005, http://www.completestreets.org/policies.html.

National Highway Traffic Safety Administration and Bureau of Transportation Statistics. *National Survey of Pedestrian & Bicyclist Attitudes and Behaviors: Highlights Report.* Washington, D.C.: U.S. Department of Transportation, 2003, http://www.bts.gov/programs/omnibus_surveys/targeted_survey/2002_national_survey_of_pedestrian_and_bicyclist_attitudes_and_behaviors/survey_highlights/entire.pdf.

Oregon Department of Land Conservation and Development. *Statewide Planning Goals.* Salem, Oregon, 2007, http://www.oregon.gov/LCD/goals.shtml.

Puentes, R. and L. Bailey. "Increasing Funding and Accountability for Metropolitan Transportation Decisions," in B. Katz and R. Puentes (eds.), *Taking the High Road: A Metropolitan Agenda for Transportation Reform.* Washington, D.C.: Brookings Institution, 2005, pp. 139–167.

Regional Greenhouse Gas Initiative. "Memorandum of Understanding," 2005, http://www.rggi.org/docs/mou_12_20_05.pdf.

Rell, M.J. Executive Order 15. Hartford, Connecticut: Office of the Governor, 2006, http://www.ct.gov/governorrell/cwp/view.asp?A=1719&Q=320908.

Rube, K. "Out of Reach: The Low Income Housing Tax Credit (LIHTC) and Public Transportation Access in Washington, D.C." unpublished, 2008.

Sacramento Area Council of Governments (SACOG). Preferred Blueprint Alternative. Sacramento, California, 2005, http://www.sacregionblueprint.org/sacregionblueprint/the_project/BP_Insert_JAN_2005.pdf.

——. *Metropolitan Transportation Plan: Summary of Plan Performance.* Sacramento, 2007, p. 4-1.

San Diego Association of Governments (SANDAG). "Smart Growth Concept Map." San Diego, California, 2006, http://www.sandag.org/index.asp?projectid=296&fuseaction=projects.detail.

San Joaquin Valley Air Pollution Control District (SJVAPCD). *2007 Annual Report on the District's Indirect Source Review Program.* Fresno, California, 2007, http://www.valleyair.org/ISR/Documents/ISRAnnualReport2007.pdf.

Seattle Climate Action Plan. "Seattle's Community Carbon Footprint: An Update." Seattle, Washington, 2007, http://www.seattle.gov/climate/docs/Seattle%20Carbon%20Footprint%20Summary.pdf.

Smart Growth Leadership Institute. "Smart Growth Implementation Tools." Washington, D.C.: Smart Growth America, 2006, http://www.sgli.org/implementation.html.

Thomas, J. "Dividing Lines and Bottom Lines: The Forces Shaping Local Development Patterns." *Journal of Planning Education and Research,* Vol. 25, 2006, pp. 275–293.

U.S. Department of Housing and Urban Development. Low-Income Housing Tax Credits. Washington, D.C., 2008, http://www.huduser.org/datasets/lihtc.html.

U.S. Department of Transportation. *2001 National Household Transportation Survey.* Washington, D.C., 2001, http://www.bts.gov/programs/national_household_travel_survey/.

Weiner, E. *Urban Transportation Planning in the United States: An Historical Overview.* Westport, Connecticut: Praeger, 1999.

Western Climate Initiative (WCI). "The Western Climate Initiative," 2008, http://www.westernclimateinitiative.org/Index.cfm.

Winkelman, S., T. Hargrave, and C. Vanderlan. *Transportation and Domestic Greenhouse Gas Emissions Trading.* Washington, D.C.: Center for Clean Air Policy, 2000, http://www.ccap.org/pdf/TGHG.pdf.

Wolf J., R. Puentes, T. Sanchez, and T. Bryan. "MPOs in the Post-ISTEA Era: What Went Wrong?" Eno Transportation Foundation 2007 Forum on the Future of Urban Transportation. Washington, D.C., September 2007.

Related ULI Publications

Beyard, Michael D. et al. *Ten Principles for Developing Successful Town Centers*. Washington, D.C.: ULI–the Urban Institute, 2007.

——. *Ten Principles for Rebuilding Neighborhood Retail*. Washington, D.C.: ULI–the Urban Land Institute, 2003.

Beyard, Michael D. and Michael Pawlukiewicz. *Ten Principles for Reinventing America's Suburban Strips*. Washington, D.C.: ULI–the Urban Land Institute, 2001.

Bohl, Charles. *Place Making and Town Center Development*. Washington, D.C.: ULI–the Urban Land Institute, 2003.

Booth, A. Geoffrey. *Transforming Suburban Business Districts*. Washington, D.C.: ULI–the Urban Land Institute, 2001.

Booth, Geoffrey et al. *Ten Principles for Reinventing Suburban Business Districts*. Washington, D.C.: ULI–the Urban Land Institute, 2002.

Dunphy, Robert T. *Developing Around Transit: Strategies and Solutions That Work*. Washington, D.C.: ULI–the Urban Land Institute, 2004.

Gause, Jo Allen. *Great Planned Communities*. Washington, DC: ULI–the Urban Land Institute, 2002.

Gause, Jo Allen and Richard Franko. *Developing Sustainable Planned Communities*. Washington, D.C.: ULI–the Urban Land Institute, 2007.

Gupta, Prema Katari. *Compact Development: Changing the Rules to Make it Happen*. Washington, D.C.: ULI–the Urban Land Institute, 2007.

——. *Creating Great Town Centers and Urban Villages*. Washington, D.C.: ULI–the Urban Land Institute, forthcoming (2008).

Haughey, Richard. *Urban Infill Housing: Myth and Fact*. Washington, D.C.: ULI–the Urban Land Institute, 2001.

——. *Higher-Density Development: Myth and Fact*. Washington, D.C.: ULI–the Urban Land Institute, 2005.

——. *Getting Density Right: Tools for Creating Vibrant Compact Development*. Washington, D.C.: ULI–the Urban Land Institute, forthcoming (2008).

Heid, James M. *Greenfield Development Without Sprawl: The Role of Planned Communities*. Washington, D.C.: ULI–the Urban Land Institute, 2004.

Pawlukiewicz, Michael. *Ten Principles for Smart Growth on the Suburban Fringe*. Washington, D.C.: ULI–the Urban Land Institute, 2003.

Peiser, Richard B. and Adrienne Schmitz. *Regenerating Older Suburbs*. Washington, D.C.: ULI–the Urban Land Institute, 2007.

Porter, Douglas R. *Making Smart Growth Work*. Washington, D.C.: ULI–the Urban Land Institute, 2003.

——. *Smart Growth Transportation for Suburban Greenfields*. Washington, D.C.: ULI–the Urban Land Institute, 2003.

Schmitz, Adrienne. *The New Shape of Suburbia: Trends in Residential Development*. Washington, D.C.: ULI–the Urban Land Institute, 2003.

Schmitz, Adrienne and Jason Scully. *Creating Walkable Places: Compact Mixed-Use Solutions*. Washington, D.C.: ULI–the Urban Land Institute, 2006.

Schwanke, Dean. *Mixed-Use Development Handbook*. Washington, D.C.: ULI–the Urban Land Institute, 2003.

Suchman, Diane R. *Developing Successful Infill Housing*. Washington, D.C.: ULI–the Urban Land Institute, 2002.